ISSUES OF
WESTWARD EXPANSION

ISSUES OF WESTWARD EXPANSION

Mitchel Roth

Major Issues in American History
Randall M. Miller, Series Editor

GREENWOOD PRESS
Westport, Connecticut • London

Library of Congress Cataloging-in-Publication Data

Roth, Mitchel P., 1953–
    Issues of westward expansion / Mitchel Roth.
        p. cm.—(Major issues in American history, ISSN 1535–3192)
    Includes bibliographical references (p.).
    ISBN 0–313–31167–6 (alk. paper)
    1. United States—Territorial expansion.   2. United States—Territorial
expansion—Sources.   3. West (U.S.)—History.   4. West (U.S.)—History—Sources.   5.
Frontier and pioneer life—West (U.S.)   6. Frontier and pioneer life—West (U.S.)—
Sources. I. Title. II. Series.
   E179.5.R68   2002   2001058640
   978—dc21

British Library Cataloguing in Publication Data is available.

Library of Congress Catalog Card Number: 2001058640
ISBN: 0–313–31167–6
ISSN: 1535–3192

First published in 2002

Greenwood Press, 88 Post Road West, Westport, CT 06881
An imprint of Greenwood Publishing Group, Inc.
www.greenwood.com

Printed in the United States of America

∞™

The paper used in this book complies with the
Permanent Paper Standard issued by the National
Information Standards Organization (Z39.48–1984).

10 9 8 7 6 5 4 3 2 1

ADVISORY BOARD

Julia Kirk Blackwelder, Chair
Department of History
Texas A&M University

Louisa B. Moffitt
Marist School
Atlanta, Georgia

Marion Roydhouse
Department of History
Philadelphia College of Textiles and Sciences

Carl Schulkin
The Pembroke School
Kansas City, Missouri

Victor Taylor
Sacred Heart Country Day School
Bryn Mawr, Pennsylvania

To
Leila and Valerie

Contents

Series Foreword

This series of books presents major issues in American history as they have developed since the republic's inception to their present incarnation. The issues range across the spectrum of American experience and encompass political, economic, social, and cultural concerns. By focusing on the "major issues" in American history, the series emphasizes the importance of an issues-centered approach to teaching and thinking about America's past. *Major Issues in American History* thus reframes historical inquiry in terms of themes and problems rather than as mere chronology. In so doing, the series addresses the current, pressing need among educators and policymakers for case studies charting the development of major issues over time, so as to make it possible to approach such issues intelligently in our time.

The series is premised on the belief that understanding America demands grasping the contentious nature of its past and applying that understanding to current issues in politics, law, government, society, and culture. If "America" was born, and remains, as an idea and an experiment, as so many thinkers and observers have argued, issues inevitably have shaped whatever that America was and is. In 1801, in his presidential inaugural, Thomas Jefferson reminded Americans that the great strength of the new nation resided in the broad consensus citizens shared as to the rightness and necessity of republican government and the Constitution. That consensus, Jefferson continued, made dissent possible and tolerable, and, we might add, encouraged dissent and debate about critical issues thereafter. Every generation of Americans has wrestled with such issues as defining and defending freedom(s), determining America's place in the world, waging war and making peace, receiving and assimilating new peoples, balancing church and state, forming a "more perfect union," and pursuing "happiness." American identity(ies) and interest(s) are not fixed. A nation of many peoples on the move across space and up and down the socioeconomic ladder cannot have it so. A nation charged with ensuring that, in Lincoln's words, "government of the people, by the people, and for the people shall not perish from the earth" cannot have it so. A nation whose heroes are not only soldiers and statesmen but also ex-slaves, women reformers, inventors, thinkers, and cowboys and Indians cannot have it so. Americans have never rested content locked into set molds in thinking and doing—not so long as dissent and difference are built into the character of a people that dates its birth to an American Revolution and annually celebrates that lineage. As such, Americans have been, and are, by heritage and habit an issues-oriented people.

We are also a political people. Issues as varied as race relations, labor organizing, women's place in the work force, the practice of religious beliefs, immigration, westward movement, and environmental protection have been, and remain, matters of public concern and debate and readily intrude into politics. A people committed to "rights" invariably argues for them, low voter turnout in recent elections notwithstanding. All the major issues in American history have involved political controversies as to their meaning and application. But the extent to which issues assume a political cast varies.

As the public interest spread to virtually every aspect of life during the twentieth century—into boardrooms, ballparks, and even bedrooms—the political compass enlarged with it. In time, every economic, social, and cultural issue of consequence in the United States has entered the public realm of debate and political engagement. Questions of rights—for example, to free speech, to freedom of religion, to equality before the law—and authority are political by nature. So, too, are questions about war and society, foreign policy, law and order, the delivery of public services, the control of the nation's borders, and access to and the uses of public land and resources. The books in *Major Issues in American History* take up just those issues. Thus, all the books in this series build political and public policy concerns into their basic framework.

The format for the series speaks directly to the issues-oriented character of the American people and the democratic polity and to the teaching of issues-centered history. The issues-centered approach to history views the past thematically. Such a history respects chronology but does not attempt to recite a single narrative or simple historical chronology of "facts." Rather, issues-centered history is problem-solving history. It organizes historical inquiry around a series of questions central to understanding the character and functions of American life, culture, ideas, politics, and institutions. Such questions invariably derive from current concerns that demand historical perspective. Whether determining the role of women and minorities and shaping public policy, or considering the "proper" relationship between church and state, or thinking about U.S. military obligations in the global context, to name several persistent issues, the teacher and student—indeed, responsible citizens every-where—must ask such questions as "how and why did the present cir-cumstance and interests come to be as they are" and "what other choices as to policy and practice have there been" so as to measure the dimen-sions and point the direction of the issue. History matters in that regard.

Each book in the series focuses on a particular issue, with an eye to encouraging readers and users to consider how Americans at different times engaged the issue based on the particular values, interests, and political and social structures of the day. As such, each book is also necessarily events-based in that the key event that triggered public con-cern and debate about a major issue at a particular moment serves as the case study for the issue as it was understood and presented during that historical period. Each book offers a historical narrative overview of a major issue as it evolved; the narrative provides both the context for understanding the issue's place in the larger American experience and the touchstone for considering the ways Americans encountered and en-gaged the issue at different times. A timeline further establishes the chro-nology and place of the issue in American history. The core of each book is the series of between ten to fifteen case studies of watershed events that defined the issue, arranged chronologically to make it possible to track the development of the issue closely over time. Each case study stands as a separate chapter. Each case study opens with a historical overview of the event and a discussion of the significant contemporary opposing views of the issue as occasioned by the event. A selection of four to nine critical primary documents (printed whole or in excerpts and introduced with brief headnotes) from the period under review pres-ents differing points of view on the issue. In some volumes, each chapter also includes an annotated research guide of print and nonprint sources to guide further research and reflection on the event and the issue. Each volume in the series concludes with a general bibliography that provides ready reference to the key works on the subject at issue.

Such an arrangement ensures that readers and users—students and teachers alike—will approach the major issues within a problem-solving framework. Indeed, the design of the series and each book in it demands that students and teachers understand that the crucial issues of American history have histories and that the significance of those issues might best be discovered and recovered by understanding how Americans at dif-ferent times addressed them, shaped them, and bequeathed them to the next generation. Such a dialectic for each issue encourages a comparative perspective not only in seeing America's past but also, and perhaps even more so, in thinking about its present. Individually and collectively, the books in *Major Issues in American History* thereby demonstrate anew William Faulkner's dictum that the past is never past.

Randall M. Miller
Series Editor

Preface

Compared to most countries in the world, the United States has a rather short history. America has weathered revolution, civil war, sectional turmoil, and world wars, yet no experience is more indelible than the nation's westward expansion. America's westward expansion beginning in the nineteenth century is the most chronicled era of the nation's history. As a result, the events, problems, and obstacles surrounding westward expansion have contributed much to defining the national character.

Each chapter in this book examines crucial events in America's westward expansion. Documents, speeches, and other primary materials in each chapter allow students and teachers to explore controversial issues from multiple perspectives. Unlike most primary source readers, which feature a sequence of documents without an accompanying narrative, this book concentrates on twelve major events that chronicle westward expansion.

Westward expansion created a number of problems and controversies. Every segment of American society was touched by the experience. For example, Chapter 11 documents the discrimination Chinese Americans faced as they competed for jobs on the West Coast in the 1880s, while Chapter 7 demonstrates that Chinese workers played a major role in one of the greatest construction feats in American history—the building of the transcontinental railroad in the late 1860s. Students will reconcile these incongruities in the context of political, social, and economic changes that accompanied nineteenth-century westward expansion.

No group of individuals suffered more from westward expansion than

the Native American population. Although the demise of America's in-
digenous peoples in the seventeenth to nineteenth centuries has been
well chronicled, this book examines certain aspects of Indian-white relations in the context of westward expansion. Indians resorted to a variety of devices to preserve their sovereignty in the face of westward
expansion. From a legal perspective, in Chapter 3, students can examine
the plight of the Cherokees and other Indian nations attempting to stave
off removal from their ancestral homelands. When assimilation and treaties did not work, some Indian nations resorted to warfare, with mixed
results. In Colorado (Chapter 8), and again at Wounded Knee, South
Dakota (Chapter 12), peaceful Indians were massacred by citizens and
army troops. But in between these two events, Plains Indians banded
together to hand U.S. troops their worst defeat of the Indian wars at the
Battle of the Little Big Horn (Chapter 9).

As students examine the episodes on Native American–white relations
in the nineteenth century, they will find that these events were influenced by factors much more complicated than simple mutual antago-
nism. Behind these episodes were a host of other issues that were too
complicated to resolve in each particular time period. Documents and
speeches offer students an opportunity to listen to both sides and make
their own decisions as to what alternatives may have been used if conditions had been different.

Other chapters are dedicated to issues involving farmers and the acquisition of land (Chapter 6), the Mormon settlement of the West (Chapter 5), and America's war with Mexico (Chapter 4). Still others focus on
the most underappreciated victim of westward expansion—the public
domain. Chapter 10 recounts the battle to preserve the nation's natural
scenery by creating national parks, beginning with Yellowstone. The con-
cluding chapter examines the price paid by farmers on the Great Plains
after years of abusing the land. It also offers another West, one of un-
fulfilled expectations. As Americans moved beyond the Mississippi River
and then the 100th meridian, they found a West that contrasted with
their expectations, where there was little rain and few alternatives if one
wanted to become a farmer.

The federal government plays an important part in the story of westward expansion as well—from the first government-sponsored expedition in Chapter 2, to President Franklin Roosevelt's New Deal
agricultural policies in the final chapter.

While other issues in westward expansion certainly could have been
presented in this book, limitations on the scope of this project made it
necessary to pare it down to twelve prominent issues and an introduction. To help students and teachers, the book includes a timeline, an
annotated bibliography in each chapter, recommended readings, and Internet and video resources to complement classroom instruction.

This book could not have been completed without the help of several individuals. First and foremost I would like to acknowledge the contributions of Professor Randall Miller at St. Joseph's University, who offered me this project and shepherded it through its various incarnations. He is without a doubt one of the finest editors I have ever worked with. I am indebted to Greenwood editor Barbara Rader for her helpful comments and patience as she prodded me along on the manuscript. Professor Ty Cashion from Sam Houston State University's history department demonstrated why he is one of America's top scholars on Texas history, as he carefully proofread several chapters on the Texan West. Special Collections Librarian Paul Culp supplied me with several hard to find resources. This book could not have been completed without the inspiration and support of Ines Papandrea.

Chronology of Events

1536   Cabeza de Vaca's epic trek across the Southwest inspires subsequent Spanish forays into the area

1540   Coronado expedition travels through present-day Texas, Oklahoma, and Kansas

1680   Pueblo revolt drives Spanish from New Mexico until 1692

1720s   Horse widely adopted by Plains Indians

1764   French fur traders establish St. Louis on Mississippi River

1770   Virginia colony acquires western lands from Cherokees

1775–83 American Revolutionary War

1783   Treaty of Paris: Great Britain recognizes U.S. territory as extending west to Mississippi River

1787   Northwest Ordinance outlines how territories can eventually be admitted to Union as states; slavery banned from territory formed from Old Northwest

1803   Louisiana Purchase extends western border of United States to Rocky Mountains and gives United States control of Mississippi River

1804–6   Jefferson sends Lewis and Clark to explore Louisiana Territory

1805   Zebulon Pike leads U.S. Army expedition up Mississippi River
            to present-day Minnesota

1806–7   Pike expedition crosses into Spanish territory

1807   Yellowstone Park explored by mountain man John Colter

1820   Major Stephen Long leads U.S. Army exploration into eastern
            Rocky Mountains and characterizes Great Plains as the "Great
            American Desert" in his official report

1821   Mexico wins independence from Spain

1821   Santa Fe Trail opened from Independence, Missouri

1821   Stephen Austin establishes American colony in Texas

1823   Jedediah Smith leads party of mountain men overland to
            Rocky Mountains

1824   Mountain man James Bridger comes upon Great Salt Lake

1825   First annual rendezvous of fur trappers

1825   Indian territory created in Oklahoma Territory

1825   Jedediah Smith crosses the Great Basin to California

1830   Congress passes the Indian Removal Act

1831   *Cherokee Nation v. State of Georgia*

1832   *Worcester v. State of Georgia*

1835–36   Texas war for independence from Mexico

1838   Trail of Tears to Indian territory in Oklahoma begins

1839   Most of remaining Five Civilized Tribes removed to Oklahoma
            and Arkansas

1841   Settlers start moving west on Oregon Trail

1842   First accurate map of the West produced by John C. Frémont
            and the U.S. Corps of Topographical Engineers

1845   United States annexes Texas as twenty-eighth state

1845   John O'Sullivan coins phrase "manifest destiny"

1846–47   Brigham Young leads Mormon trek to Utah

1846–48   War with Mexico

1848   Treaty of Guadalupe Hidalgo cedes much of the Southwest to
            the United States

1848   Gold discovered in California

1850   Compromise of 1850; California becomes thirty-first state

1851   Treaty of Fort Laramie with northern plains tribes

1853   Gadsden Purchase adds southern New Mexico to U.S. territory

1854   Congress enacts Kansas-Nebraska Act

1859   Discovery of gold and silver in the Comstock lode leads to mining rush in Nevada

1859   '59ers rush for gold fields of Colorado

1859   Oregon becomes thirty-third state

1860   Inauguration of Pony Express

1861–65.   American Civil War

1862   Homestead Act signed into law by President Lincoln

1862   Congress passes Pacific Railroad Act to aid construction of transcontinental railroad

1862   Sioux war in Minnesota

1864   Colorado militia massacres Southern Cheyennes at Sand Creek

1864   Congress passes Immigration Act in order to recruit Chinese labor to build the transcontinental railroad

1864   Nevada becomes thirty-sixth state

1866   Captain William Fetterman's command wiped out by Sioux

1866–67   Red Cloud War along Bozeman Trail

1867   First major cattle drive from Texas to Abilene, Kansas

1867   Nebraska becomes thirty-seventh state

1867   Treaty of Medicine Lodge with southern plains tribes

1867   Purchase of Alaska from Russia, better known as "Seward's Folly"

1867–83   Decimation of buffalo herds

1868   Custer destroys Cheyenne village on Washita River

1868   Fort Laramie Treaty creates Great Sioux Reservation

1869   Completion of transcontinental railroad

1869   John Wesley Powell explores Grand Canyon

1869   Wyoming Territory grants women right to vote

1871   Largest number of cattle driven from Texas to Kansas in one year—600,000

1871   Anti-Chinese rioting in Los Angeles

1871   Indian Appropriation Act ends recognition of Indian tribes as sovereign nations

1872   Yellowstone becomes nation's first national park

1872   Congress passes Mining Law

1873   Congress passes Timber Culture Act

1874–75 Red River War on southern plains

1875   Beginning of "Great Sioux War"

1876   Custer and his Seventh Cavalry wiped out at Battle of the Little Big Horn

1876   Colorado becomes thirty-eighth state

1877   Passage of Desert Land Act

1880   Chinese Exclusion Treaty

1881   Surrender of Sitting Bull

1881   Publication of Helen Hunt Jackson's *A Century of Dishonor*

1882   Chinese Exclusion Act

1887   Congress passes Dawes Severalty Act

1889   Washington, Montana, North Dakota, and South Dakota admitted to Union as states

1889–90 Ghost Dance spreads from Nevada to Great Plains

1890   Sitting Bull killed

1890   Wounded Knee Massacre at Pine Ridge Reservation

1890   Yosemite National Park established

1890   Wyoming and Idaho admitted as states

1890   Mormons prohibit polygamy in order to win statehood

1893   Utah becomes forty-fifth state

1893   Great Northern Railroad completed

1902   Publication of Owen Wister's *The Virginian*

1907   State of Oklahoma formed by union of Oklahoma and Indian territories

1912   Arizona and New Mexico granted statehood

1931   Nevada legalizes gambling

1933–34 Dust Bowl sends "Okies" and "Arkies" to California

1934   Taylor Grazing Act sets aside public lands for livestock grazing

1936   Completion of Boulder Dam (renamed Hoover Dam)

1941–45 World War II

1942   President Roosevelt authorizes relocation of Japanese Americans on West Coast to internment camps

1943   Zoot Suit riots in Los Angeles

1945   First successful atomic bomb test near Alamogordo, New Mexico

1955   Disneyland opens in Anaheim, California

1958   Brooklyn Dodgers move to Los Angeles and New York Giants to San Francisco

1963   California surpasses New York as most populous state

1965   Watts riots

1972   FBI arrests Indian occupants of Wounded Knee, South Dakota

1992   Los Angeles riots

1

Introduction

Between the early seventeenth and the twentieth centuries, the United States made the transition from thirteen loosely allied British colonies along the Atlantic coast to a republic of states stretching across mountain ranges, deserts, rivers, canyons, and through Native American nations more varied than the cultures of the Old World. Behind the territorial expansion toward western shores was an almost unspoken confidence that it was predestined to occur. Expansionism was a force in America as early as the seventeenth century, when Massachusetts Bay Puritans embarked on a campaign to seize Indian lands. Over the next three centuries territorial expansion proceeded by appropriating Indian lands either through force or subterfuge. As a result, today's Indians have a land base of only 52 million acres, which is less than the size of Minnesota.

In the middle of the eighteenth century, most of the non-Indian population in North America was crowded along a narrow strip of land along the Atlantic seaboard. American territorial expansion had its roots in the conflict between France and Great Britain over which country would dominate the continent. Following the French and Indian War and the American Revolution, the new nation inherited a desire for territorial expansion, and through a series of Indian treaties and campaigns of conquest, the United States acquired more and more land.

Rudimentary policies governing land sales were established soon after the American Revolution. Over the next century, the national land system was gradually modified. Minimum prices for lands were established, and public lands were to be surveyed and then put up for sale at public auctions. One rule that was established early on, but was often violated, was the prohibition against squatting on public lands prior to purchase.

Into the nineteenth century, the United States remained a nation of land-hungry farmers. For them, the seemingly "unsettled" wilderness lands represented wealth and optimism. Western expansion continued with few interruptions following the American Revolution. Between 1781 and 1802 (the year before the Louisiana Purchase) the United States gained 225 million acres of public lands thanks to the Treaty of Paris (1783) with Great Britain and the western cessions of land claims by the states to the national government.

The encroachment of American settlement into the trans-Appalachian region between 1790 and 1800 led indirectly to the purchase of the Louisiana Territory in 1803 from France. The acquisition of this vast area spurred an expansionist psychology among the American people that found its greatest expression in the late 1840s, culminating in the U.S.-Mexican War. The purchase of Louisiana set a precedent for the new government under the Constitution to acquire land by purchase and ended the presence of powerful foreign adversaries on the western frontier.

Before the Louisiana Purchase, little was known about the lands west of the Mississippi River. Over the next century a procession of fur traders, mountain men, scientists, artists, and federally sponsored expeditions surveyed, publicized, and sometimes exaggerated the potential of these lands for settlement. The first and most famous of these expeditions was the Lewis and Clark expedition (1804–1806). Plans for this undertaking had already been made by the ever-curious President Thomas Jefferson even before the consummation of the purchase.

The Lewis and Clark expedition, or "Corps of Discovery," achieved more than anyone could have imagined, and in doing so opened the door to the West. Their success inaugurated the western fur trade when it was reported that they had traversed the richest beaver country in the nation. All of the colonial powers had been involved in the mass commercial exploitation of animal pelts and skins at one time or another. Competition between European nations and among Indian tribes for the fur trade was a major factor in many of the intertribal and colonial wars, including the French and Indian War. But when fur trading expanded into the Rocky Mountains in the 1820s, the old systems of fur trading became obsolete because the Indians in this region were unconcerned with trapping. Although the fur traders and mountain men left few journals, diaries, or maps, they laid the groundwork for future commerce, settlement, and emigration routes. Their contributions to the geographical and scientific knowledge of the West should not be underestimated.

People moved west for many different reasons. The gold seekers of 1849 were drawn by the lure of wealth. Irish and Chinese immigrants worked on the railroads and in the mines. Indians were forced west either by federal removal policies or by stronger Indian nations. Other groups, such as the Mormons, went west to escape the United States by settling in the remote reaches of Utah. And still others sought land for farming, slavery, and timber, or headed west because of climatic factors, as did the Dust Bowl farmers of the 1930s.

In the early nineteenth century the idea of moving the Indians west of the Mississippi began to take root in the minds of American leaders. American expansion during this period is inextricably linked with the life of Andrew Jackson, the first president from a "western" state. Jackson's policies during his presidency (1829–1837) resulted in the opening of new lands for settlement, but this time at the expense of Indian peoples rather than foreign nations. Following his first presidential address in 1829, Jackson supported the campaign to remove Indians from the Southeast to west of the Mississippi River in 1830.

The federal government had arbitrated several removal treaties prior to Jackson's Indian Removal Act of 1830. But the most infamous of the removals was that of the Five Civilized Tribes, which included the Choctaws, Creeks, Chickasaws, Cherokees, and Seminoles residing in Alabama, Georgia, Florida, and Mississippi. The Cherokees had taken the greatest steps toward assimilation in an attempt to escape removal. In addition to establishing a written alphabet and a constitution modeled after the U.S. Constitution, they created a newspaper, founded schools, and sometimes owned slaves. In 1831 they took their case to the U.S. Supreme Court, where Chief Justice John Marshall upheld their sovereignty as a separate nation, ruling in *Cherokee Nation v. Georgia* that the federal government had no right to remove them. Despite several rulings that favored the Cherokees, President Jackson and Georgia officials refused to honor the decisions, and in 1838 federal troops led the eviction of the Cherokee to lands west of the Mississippi River, in a forced march that became known as the Trail of Tears.

A substantial number of sympathetic Americans saw removal as the only way to save Indians from extinction and from the ravages of white diseases, poverty, and alcoholism. Others hoped to assimilate the Indians apart from white society as a way of preparing them for coexistence. Regardless of motivation, the overwhelming goal of removal was to take ancestral Indian lands, a pattern that would follow as Americans moved west. With each stage of westward expansion, immense areas of land and the Indian peoples of the region came under United States dominion. Whenever the process of admitting new territories and states to the Union was considered, Indians were given little if any say in the process. From the Louisiana Purchase to the annexation of Texas and the U.S.-Mexican War, each land acquisition only accelerated the pace of expansion.

During the first half of the nineteenth century, members of the Church of Jesus Christ of Latter-day Saints, better known as the Mormons, were persecuted for religious reasons and driven from New York to Ohio and then to Missouri and Illinois. After their founder, Joseph Smith, was assassinated in 1844, Brigham Young assumed Mormon leadership and led the Latter-day Saints across the continent, where they settled in the isolated valleys of northern Utah. Following the end of the U.S.-Mexican War, the Great Basin and its Mormon stronghold at Salt Lake City became part of the United States.

With the discovery of gold in California in 1848, the Mormon lands in Utah reaped the economic benefits from the overland traffic to California. Mormon settlers, skilled in the techniques of irrigation, had made this arid region prosper since their arrival in 1847, but were still considered squatters by the federal government. Until the United States opened up a land office in the Utah Territory in 1869, officials of the Mormon Church managed land distribution and settlement. By the end of the 1860s Mormon settlers sought to formalize their occupation of the Great Basin using procedures established by the Preemption Act (1841) and the Homestead Act (1862).

At the turn of the nineteenth century, today's Pacific Northwest was known as the Oregon Country. In the 1790s, no less than four nations laid claim to the region, including Spain, Great Britain, Russia, and the United States. Due to several international treaties, by 1825 only the United States and Great Britain controlled the territory, agreeing to "joint occupation," though in practice Americans confined their settlement and interests below the 54°40' line, which became the de facto border between the Americans and the British. It was not long before a congressional committee was exploring options to annex the territory before much of it fell under the domination of Great Britain, though few Americans thought that it would be worth going to war over the distant land at this point. Still, the public debate continued to resonate in the halls of Congress.

In the 1820s and 1830s American settlers began to trickle into the fertile Willamette Valley of Oregon. In 1836 Presbyterian and Congregationalist missionaries, including Marcus and Narcissa Whitman, made the overland journey, but missionaries like the Whitmans were better at attracting new settlers to the region than they were at converting Native Americans to Christianity. The lure of the West was partly a product of conditions in the East. During the panic of 1837 American farmers faced economic hardships due to plunging farm prices and land values. It was not long before emigrants began forming wagon trains and heading for the Pacific coast. While some went to California, the majority in the early 1840s targeted Oregon and its fertile alluvial soil. By 1845 more than 6,000 Americans had put down roots in the Willamette Valley.

In 1844 James K. Polk was elected president, running on an expansionist platform that called for the "re-annexation of Texas and the re-occupation of Oregon." One of his first acts was to ask Congress to approve the end of joint occupation of Oregon. However, with war about to break out on the Mexican border, Polk was in no position to back up the threat of "Fifty-Four Forty or Fight," referring to American claims to the territory. In June 1846, both sides worked out a compromise that settled on a boundary along the 49th parallel that extended to the Pacific coast. The resolution of the Oregon question brought 280,000 square miles of territory into the American domain. In August 1848, the Oregon Territory was formally authorized by Congress. Over the next two decades the territories of Washington, Idaho, Montana, and Wyoming would be carved out of the former British possessions.

During the mid-1840s the United States experienced its most rapid territorial expansion. Westward expansion and land acquisition in the 1840s was fueled by a variety of motives, rationalizations, and federal land policies. In 1845 journalist John L. O'Sullivan coined the phrase "manifest destiny," a slogan linked to the westward expansion of the era, when the United States annexed Texas, acquired Oregon from Great Britain, and purchased California and the Southwest from Mexico. Although it is not a sharply defined concept, inherent in the idea of manifest destiny is the notion that Americans were destined by divine providence to expand the national domain to its natural borders. This expansion was justified by rhetoric heralding American racial superiority that ultimately led to fateful consequences for non-Anglo cultures. American expansionists ignored Indian and Mexican land claims as well as countless treaties as they carved out an empire that would expand from coast to coast. The ideological underpinnings of expansionism had repercussions that would reverberate into the 1880s, when Californians led a successful campaign to end further Chinese immigration.

Prior to the U.S.-Mexican War (1846–1848), the Missouri Compromise line, established in 1820, determined which territories would be open for slavery. The nation at that time still responded to the American Revolutionary impetus to restrict the growth of slavery. All western territory north of the southern boundary of Missouri (36°30') would be "forever" closed to slavery, but the prohibition by implication left the area south of 36°30' open to slavery. At the time this line was drawn, most of the western lands south of the dividing line were owned by Spain. With Mexico's independence from Spain in 1821, the only way to open these lands for slavery was to acquire them somehow from Mexico.

In the early 1820s, white southerners began migrating into East Texas at the invitation of the Mexican government. With their slaves in tow, they transplanted the cotton culture of the Old South as best they could. But during the next decade, the immigrants, now known as Texicans, became increasingly restive under Mexican sovereignty, and in 1836 they rebelled, fighting the famous battles of the Alamo and San Jacinto, and declaring their independence from Mexico. The Texans won their independence but sought annexation by the United States. Congress refused to allow Texas into the Union as a slave state, fearing this would disrupt the Union by forcing the expansion of slavery into politics. For almost ten years, Texas existed as the independent Lone Star Republic. But Polk's election on an expansionist platform in 1844 opened the door to annexation. With American-Mexican relations deteriorating, Congress, by joint resolution of the two houses, moved ahead and finally approved the annexation of Texas in 1845.

Many northerners blamed the outbreak of war between Mexico and the United States in 1846 on the annexation of Texas, which they viewed as a proslavery conspiracy. The Texas Revolution of 1836 was prompted in part by the Mexican prohibition of slavery in Texas. Settled primarily by southern emigrants, Texas was, one observer remarked, an "Empire for Slavery." Many northerners viewed the subsequent aggressive diplomacy on the part of the Polk administration to secure the U.S. hold on Texas and acquire further land south of the 36°30' Missouri Compromise line, while settling for the 49th parallel as the border between the United States and British Canada in the Northwest, as part of a proslavery conspiracy by a slaveowning, proslavery southern president. Polk seemed willing to fight for territory open to slavery but not to do so for areas closed to it.

The year 1848 proved a seminal one in the history of westward expansion. James W. Marshall discovered gold in California in January, leading tens of thousands of Americans to uproot themselves and move to a part of the country that would otherwise have been left to native cultures or the most intrepid pioneers. A nation of farmers, there was little justification or reason for them to relocate or travel through the arid Great Plains and the even more arid and remote lands of the Far West. Even the best farming lands in valleys of central California and the Willamette Valley of Oregon drew few settlers prior to the Gold Rush. In February 1848, the war with Mexico ended when the vanquished nation ceded 1.2 million square miles of territory to the United States. Most gold seekers followed a central overland route, while others opted for more southern routes through northern Mexico. By the end of 1849, more than 80,000 Forty-Niners reached California.

Closely linked with the U.S.-Mexican War and the controversy over westward expansion was the issue of slavery. As noted above, many northerners and opponents of slavery's expansion into the western territories believed that slavery was the major cause of the war. Some critics even went as far as to claim that President Polk's administration deliberately followed a policy designed to acquire more territory for the slave states. During the war, northerners argued for a policy that would prevent expansion into the territories acquired from Mexico, while southerners demanded that these lands be open for slavery.

The debate continued in the years following the war, ultimately exacerbating the sectional tensions that would lead to the Civil War. The ratification of the Treaty of Guadalupe Hidalgo, ending the war with Mexico, dictated difficult terms to Mexico. And with it, President Polk achieved his objective of expanding American sovereignty to the Pacific Ocean. In return for payment of $15 million, Mexico ceded to the United States what today comprises the states (or parts thereof) of New Mexico, Arizona, California, Utah, Nevada, and Colorado.

The problem of slavery in the territories was finally addressed by the Compromise of 1850, which ended for a time the debate over the status of the new territories. Ultimately, California was admitted to the Union as free state, the sale of slaves was outlawed in Washington, D.C., a harsh federally enforced fugitive slave law was enacted, and the Utah and New Mexico territories were organized with popular sovereignty, meaning the voters in the territories could decide the issue of slavery.

Sectional politics proved an obstacle for other aspects of westward expansion, most notably the building of a transcontinental railroad. Between 1845 and 1852, legislation pertaining to the building of the transcontinental railroad was debated in both houses of Congress. Each region had its spokesman. Among the most outspoken proponents for a rail system linking the East with the West was Jefferson Davis, one of Mississippi's richest planters and a veteran of the U.S.-Mexican War. An engineer, a stalwart supporter of slavery, and the future president of the Confederacy, Davis wanted the eastern terminus of the railroad to be in the South. He knew well that whichever city achieved this objective would profit from the California trade and would become economically tied to the West. As an engineer, Davis argued that the best route was a southern one, with few major physical barriers or mountain ranges of consequence. However, here he allowed his sectional leanings to obscure the major problem with this route—the almost utter lack of water. Also, in order to keep the flat line that Jefferson Davis envisioned, the projected railroad would have to travel through Mexican territory. As secretary of war (the War Department directed the land surveys) under President Franklin Pierce (1853–1857), Davis sent railroad agent James Gadsden to Mexico City to purchase 30,000 square miles of land for $10 million, and Gadsden negotiated the purchase. Except for the purchase of Alaska in 1867, with the Gadsden Purchase in 1853 the United States had expanded to its present boundaries on the continent.

Davis never imagined that farming, let alone the plantation economy, could make the transition to the Great Plains—"the Great American Desert." Ever the military man, and as head of the War Department, Davis was primarily concerned at this point with having a source of transportation that would enable the rapid deployment of troops west in the event of hostilities with the Indians or threats from foreign powers to America's Pacific territory. Early explorers of the lands between the 98th meridian and the Rocky Mountains such as Zebulon Pike and Stephen Long compared this region to the Sahara Desert of North Africa. Because of their reports, mapmakers between the early 1800s and the 1860s distinguished this area of the Great Plains as the Great American Desert. For years this misnomer proved a barrier to western expansion. California-bound settlers and gold seekers added to the legend, describing the Great Plains in their many letters and journals as unfit for white settlement and traditional farming techniques.

The most prominent alternative to the southern railroad route was a central one, with its eastern terminus at Chicago. The proposed route would run through Iowa and across the Plains and then climb both the Sierra and Rocky Mountain ranges up to 8,000 feet before reaching the coast. It ran through part of the Louisiana Purchase that had never been organized as a territory. In May 1854, eager to organize the territory and establish the central route for a transcontinental railroad, Senator Stephen A. Douglas of Illinois proposed a plan that would create two new federal territories—Kansas and Nebraska. In doing so, Douglas allowed the issue of slavery and westward expansion once more to reach the national stage because the new territories were to be organized without prohibitions on slavery, which in effect opened land to slavery that had been "forever closed" to it in the Missouri Compromise. His solution to the expansion of slavery into federal territory was to allow territorial residents themselves to decide the issue. The passage in 1854 of what became known as the Kansas-Nebraska Act added more fuel to the fire that would ignite the Civil War seven years later. Hostility to the bill's provisions led to early bloodshed in Kansas, as settlers from proslavery Missouri and neighboring free states rushed into Kansas attempting to influence the outcome of the vote over slavery. Free-state men and proslavery factions established separate governments and organized militias, and in one of the most notorious examples of sectional violence in the West, the abolitionist John Brown and several followers hacked five proslavers to death near Pottawatomie Creek in 1856.

At the heart of the Kansas-Nebraska Act was Douglas's intention to connect the imminent transcontinental railroad to his home state of Illinois. He gave little consideration to the fact that this land had already been promised to Indian tribes just recently forcibly relocated from the East. In one fell swoop, the Kansas-Nebraska Act repealed the Missouri Compromise, upset the political balance between the North and the South, and created the Republican Party from Free Soilers, anti-Nebraska

Democrats, and former Whigs united to prevent any further extension of slavery into the territories.

The passage of the Kansas-Nebraska Act should have removed most objections to a central railroad. Northerners would never support a railroad that would tie the West to the South, but with the South holding the upper hand in Congress, the debate over which route to use would only be resolved in the 1860s, after the southern states seceded from the Union. Once southern opposition disappeared, the central route was easily approved by Congress.

By 1865 financing was in place, and the Union Pacific (from the West Coast) and the Central Pacific (from the Midwest) began the frantic race to see which could build the fastest, capture the most subsidies, and capture the most future commerce. Following the symbolic joining of the rails at Promontory, Utah, in 1869, transcontinental service began almost immediately, although much of the construction work was so shoddy most of the rails had to be relaid. In the rush to complete the railroad workers improperly laid the gravel and broken stones between and under railroad ties. This ballast gave stability, provided drainage, and helped distribute loads. The hastily built roadbeds collapsed, and curves that had been engineered too sharply derailed trains. Repairing the defective construction eventually cost almost $10 million and sent the railroads reeling into bankruptcy.

Poor construction notwithstanding, the Union Pacific lost no time in distributing posters advertising coast-to-coast travel, promising passengers the luxury of palace sleeping cars as they made the four-day trip from Omaha to San Francisco. The transcontinental railroad brought mining engineers and investment bankers to the Southwest, and proved the key ingredient for making the transition from preindustrial economic activity into a more modern technological era. The railroads changed the character of western settlement, as trains hauled products of western mines, farms, ranches, and forests directly to the East. In return, westerners gained access to the most recent eastern commodities. With railroad linkages spanning the continent, the West also hitched its fortunes to markets in both the Pacific and Atlantic commercial worlds.

By 1885 three more transcontinental railroads were in operation. By 1890 Kansas and Nebraska boasted populations of more than 1 million. Even the desert Arizona Territory saw its population grow to almost 100,000, before the advent of air conditioning. In many respects, the railroads filled the empty spaces and generated the population explosion. Railroads established land offices in major American cities and sent agents to Europe to recruit immigrants. To attract settlers to the most arid reaches of the Plains, railroad boosters produced lavish brochures heralding the Eden-like qualities of Kansas and the Dakotas, and railroad companies provided credit to prospective settlers.

The onset of the twentieth century witnessed one of the most vigorous campaigns of railroad expansion in the nation's history. It had been less than fifty years since the completion of the transcontinental railroad, yet between 1890 and 1917 railroad systems across America were already being reengineered and rebuilt, especially in the West.

The outbreak of the Civil War also removed southern obstacles to federal land sales policy. Beginning in the 1830s and 1840s, the sale of western lands to finance internal improvements was seen by many in Congress as a remedy to federal financial shortfalls. Cheap land sales would encourage westward expansion, and the money from those land sales would improve the national infrastructure. Southerners generally opposed the idea because they were convinced, and not without reason, that most of the improvements would take place in the North and the West, not in the South. In 1841 Congress had passed the Preemption Act over southern objections. The law allowed a prospective settler to stake out a land claim before the sale and then pay $1.25 per acre for the same land when the sale commenced. Proceeds would then be distributed to the states for internal improvements. The following year the distribution part of the law was repealed, but the preemption provisions continued, greatly accelerating the westward movement. Northern politicians competed for votes by promising lower land prices in the public domain. With the passage of the Homestead Act in 1862, any American citizen could stake out a claim to 160 acres of federal land, inaugurating an era of free land.

Westward expansion was not accomplished without violence and bloodshed. The classic image of western violence remains the clash of cultures between Indians and whites. Indeed, between 1840 and 1890, the West was the scene of more than sixty Indian wars. However, violence came in a variety of incarnations. The American West was the stage for vigilante activity, range wars, labor conflict, racial violence, and personal confrontations between young men carrying weapons and under the influence of alcohol.

In the early 1840s Indians aided overland pioneers on the western trails, with bloody conflict being the exception rather than the rule. Conflict between Indian and white settlers began in earnest after the passage of the Homestead Act, which added to the tensions as thousands competed for the shrinking Indian lands.

Although most of the western Indian wars began with the increased expansion following the American Civil War (1861–1865), conflict began soon after the Indian Removal Act of 1830, which established a "permanent" Indian frontier west of the Mississippi River. In 1836, after Texas declared itself an independent republic from Mexico, the Texas Rangers were organized to protect settlers from Comanche and Kiowa raiders, and in the West settlers and ranchers waged their own wars against Indian peoples. During the 1840s conflict intensified. Following the U.S.-Mexican War, federal troops clashed with the Navajo and Tiwa Indians in New Mexico, a region newly won from Mexico and now part of the United States. Fighting also broke out in the Pacific Northwest, in lands formerly shared with Great Britain, after the killing of the Whitmans and ten others in 1847.

During the 1850s white migration westward dramatically increased and war spread to most parts of the American West. Chiefly to blame for this was a rising tide of white emigration following the takeover of the Southwest from Mexico and the California Gold Rush. Accompanying westward expansion was an increased military presence, as forts and roads were built to protect the traders, trappers, and other entrepreneurs who followed American expansion.

Between 1865 and the Wounded Knee Massacre of 1890, the final stage of the Indian wars was acted out on the Great Plains and in the Southwest. During the Civil War, Indian warriors probably outnumbered white soldiers, particularly after many soldiers were pulled out of frontier forts to serve in the Civil War, fought mainly east of the Mississippi River. With the end of the Civil War, more troops were freed up to serve in the Indian wars.

Violence often overstepped the boundary between war and atrocity as fighting escalated in the 1860s. While massacres were carried out by both sides, and while whites made much of Custer's "Last Stand" at the Battle of the Little Big Horn in 1876, most often it was the Indians who took the brunt of the casualties. The Sand Creek Massacre in 1864 left more than 200 Indian men, women, and children butchered to death in eastern Colorado. And in one of the last violent episodes of the Indian wars, more than 150 Sioux were slaughtered at Wounded Knee, South Dakota, in 1890.

At the outbreak of the Civil War, half of the nation's land area was located in unsettled or sparsely populated territory in the West. Exceptions included the 440,000 people on the West Coast, 40,000 Mormons near the Great Salt Lake, and 94,000 mostly Spanish-speaking citizens in New Mexico. Settlers had barely spilled over the far boundaries of Minnesota, Iowa, Missouri, and Arkansas.

By the time the Homestead Act was passed in 1862, most of the arable lands in the trans-Mississippi West already had been claimed by speculators or granted to railroads. The 160-acre units provided by the act proved too small for the extensive type of farming required in the drier portions of the West. The only way successfully to cultivate the land in the arid regions was through irrigation. With the completion of the transcontinental railroad, land speculators and railroad builders convinced ranchers and farmers to relocate to the Great Plains and farther west to take advantage of the Homestead Act.

The late nineteenth century was a volatile era in western politics. During the 1880s and 1890s, farmers faced desperate conditions. A series of farming booms came to a crashing halt in a region extending down through Nebraska, Kansas, and Texas. Farm production often outpaced demand, which led to steadily falling crop prices. Tens of thousands of farmers had a difficult, if not impossible time making ends meet. In searching for culprits, farmers focused on eastern banks and railroads, which they felt exploited poor people. The farming collapse triggered the creation of the People's Party, a designation that would lead to the derivation "Populism." During the 1890s the Populist Party grew into the most significant third-party movement of its time.

Populist orators campaigned across the Great Plains. Mary Elizabeth Lease (1853–1933), who taught school, farmed, and then practiced law, made a particular impression on Kansas residents during her more than 150 speeches and with her slogan "What you farmers need is to raise less corn and more hell." Even more popular was Kansas Populist politician "Sockless Jerry" Simpson (1842–1905), whose wit and down-home humor led to three terms in Congress (1890, 1892, and 1896). When his opposition accused him of not wearing any socks and of being a country bumpkin, Simpson took advantage of this caricature. He was a skilled campaigner but a poor writer, and some observers believe he could have been a serious presidential candidate if he had not been born in Canada.

It took more than a bit of ingenuity for homesteaders to survive and flourish on the Great Plains. The sod house was one of the greatest adaptations made by settlers to the inhospitable environment. Settling in a region lacking wood, rock, and brick clay, early pioneers first borrowed features from Indian earth-covered lodges and English turf shelters. Over time they improved on this design. Plainsmen used special plows to cut the turf into blocks that became known in some areas as "Nebraska marble." In a day before air conditioning and central heating, sod houses were cheap (costing only pennies), cool in summer, warm in winter, and almost impervious to bullets, fire, and wind. Although sod houses were known to withstand even tornados, to many a settler's despair they also proved to be dark, leaky, smoky, and hospitable to bugs.

Nothing distinguished the western United States from the rest of the nation more than the region's lack of water. West of the 100th meridian, water was in short supply. Techniques of dry farming were developed on the Plains to utilize every drop of moisture in combination with especially sturdy strains of wheat. Introduced in the late nineteenth century, dry farming involved the conservation of soil moisture during dry weather by special tilling methods. The Mormons used this method to great success in Utah early on, although it reached an apogee of sorts in Nebraska, where Hardy W. Campbell, its most stalwart advocate, popularized the principles of dry farming. As the evangelistic voice of dry farming, Campbell recommended that farmers keep half their land fallow each year to accumulate moisture in packed undersoil. According to Campbell, dry farming was a "climate-free" system of land use, involving a cycle of deep plowing in the fall, packing the subsoil with an implement known as the subsurface packer, and then frequently stirring up a dust mulch.

Innovations such as dry farming ushered in an era of large-scale agriculture on the Great Plains. In 1909 Congress passed the Enlarged Homestead Act, by which settlers were given 320 acres. Thousands more farmers rushed to grab their share of the last agricultural frontier. Thousands of farmers from the Texas and Oklahoma panhandles as well as parts of Kansas, Colorado, and New Mexico were drawn west in a new wave of migration to improve economic prospects after World War I. According to historian Donald Worster, this "latest surge of settlement" between 1910 and the 1930s laid the groundwork for the Dust Bowl years on the horizon. Unlike earlier eras of farming, successful dry farming required big machines and new technology as one-crop farming (usually drought-resistant grains such as sorghum and hard winter wheat) became routine. For Dust Bowl authority Worster, "the new-style sodbuster was an expansionist, feeling all the old land hunger of an opportunity-seeking democrat, but adding an intense desire to make his new machines profitable that would have shocked Thomas Jefferson's agrarian idealism."[1]

Although boosters and pseudo-scientists promoted the adage that "rains follow the plow," the Dust Bowl of the 1930s would completely discredit the theory. The publication of John Wesley Powell's *Report on the Lands of the Arid Regions of the United States* in 1879 contended that agriculture would prove destructive to the semiarid lands, but his various recommendations went unheeded. His battle to reform land settlement laws often brought him into conflict with mining, cattle, and timber interests, who feared that land laws would bring an end to an era of exploitation. Powell seemed almost sagelike after a series of droughts, blizzards, and dust storms hit the region in the 1880s.

Millions of buffalo once roamed the Great Plains from southern Canada to Texas. The Plains Indians built their culture around the animal. But like the beaver in the 1820s, a fashion craze signaled the destruction of the great buffalo herds. This time, instead of the beaver hat being all the rage, hunters targeted buffalo hides for coats. Hunters reduced the buffalo population from almost 10 million in 1800 to less than 10,000 in 1900. The decimation of the buffalo also spelled the end of Plains Indian culture.

Attempts were made to reverse the environmental destruction of the West beginning in 1872, with the creation of the world's first national park at Yellowstone. America seemed to have finally reversed course by introducing the concept of protecting unique natural "monuments" and environments from commercial exploitation after generations of plundering the wilderness. Wilderness conservation became increasingly politicized in the decades following the creation of Yellowstone National Park.

The twentieth century was particularly fraught with battles over federal land and wilderness policy, and the increased access to the West in the automobile and airplane culture of the post–World War II era added to physical stresses on the land and led to more conflict in politics. No uniform environmental policy emerged. But the organization of new "pro-environment" interest groups and the expanded influence of older ones such as the Sierra Club in the 1970s and afterward ensured that oil, mining, and timber interests would not go unchallenged.

The West became the battleground of national environmental policy. In 1981 President Ronald Reagan appointed anti-environmentalist James G. Watt as secretary of the interior. During his two-year tenure as caretaker of the American wilderness, public lands came under rapid development and public resources were sold at bargain prices. Environmental groups rallied opposition and made the environment a major political issue in the 1980s.

During the last decades of the twentieth century an increasing number of environmental controversies over public lands in the West became inextricably linked to political partisanship. In 1996, for example, President William Clinton used the Antiquities Act of 1906, intended to protect native artifacts and sacred grounds, to declare 1.7 million acres of south central Utah the Grand Staircase-Escalante Monument, making it the largest national park in the contiguous forty-eight states. Almost immediately Republican opponents proclaimed this action an abuse of federal power. Senator Orrin Hatch (R-UT) favored an acreage limitation to any future presidential national monument proclamation. Also vocal in their dissent were developers who considered the park home to the nation's largest unmined coal reserve. Among the president's supporters was a link to the recent past, as Theodore Roosevelt IV, representing the National Parks and Conservation Association, argued in favor of preserving the presidential authority to create national monuments.

No region of the United States escaped the Great Depression unscathed. This era coincided with a persistent drought made worse by poor farming techniques and overgrazing on the Plains. In the 1930s it became clear that western problems could not all be resolved through state or regional action alone. It would take the intervention of the federal government to lead the sector back to prosperity. For a region so identified with rugged individualism, it came as a shock to many that the West had become reliant on the government dole.

Before 1934 the grazing capacity of the open rangelands was rapidly being diminished because of overgrazing and poor management. Congress stepped in and withdrew much of this land from public domain status. With the passage of the conservation-oriented Taylor Grazing Act of 1934, the federal government removed 142 million acres of western lands from future speculation and placed them under federal control. The new policy ended land sales and homesteading on much of the Great Plains, as the land came under the bureaucratic stewardship of the federal government. Thus began a new era in which the public domain was placed under federal management instead of being for sale to the highest bidder.

The onset of the Great Depression left no segment of society untouched. Western Mexican American communities were particularly hard hit, since their residents were typically the first to be fired and the last to be hired in hard economic times. Like other immigrant groups before them, Mexican Americans were targeted by repatriation drives. Such employment opportunities as Mexicans and Mexican Americans had in the West were typically as seasonal agricultural laborers. Mexican labor produced a significant percentage of twentieth-century harvests. During World War II, a labor shortage in agricultural and wartime industries led to the Bracero Program, in which Mexican labor was imported to American farms on a contract basis. Farmers were so dependent on this system that it continued after the war ended.

The New Deal (1933–1943) saw a dramatic shift of federal dollars to the western states. Among the many programs targeting the western states were dam building projects and the construction of courthouses and other public structures. Among the most prominent New Deal programs was the Civilian Conservation Corps, most of whose work of resource conservation was done in the West.

Dam building was given greater urgency in the 1930s. Dam construction on the Colorado and Columbia Rivers helped supply electricity to produce ships and planes for the American war effort. In 1936 Boulder Dam was completed on the Colorado River, and five years later the Grand Coulee Dam, which was for a time the world's largest hydroelectric installation, began operating on the Columbia River. Western dams not only altered the landscape, but also provided the growing urban populations in the West with water supplies, hydroelectric power, flood control, and recreation facilities. The control of water opened much new area to settlement after World War II.

At the dawning of the twentieth century, the West was undergoing growing pains along with the rest of the nation. One of the West's greatest strengths and sources of vitality has always been its multicultural population. With Chinese, Japanese, and African American newcomers joining the hundreds of different native cultures, including

Mexicans and Mexican Americans, the West seemed as much a melting pot of cultures as the East.

Racialism once more entered western politics in the 1940s after the Japanese attack on Pearl Harbor. Believing that Japanese Americans posed a threat to national security, President Franklin Roosevelt ordered the 100,000 Japanese Americans who were living on the Pacific Coast to be removed inland to detention camps.

Following World War II, technology and immigration transformed the West as never before. The invention and mass marketing of air conditioning enabled large population centers such as Phoenix, Arizona, to flourish in inhospitable climates. Wartime industries subsidized by the federal government launched western state economies into an era of unprecedented growth. But many of the technological advances that allowed life in the West to prosper contained the seeds of environmental and human catastrophe. Unlike gold and silver mining in years past, uranium prospecting and nuclear testing brought the threat of cancer to communities in proximity to atomic test zones. Pesticides that helped agriculture flourish have been linked to higher mortality rates and increased health risks among farm workers.

Between 1940 and 1970 some 20 million people relocated to the Far West. Demonstrating a significant shift in population, in 1963 California surpassed New York as the nation's most populous state. By the early 1960s, between 250,000 and 500,000 people lived in cities as disparate as Salt Lake City, Tucson, Albuquerque, and Omaha. Phoenix, Denver, and Oklahoma City boasted more than a half million inhabitants each.

In the postwar era immigrants from the Northeast and Snow Belt states came west to live in the burgeoning cities of what became known as the Sun belt. California received the lion's share of population (22.7 million) between 1970 and 1980, while millions more flocked to Texas, Arizona, and New Mexico. These newcomers moved into urban centers with more than 1 million inhabitants in the West, but they also staked out new lives in mountain "retreats," desert "ranches," and suburban areas sprawling everywhere. The migration continued into the 1990s as many Anglo Americans and Asian immigrants moved into the traditionally Hispanic Southwest, creating a New West that was more Spanish, Asian, and African American, and less Anglo.

Looking back at westward expansion from a twenty-first-century vantage point provides a tantalizing contrast with the past to the student of western history. Not long ago Native Americans and buffalo, the two most indelible symbols of the American West, were supposedly headed toward extinction. If one were to look at the Great Plains today, it would seem that the reverse was true. According to the 2000 census, the white population of the Great Plains—from eastern Montana and North Dakota down through the semiarid reaches of South Dakota, Nebraska,

Kansas, Oklahoma, and West Texas—has been shrinking. In some counties, population depletion since the early twentieth century has been so dramatic that much of the terrain has no human habitation. Accompanying the dramatic decrease in Anglo population is a tremendous increase in the Native American population, rising by 200 percent. As if fulfilling a prophecy from the Ghost Dance era, today, along with the jump in the Indian population, perhaps 300,000 bison now graze the Plains, reaching numbers not seen since the early 1870s. The West remains ever changing and changeful.

NOTE

1. Donald Worster, *Dust Bowl: The Southern Plains in the 1930s* (New York: Oxford University Press, 1979), p. 87.

2

Lewis and Clark and the Louisiana Purchase: Government-Sponsored Expeditions to Western Lands

The Lewis and Clark expedition (1804–1806) became the most famous exploratory undertaking in American history. By opening "the West" to settlement and commerce, it had a tremendous impact on the western Indian nations, the fur trade, and the future of the American West. More important, by bringing back accounts and specimens of the previously "unknown" West beyond the wide Missouri River and by mapping their routes, Lewis and Clark opened the Far West to the American imagination. But the expedition was not an isolated venture. Its significance was also derived from its relationship to government. The expedition was a government-sponsored effort to know and claim the West, and the success of the Lewis and Clark expedition led the government to sponsor other forays across a wide expanse. Armed with knowledge from such efforts, the United States reached across the continent to build an American empire. Over the nineteenth century, the federal government shaped American territorial boundaries through land purchases, treaties, annexation, and warfare.

The author and strategist of the Lewis and Clark expedition, President Thomas Jefferson, had considered the prospect of a water route across the continent since the 1780s. Jefferson demonstrated great foresight in his interest in the Far West at a time when few of his contemporaries took notice. Since the sixteenth century quixotic explorers had yearned for such a route, but had little success. As secretary of state in the 1790s, Jefferson had twice tried to send out transcontinental expeditions, but it was not until his ascendence to the presidency in 1801 that he would have the opportunity to act on his interest.

In a secret message to Congress for support on January 18, 1803, Jefferson noted that the appropriations for the proposed expedition were "for a venture whose meaning and propriety were then and still remain uncertain." These expenditures were unprecedented, particularly for a fledgling nation still grappling with financial problems. However, for Jefferson and his supporters the commercial, military, and scientific rewards that were anticipated would more than make up for the initial hostility to the expedition by some congressmen and others who doubted the legality or logic of such a new errand into the wilderness.

At the time Jefferson petitioned Congress for funding to send an expedition to the Pacific in January 1803, Louisiana still belonged to France, while Great Britain, Spain, Russia, and the United States claimed the Pacific Northwest. The United States was already one of the world's largest nations by the nineteenth century, and few could have predicted the scope of its expansion in the next half century. When Jefferson became president he brought with him his republican vision of a land of small independent farmers. According to his idea, the East and the West would be intertwined in a market and transportation network. Crucial to this market was control of the Mississippi River, which in 1800 still resided in Spanish lands, and then in 1801 was acquired by France, a more dangerous imperial power than Spain. Even after the United States bought the territory from France, few had any idea whether the lands could sustain Jefferson's agricultural vision. Jefferson was apparently aware that the purchase did not extend to the Pacific Ocean, but ever the naturalist, he wondered whether the South American llamas or great hulking mammoths might still exist in this wilderness unknown to the white man. To help find out, Jefferson commissioned Meriwether Lewis (1774–1809) to mount an expedition across the continent.

Lewis had been a frontiersman and river boatman on the Georgia frontier while still in his teens. Well educated and a friend and neighbor of Thomas Jefferson, Lewis shared many of the president's interests, particularly about the American West. Lewis was living in Jefferson's house, serving as his secretary in 1802, when they received word that the British fur trader Alexander Mackenzie had completed the first transcontinental trip to the Pacific Ocean in the 1790s. Reading Mackenzie's published account galvanized Jefferson into action. Concerned with British presence in the northwestern territories, two decades after the end of the American Revolution, Jefferson recognized that Mackenzie's route across Canada would not immediately jeopardize American interests. What did concern the president was the fur trader's recommendation to the British to open a series of trading posts across the West in order to seize the initiative in controlling trade between the Atlantic and Pacific Oceans.

Hoping to beat the British in this endeavor, Jefferson dispatched an American expedition ahead of them to find an all-water route to the Pacific. Jefferson selected Lewis, who then enlisted William Clark (1770–1838), to lead a Corps of Discovery from St. Louis to the Pacific Ocean and back. The subsequent 8,000-mile, twenty-eight-month journey did much more than explore the western lands. The ever-inquisitive Jefferson charged the expedition with a multitude of goals, which included acquiring as much information as possible about the Indian tribes, minerals, geography, topography, flora and fauna, and climate of the lands they traversed. Not only did Jefferson want to break the British orientation of the Indian tribes, but he wanted to find out whether the lands had the ability to support a large population. In order to prepare them for the trek, Jefferson sent Lewis to Philadelphia, where some of the nation's finest minds would give him a crash course in map-making, botany, anatomy, and astronomy.

To finance the journey, Jefferson had to win congressional approval for the unprecedented expenditure. According to popular knowledge the Lewis and Clark expedition was conceived as a sequel to the Louisiana Purchase. In fact, it was the converse, in that Jefferson was still deep in negotiations with the French to purchase the Louisiana Territory at the time he proposed the expedition to Congress.

The purchase followed almost twenty years of diplomatic intrigue with powerful neighbors in the Mississippi Valley (first the Spanish and then the French) as well as the British to the north as these nationalities played an endgame for control of the western territories. As secretary of state in 1790, Jefferson offered American assistance if England sent a force down the Mississippi River from the Great Lakes to take New Orleans from Spain. Jefferson's foresight won accommodations from the Spanish in Florida and Louisiana to checkmate England's moves in the West.

The Lewis and Clark expedition and the Louisiana Purchase were precipitated by a number of factors besides Jefferson's foresight. Frontier pressures on the federal government increased dramatically between 1790 and 1800 as western pioneers looked increasingly to the Mississippi River to transport produce and other goods via the Gulf of Mexico to the Atlantic Ocean to markets in Europe and in the eastern states. In these years the population of Kentucky alone rose from 73,677 to 220,955. In the last decade of the eighteenth century the non-Indian population of the entire Old Northwest was about 3,000. Ten years later the non-Indian population of Ohio alone had reached 43,365. As the Mississippi River became an economic lifeline for the burgeoning population along the river by the late eighteenth century, there were fears in the West that the Spanish, who then owned Louisiana, could block access to the great river. The French Revolution and the emergence of Napoleon led to a treaty between Spain and France by which Louisiana was ceded to France in 1801 with the promise that France would not sell the land to a third party. With the looming outbreak of war between Great Britain and France, and his dreams of an American empire shattered by the Haitian revolt, Napoleon decided to sell the territory to the United States to get money for his European ambitions and to keep Louisiana out of British hands.

By the time Lewis and Clark pushed off on the Missouri River, Louisiana had become American territory, more than doubling the size of the country. But the exact boundaries of the Louisiana Purchase and the nature and prospects of its lands and resources remained unknown. The Lewis and Clark expedition would be the first of several government-sponsored efforts to chart the expanse of the new acquisition—828,000 square miles of territory between the Mississippi River and the Rocky Mountains that contained lands that would later form Missouri, Nebraska, Iowa, Arkansas, North Dakota, South Dakota, Kansas, Minnesota, Montana, Wyoming, Oklahoma, and parts of Colorado and Louisiana. The purchase of these lands ignited an expansionist psyche among the American people and removed the presence of strong powers on much of the western frontier.

The members of the Lewis and Clark expedition reflected the demographics of the early nineteenth-century frontier. The expedition was probably the most racially diverse exploration party of its time; included among its number was the Shoshone woman Sacajawea, Clark's slave York, and an assortment of American soldiers, French trappers, and *meti* guides, who were of mixed Indian and French ancestry. Although more than forty men participated in the initial ascent of the Missouri River, besides Lewis and Clark, only twenty-seven served as permanent members of the Corps of Discovery. Seven members of the expedition kept journals during the journey, while Lewis and Clark studied Indian tribes, arranged trade agreements, asserted the government's influence, offered gifts, and recorded manners and customs. They would identify 300 new plants and animals and would come back with drawings, maps, and field notes that would help other subsequent expeditions. One of the greatest wonders of the expedition was that in an era of rather primitive medical knowledge only one man died. But he might have perished from the ruptured appendix even if he had stayed in Philadelphia.

When the Corps of Discovery returned to St. Louis on September 23, 1806, almost everyone had given up hope that they were still alive. Despite encountering hundreds if not thousands of Indians on the trip, there was little hostility between the Corps and the various native peoples they met. According to the explorers' accounts, they had only one violent encounter, which resulted in the deaths of two Indians.

Although the Lewis and Clark expedition ended up costing more than fifteen times the original estimate of $2,500, its success inaugurated an era of federally funded exploration and expansion. The government-sponsored expeditions of the early 1800s both heightened and dampened the American resolve to expand westward. Historian William Goetzmann has suggested that, contrary to the myth of rugged frontiersmen, a large part of the exploration of the West was conducted under federal sponsorship beginning with the Lewis and Clark expedition. Over the following half century, government support of scientific exploration in the trans-Mississippi West led to extensive land acquisitions beyond the boundaries of Louisiana, the annexation of Texas, and war with Mexico.

Prior to the return of the Lewis and Clark expedition, President Jefferson had dispatched a second major exploring party into the Far West, under the command of Zebulon Pike, in 1805. Pike undertook two expeditions, in 1805 and 1806. Anxious to justify to Congress and the nation his purchase of the Louisiana lands, Jefferson selected Pike to explore the unknown lands between the Arkansas and Red Rivers, make peace with Indian tribes, select hospitable sites for military posts, and find out to what extent British fur traders were still occupying lands recently acquired from France.

During Pike's second expedition, his force of twenty-three men was arrested by Spanish troops when it crossed the border into Spanish lands. Pike's men were taken first to Santa Fe and then into Mexico. Escorted by Spanish soldiers back and forth through Spanish territory, they were inadvertently enlightened by their captors about the Spanish Southwest, military installations, and potential business opportunities. The Americans were eventually turned loose on the Red River. Although many of Pike's notes were confiscated, he and his men kept miniature diaries and notes which they hid inside their gun barrels. Pike later wrote a widely disseminated report on his expedition, by which he did much to create one of the most influential myths of the early American West, namely, that the western Great Plains as Stephen Long later called it, was a "Great American Desert." Pike compared the central plains of North America to the deserts of North Africa, describing them as incapable of cultivation. Other observers of the Plains echoed Pike's term and fixed the image of a trackless barren plain in the American mind. Pike did make keen observations as to the commercial opportunities that would soon be gained by the Santa Fe trade. From a modern perspective it is easy to criticize Pike and others for creating the image of the "American Desert." But, given the agricultural know-how of the early 1800s, there were few if any opportunities for settlement in a land without timber, fuel, and surface water, and before the invention of water pumps and light windmills. Recent historians suggest that the Dust Bowl and other calamities of the twentieth century may lend some credence to the claims of the early explorers as well.

In 1820 the federal government dispatched a new expedition under Major Stephen H. Long to find the source of the Red River. Long failed in his pursuit, but his journey left an indelible impression on him of a land so barren it could never be suitable for settlement. His report, together with Pike's impressions, served to dissuade settlers from occupying the Far West for a generation. But subsequent expeditions would cast doubts on these views.

The pace of federal exploration increased during the 1840s, stimulated by the imperialist zeal of the period together with the search for a suitable transcontinental railroad route. The reorganization of the army's Corps of Topographical Engineers in 1838 saw scientific goals merge with expansionist ones that included not only noting natural resources and Indian cultures, but also gathering information that would help accommodate settlers in the Far West. In this phase of exploration, explorers and scientists were often under military sponsorship.

Although Lewis and Clark never found Jefferson's much sought after all-water route to the Pacific, nor the agricultural lands that would support a land of yeoman farmers, the Corps of Discovery stimulated interest among fur traders and others. In the process they accumulated a huge store of scientific, geographical, and anthropological knowledge and laid the groundwork for America's claim to the Oregon Territory. The fur trappers and traders who followed trails blazed by Lewis and Clark, Pike, Long, and others would themselves add to the growing knowledge of the American West and made possible trade and more sustained contact with it.

By 1821 a road was opened from St. Louis to Santa Fe to Chihuahua, Mexico, to feed the clamor for American goods in the Southwest following Mexico's independence from Spain. In the process the Santa Fe trade became an important outlet for American manufacturers. Although most of the trappers and traders from this era did not keep written records, their efforts opened up the heart of the Rockies and the Great Salt Lake region, trails to California, and routes to much of the Southwest, and information and goods traveled together.

Initially, Jefferson was seen as breaking the law with the Louisiana Purchase. As the nation's first territorial purchase, it set a precedent for how the new government under the U.S. Constitution should acquire new lands and in the process opened the door into the heart of the West. The purchase of Louisiana and the Lewis and Clark expedition were an overture to an era of expansion in the 1840s that would drastically alter the history of the American West.

DOCUMENTS

2.1.   Objection to the Purchase of Louisiana (1803)

The following argument by a United States senator against the purchase of the Louisiana Territory accompanied similar discussions concerning westward expansion during the nineteenth century. The senator expresses concerns that the settlers in the Louisiana Territory will be so far from Washington, D.C., that they will become alienated enough to form closer connections with other nations and trading partners. The lack of foresight by the senator was indicative of the westward expansion policy of the early nineteenth century, which was predicated on Indian and commercial policies.

I wish not to be understood as predicting that the French will not cede to us the actual and quiet possession of the territory. I hope to God they may, for possession of it we must have—I mean of New Orleans, and of such other positions on the Mississippi as may be necessary to secure to us forever the complete and uninterrupted navigation of that river. This I have ever been in favor of; I think it essential to the peace of the United States, and to the prosperity of our Western country. But as to Louisiana, this new, immense, unbounded world, if it should ever be incorporated into this Union, which I have no idea can be done but by altering the Constitution, I believe it will be the greatest curse that could at present befall us; it may be productive of innumerable evils, and especially of one that I fear even to look upon. Gentlemen on all sides, with very few exceptions, agree that the settlement of this country will be highly injurious and dangerous to the United States; but as to what has been suggested of removing the Creeks and other nations of Indians from the eastern to the western banks of the Mississippi, and of making the fertile regions of Louisiana a howling wilderness, never to be trodden by the foot of civilized man, it is impracticable.... you had as well pretend to inhibit the fish from swimming in the sea as to prevent the population of that country after its sovereignty shall become ours. To every man acquainted with the adventurous, roving, and enterprising temper of our people, and with the manner in which our Western country has been settled, such an idea must be chimerical. The inducements will be so strong that it will be impossible to restrain our citizens from crossing the river. Louisiana must and will become settled, if we hold it, and with the very population that would otherwise occupy part of our present territory. Thus our citizens will be removed to the immense distance of two or three thousand miles from the capital of the Union, where they will scarcely ever feel the rays of the General Government; their affections will become alienated; they will gradually begin to view us as strangers; they will form other commercial connexions, and our interests will become distinct.

These, with other causes that human wisdom may not now foresee, will in time effect a separation, and I fear our bounds will be fixed nearer to our houses than the waters of the Mississippi. . . . And I do say that under existing circumstances, even supposing that this extent of territory was a desirable acquisition, fifteen millions of dollars was a most enormous sum to give. Our Commissioners were negotiating in Paris—they must have known the relative situation of France and England—they must have known at the moment that a war was unavoidable between the two countries, and they knew the pecuniary necessities of France and the naval power of Great Britain. These imperious circumstances should have been turned to our advantage, and if we were to purchase, should have lessened the consideration.

Source: *Annals of Congress*, 8th Congress, 1st session (Washington, DC: Gales and Seaton, 1852), pp. 31–58.

2.2.   Debate over Constitutionality of Louisiana Purchase (1803)

One of the main debates over the Louisiana Purchase revolved around the constitutionality of purchasing lands from other nations. By purchasing this vast territory, President Jefferson had greatly expanded the powers of the executive office. Since the end of the American Revolution, first the Confederation, and then the United States, was determined to secure free navigation on the Mississippi River. Supporters of the purchase saw this as essential for the survival and expansion of the new nation. Whoever controlled the river had access to the important port of New Orleans. In the following excerpt, Senator John Breckinridge of Kentucky supports the purchase, basing his argument on the "uninterrupted use of the Mississippi [River]," countering the argument of Uriah Tracy of Connecticut that Congress "may acquire territory . . . but cannot incorporate it into the Union."

SENATOR BRECKINRIDGE.—No gentleman has yet ventured to deny that it is incumbent on the United States to secure to the citizens of the western waters the uninterrupted use of the Mississippi. Under this impression of duty what has been the conduct of the General Government, and particularly of the gentlemen now in the opposition, for the last eight months? When the right of deposit was violated by a Spanish officer without authority from his government, these gentlemen considered our national honor so deeply implicated, and the rights of the western people so wantonly violated, that no atonement or redress was admissible, except through the medium of the bayonet. Negotiation was scouted at. It was deemed pusillanimous, and was said to exhibit a want of fellow-feeling for the western people, and a disregard to their essential rights. Fortunately for their country the counsel of these gentlemen was rejected, and their war measures negatived. The so much scouted process of negotiation was, however, persisted in, and, instead of restoring the right of deposit and securing more effectually for the future our right to navigate the Mississippi, the Mississippi itself was acquired, and everything which appertained to it. I did suppose that those gentlemen who, at the last session, so strongly urged war measures for the attainment of this object, upon an avowal that it was too important to trust to the tardy and less effectual process of negotiation, would have stood foremost in carrying the treaty into effect, and that the peaceful mode by which it was acquired would not lessen with them the importance of the acquisition.

Permit me to examine some of the principal reasons which are deemed so powerful by gentlemen as to induce them to vote for the destruction of this treaty. Unfortunately for the gentlemen, no two of them can agree on the same set of objections; and, what is still more unfortunate, I believe there is no two of them concur in any one objection. In one thing only they seem to agree, and that is to vote against the bill. An honorable gentleman from Delaware [Mr. White] considered the price to be enormous. An honorable gentleman from Connecticut, who has just sat down [Mr. Tracy], says he has no objection whatever to the price; it is, he supposes, not too much. An honorable gentleman from Massachusetts [Mr. Pickering] says that France acquired no title from Spain, and therefore our title is bad. The same gentleman from Connecticut [Mr. Tracy] says he has no objection to the title of France; he thinks it a good one. The gentleman from Massachusetts [Mr. Pickering] contends that the United States cannot, under the Constitution, acquire foreign territory. The gentleman from Connecticut is of a different opinion, and has no doubt but that the United States can acquire and hold foreign territory; but that Congress alone have the power of incorporating that territory into the Union. Of what weight, therefore, ought all their lesser objections be entitled to when they are at war among themselves on the greater one?

The same gentleman has told us that this acquisition will, from its extent, soon prove destructive to the Confederacy.

This is an old and hackneyed doctrine: that a republic ought not to be too extensive. But the gentleman has assumed two facts and then reasoned from them: First, that the extent is too great; and, secondly, that the country will be soon populated. I would ask, sir, what is his standard extent for a republic? How does he come at that standard? Our boundary is already extensive. Would his standard extent be violated by including the island of Orleans and the Floridas? I presume not, as all parties seem to think their acquisition, in part or in whole, essential. Why not, then, acquire territory on the west as well as on the east side of the Mississippi? Is the Goddess of Liberty restrained by water courses? Is she governed by geographical limits? Is her dominion on this continent confined to the east side of the Mississippi? So far from believing in the doctrine that a Republic ought to be confined within narrow limits, I believe, on the contrary, that the more extensive its dominion the more safe and more durable it will be. In proportion to the number of hands you intrust the precious blessings of a free government to, in the same proportion do you multiply the chances for their preservation. I entertain, therefore, no fears for the Confederacy on account of its extent.

The gentleman from Connecticut [Mr. Tracy] admits explicitly that Congress may acquire territory and hold it as a territory, but cannot incorporate it into the Union. By this construction he admits the power to acquire territory, a modification infinitely more dangerous than the unconditional admission of a new State; for, by his construction, territories and citizens are considered and held as the property of the Government of the United States, and may consequently be used as dangerous engines in the hands of the Government against the States and people.

The same gentleman, in reply to the observations which fell from the gentleman from South Carolina as to the admission of new States, observes that, although Congress may admit new States, the President and Senate, who are but a component part, cannot. Apply this doctrine to the case before us. How could Congress by any mode of legislation admit this country into the Union until it was acquired? And how can this acquisition be made except through the treaty-making power? Could the gentleman rise in his place and move for leave to bring in a bill for the purchase of Louisiana and its admission into the Union? I take it that no transaction of this or any other kind with a foreign power can take place except through the executive department, and that in the form of a treaty, agreement, or convention. When the acquisition is made Congress can then make such disposition of it as may be expedient.

Source: Marion Mills Miller, ed., *Great Debates in American History*, Vol. 2 (New York: Current Literature Publishing Co., 1913), pp. 108–110.

2.3.   President Thomas Jefferson's Directions to Meriwether Lewis (1803)

In June 1803, President Jefferson signed the following letter to Meriwether Lewis, detailing the goals of his mission to explore the Louisiana Territory. By this time Jefferson knew that these lands belonged to the United States and could be more open about his plans for commercial development and trade with Asia.

Your mission has been communicated to the ministers here from France, Spain, and Great Britain, and through them to their governments; and such assurances given them as to its objects, as we trust will satisfy them. The country of Louisiana having been ceded by Spain to France, the passport you have from the minister of France, the representative of the present sovereign of the country, will be a protection with all its subjects; and that from the minister of England will entitle you to the friendly aid of any traders of that allegiance with whom you may happen to meet.

The object of your mission is to explore the Missouri river, and such principal streams of it, as, by its course and communication with the waters of the Pacific ocean, whether the Columbia, Oregan, Colorado, or any other river, may offer the most direct and practicable water-communication across the continent, for the purposes of commerce.

Beginning at the mouth of the Missouri, you will take observations of latitude and longitude, at all remarkable points on the river, and especially at the mouths of rivers, at rapids, at islands, and other places and objects distinguished by such natural marks and characters, of a durable kind, as that they may with certainty be recognised hereafter. The courses of the river between these points of observation may be supplied by the compass, the log-line, and by time, corrected by the observations themselves. The variations of the needle, too, in different places, should be noticed.

The interesting points of the portage between the heads of the Missouri, and of the water offering the best communication with the Pacific ocean, should also be fixed by observation; and the course of that water to the ocean, in the same manner as that of the Missouri.

Your observations are to be taken with great pains and accuracy; to be entered distinctly and intelligibly for others as well as yourself; to comprehend all the elements necessary, with the aid of the usual tables, to fix the latitude and longitude of the places at which they were taken; and are to be rendered to the war-office, for the purpose of having the calculations made concurrently by proper persons within the United States. Several copies of these, as well as of your other notes, should be made at leisure times, and put into the care of the most trust worthy of your attendants to guard, by multiplying them against the accidental losses to which they will be exposed. A further guard would be, that one of these copies be on the cuticular membranes of the paper-birch, as less liable to injury from damp than common paper.

The commerce which may be carried on with the people inhabiting the line you will pursue, renders a knowledge of those people important. You will therefore endeavour to make yourself acquainted, as far as a diligent pursuit of your journey shall admit, with the names of the nations and their numbers;

The extent and limits of their possessions;

Their relations with other tribes or nations;

Their language, traditions, monuments;

Their ordinary occupations in agriculture, fishing, hunting, war, arts, and the implements for these;

Their food, clothing, and domestic accommodations:

The diseases prevalent among them, and the remedies they use;

Moral and physical circumstances which distinguish them from the tribes we know;

Peculiarities in their laws, customs, and dispositions;

And articles of commerce they may need or furnish, and to what extent.

And, considering the interest which every nation has in extending and strengthening the authority of reason and justice among the people around them, it will be useful to acquire what knowledge you can of the state of morality, religion, and information among them; as it may better enable those who may endeavour to civilize and instruct them, to adapt their measures to the existing notions and practices of those on whom they are to operate.

Other objects worthy of notice will be—

The soil and face of the country, its growth and vegetable productions, especially those not of the United States;

The animals of the country generally, and especially those not known in the United States;

The remains and accounts of any which may be deemed rare or extinct;

The mineral productions of every kind, but more particularly metals, lime-stone, pit-coal, and saltpetre; salines and mineral waters, noting the temperature of the last, and such circumstances as may indicate their character;

Volcanic appearances;

Climate, as characterized by the thermometer, by the proportion of rainy, cloudy, and clear days; by lightning, hail, snow, ice; by the access and recess of frost; by the winds prevailing at different seasons; the dates at which particular plants put forth, or lose their flower or leaf; times of appearance of particular birds, reptiles or insects.

Although your route will be along the channel of the Missouri, yet you will endeavour to inform yourself, by inquiry, of the character and extent of the country watered by its branches, and especially on its southern side. The North river, or Rio Bravo, which runs into the gulf of Mexico, and the North river, or Rio Colorado, which runs into the gulf of California, are understood to be the principal streams heading opposite to the waters of the Missouri, and running southwardly. Whether the dividing grounds between the Missouri and them are mountains or flat lands, what are their distance from the Missouri, the character of the intermediate country, and the people inhabiting it, are worthy of particular inquiry. The northern waters of the Missouri are less to be inquired after, because they have been ascertained to a considerable degree, and are still in a course of ascertainment by English traders and travellers; but if you can learn any thing certain of the most northern source of the Missisipi, and of its position relatively to the Lake of the Woods, it will be interesting to us. Some account too of the path of the Canadian traders from the Missisipi, at the mouth of the Ouisconsing to where it strikes the Missouri, and of the soil and rivers in its course, is desirable.

In all your intercourse with the natives, treat them in the most friendly and conciliatory manner which their own conduct will admit; allay all jealousies as to the object of your journey; satisfy them of its innocence; make them acquainted with the position, extent, character, peaceable and commercial dispositions of the United States; of our wish to be neighbourly, friendly, and useful to them, and of our dispositions to a commercial intercourse with them; confer with them on the points most convenient as mutual emporiums, and the articles of most desirable interchange for them and us. If a few of their influential chiefs, within practicable distance, wish to visit us, arrange such a visit with them, and furnish them with authority to call on our officers on their entering the United States, to have them conveyed to this place at the public expense. If any of them should wish to have some of their young people brought up with us, and taught such arts as may be useful to them, we will receive, instruct, and take care of them. Such a mission, whether of influential chiefs, or of young people, would give some security to your own party. Carry with you some matter of the kine-pox; inform those of them with whom you may be of its efficacy as a preservative from the small-pox, and instruct and encourage them in the use of it. This may be especially done wherever you winter.

Source: Meriwether Lewis, *History of the Expedition under the Command of Captains Lewis and Clark to the Sources of the Missouri . . . Performed During the Years 1804–5–6*, prepared by Paul Allen, Vol. 1 (Philadelphia: Bradford and Inskeep, 1814), pp. xiii–xviii.

2.4.   Zebulon Pike Describes the Great American Desert (1804)

In the following passage explorer Zebulon Pike describes the Great Plains as a barrier to western expansion, comparing the vast land to the Sahara Desert. Sixteen years later, in 1820, Stephen Long gave the region the appellation "the Great American Desert."

Numerous have been the hypothesis formed by various naturalists, to account for the vast tract of untimbered country which lies between the waters of the Missouri, Mississippi, and the western Ocean, from the mouth of the latter river to the 48° north latitude. Although not flattering myself to be able to elucidate *that*, which numbers of highly scientific characters, have acknowledged to be beyond their depth of research; still, I would not think I had done my country justice, did I not give birth to what few lights my examination of those internal deserts has enabled me to acquire. In that vast country of which we speak, we find the soil generally dry and sandy, with gravel, and discover that the moment we approach a stream, the land becomes more humid with small timber; I therefore conclude, that this country never was timbered, as from the earliest age, the aridity of the soil having so few water courses running through it, and they being principally dry in summer, has never afforded moisture sufficient to support the growth of timber. In all timbered land, the annual discharge of the leaves, with the continual decay of old trees and branches, creates a manure and moisture, which is preserved from the heat of the sun not being permitted to direct his rays perpendicularly, but only to shed them obliquely through the foliage. But here a barren soil, parched and dried up for eight months in the year, presents neither moisture nor nutrition sufficient, to nourish the timber. These vast plains of the western hemisphere, may become in time equally celebrated as the sandy desarts of Africa; for I saw in my route, in various places, tracts of many leagues, where the wind had thrown up the sand, in all the fanciful forms of the ocean's rolling wave, and on which not a speck of vegetable matter existed.

But from these immense prairies may arise one great advantage to the United States, viz: The restriction of our population to some certain limits, and thereby a continuation of the union. Our citizens being so prone to rambling and extending themselves, on the frontiers, will, through necessity, be constrained to limit their extent on the west, to the borders of the Missouri and Mississippi, while they leave the prairies incapable of cultivation to the wandering and uncivilized aborigines of the country.

Source: Zebulon M. Pike, *An Account of Expeditions to the Sources of the Mississippi and the Western Territory* (Philadelphia: C. and A. Conrad, 1810), Appendix to part 2, p. 8.

2.5.   "The Great American Desert" (1820)

In 1820 Major Stephen H. Long led a government expedition to find the source of the Red River. Among the nineteen expedition members was the botanist Dr. Edwin James, who recorded his impressions of the arid region, which fostered the legend of the Great American Desert first introduced by Zebulon Pike. James describes the inhospitable environment and the region's unsuitability for settlement.

[August 3, 1820.] . . . We were becoming somewhat impatient on account of thirst, having met with no water which we could drink, for near twenty-four hours. Accordingly getting upon our horses at an early hour, we moved down the valley, passing an extensive tract, whose soil is a loose red sand, intermixed with gravel and small pebbles, and producing nothing but a few sunflowers and sand-cherries still unripe. While we should remain upon a soil of this description, we could scarcely expect to meet with water or wood, for both of which we began to feel the most urgent necessity, and as the prospect of the country before us promised no change, it is not surprising we should have felt a degree of anxiety and alarm, which, added to our sufferings from hunger and thirst, made our situation extremely unpleasant. We had travelled greater part [*sic*] of the day enveloped in a burning atmosphere, sometimes letting fall upon us the scorching particles of sand which had been raised by the wind, sometimes almost suffocating by its entire stagnation, when we had the good fortune to meet with a pool of stagnant water, which though muddy and brackish, was not entirely impotable, and afforded us a more welcome refreshment, than is often in the power of abundance to supply. Here was also a little wood, and our badger, with the addition of a young owl, which we had the good fortune to take, was very hastily cooked and eaten.

. . .

In regard to this extensive section of country, we do not hesitate in giving the opinion, that it is almost wholly unfit for cultivation, and of course uninhabitable by a people depending upon agriculture for their subsistence. Although tracts of fertile land, considerably extensive, are occasionally to be met with, yet the scarcity of wood and water, almost uniformly prevalent, will prove an insuperable obstacle in the way of settling the country. This objection rests not only against the immediate section under consideration, but applies with equal propriety to a much larger portion of the country. Agreeably to the best intelligence that can be had, concerning the country both northward and southward of the section, and especially to the inferences deducible from the account given by Lewis and Clark, of the country situated between the Missouri and the Rocky Mountains, above the river Platte, the vast region commencing near the sources of the Sabine, Trinity, Brasis, and Colorado, and extending northwardly to the forty-ninth degree of north latitude, by which the United States territory is limited in that direction, is throughout, of a similar character. The whole of this region seems peculiarly adapted as a range for buffaloes, wild goats, and other wild game, incalculable multitudes of which, and ample pasturage and subsistence upon it.

This region, however, viewed as a frontier, may prove of infinite importance to the United States, inasmuch as it is calculated to serve as a barrier to prevent too great an extension of our population westward, and secure us against the machinations or incursions of an enemy, that might otherwise be disposed to annoy us in that quarter.

Edwin James, *An Account of an Expedition from Pittsburgh to the Rocky Mountains, Performed in the Years 1819, 1820* (Ann Arbor, 1966 reprint, Americana University Microfilms International; Philadelphia: Carey & Lea, 1823), Vol. 2, pp. 93–94; Vol. 2, p. 361.

ANNOTATED SELECTED BIBLIOGRAPHY

Ambrose, Stephen E. *Undaunted Courage: Meriwether Lewis, Thomas Jefferson, and the Opening of the American West*. New York: Simon and Schuster, 1996. Best-selling account gives new life to oft-told saga of Lewis and Clark expedition.

Betts, Robert B. *In Search of York: The Slave Who Went to the Pacific with Lewis and Clark*. Boulder: Colorado Associated University Press, 1985. Historian reveals the story of the only African American member of the expedition.

Chuinard, Eldon G. *Only One Man Died: Medical Aspects of the Lewis and Clark Expedition*. Glendale, CA: Arthur Clark Co., 1980. Fascinating medical account of the journey, during which only one member died.

Coues, Elliott, ed. *The History of the Lewis and Clark Expedition*. 4 vols. New York: Francis P. Harper, 1893. Building on the original authorized history of the expedition, Coues summarizes the whole story in much more readable fashion, offering footnotes, correcting numerous errors, and providing modern locations of camps and exploration sites.

Duncan, Dayton, and Ken Burns. *Lewis and Clark: The Journey of the Corps of Discovery*. New York: Alfred A. Knopf, 1997. This illustrated history of the expedition is an excellent supplement to the 1997 PBS documentary *Lewis and Clark: The Journey of the Corps of Discovery*.

Goetzmann, William H. *Army Exploration of the American West, 1803–1863*. New Haven: Yale University Press, 1959. The first and still the best examination of the role played by the U.S. Army Topographical Engineers in the exploration of the trans-Mississippi West.

Lavender, David. *The Way to the Western Sea: Lewis and Clark Across the Continent*. New York: American Heritage Publishing, 1988. Rather straightforward account of the epic journey.

Montgomery, M. R. *Jefferson and the Gun-Men: How the West Was Almost Lost*. New York: Crown, 2000. A good history that portrays the Lewis and Clark and Zebulon Pike expeditions as parts of a larger struggle to establish power in western America.

Ronda, James P. *Lewis and Clark among the Indians*. Lincoln: University of Nebraska Press, 1984. Ronda combines historical, anthropological, and archeological research to create an ethnohistory of the Lewis and Clark expedition.

3

Indian Removal, 1803–1839

From the first Native American contact with European nations in North America, there was a tendency to treat the loosely organized Indian tribes as European nations in miniature. But the majority of Indian peoples did not have political loyalties that extended much beyond the local tribal unit. As English colonists became American citizens following the revolution, the new federal government viewed the multitude of Indian tribes as sovereign nations that existed simultaneously with the American government. As the sole arbiter of foreign affairs, so too did the federal government become the arbiter of Indian-American affairs, which included negotiations such as treaty making. Between 1789 and 1870, 370 written treaties were negotiated between the United States and various Indian tribes. In the eyes of the United States many of these treaties were legally akin to other treaties negotiated with foreign sovereign nations.

During the nation's first presidential administration under George Washington, the colonial precedent of treating Indian tribes as "nations" was a manageable federal Indian policy as long as the tribes occupied lands outside white governmental jurisdiction. With the rapid western expansion of the states after the American Revolution this policy would be challenged on several fronts. The federal government was confronted with resolving such issues as whether Indians were bound by state laws if they resided in a state.

According to the Indians, treaties were sacred and inviolate agreements between the U.S. government and the tribes, guaranteeing them their lands "for perpetuity." Although the Indians viewed the treaties as fixed agreements locked in time and nomenclature, the federal government had a somewhat different perspective, viewing treaties as dynamic political arrangements and evolving legal documents subject to winds of political, social, and economic change. These conflicting interpretations would lead to misunderstanding and conflict between the cultures over the ensuing two centuries.

Since 1803 and the purchase of Louisiana, the states repeatedly attempted to convince the Cherokee, Chickasaw, Choctaw, Creek, and Seminole peoples in the southern states, known collectively as the Five Civilized Tribes, to accept removal. While some did move west on their own, the majority resisted as the states insisted that the federal government extinguish Indian land claims. President Thomas Jefferson had supported the establishment of an "Indian country" beyond the Mississippi River several decades before the passage of the Indian Removal Act (1830) under President Andrew Jackson. Both presidents recognized that as long as Indians remained on lands coveted by settlers their lives were in danger. As long as they lived in close proximity to white communities they would be ravaged by disease, alcoholism, and poverty. Removal could insulate them from the worst that white civilization had to offer, while missionaries and educators would introduce them to the more virtuous aspects of white culture.

Beginning in the 1830s, federal control of Indian affairs was challenged when President Andrew Jackson allowed state control of Indian affairs to supersede that of the federal government, by refusing to honor federal treaty commitments in the southeastern states. The outcome of these proceedings set a precedent for future American Indian policy in the trans-Mississippi West.

Following the American Revolution, the new government faced a number of dilemmas concerning Indian-white relations. In signing the Treaty of Paris in 1783, Great Britain relinquished its former American empire, which had ranged between the Appalachian Mountains and the Mississippi River, south of Canada. After the war thousands of settlers moved across the mountains into what today comprises Ohio, Illinois, Indiana, Tennessee, Alabama, and Mississippi. The avalanche of settlers onto Indian lands precipitated a number of violent encounters.

The fact that most Indian tribes had sided with the British during the war further fragmented popular opinion concerning Indian-white relations. Unfortunately, even tribes that stayed neutral or fought alongside the colonists were viewed as having sided with the enemy. Settlers living on the margin of Indian lands took a dim view of assimilation, and after the hard-fought wars in which they emerged victorious, the frontier inhabitants were less willing to be reined in by their government than they were under the British. While the government was constantly confronted with illegal squatters on Indian lands, the Indians were generally forced to concede land. This process was repeated countless times as Indian lands continued to diminish in the Southeast.

Federal officials recognized that they could not guarantee the safety of Indians as white settlers encroached on their rapidly shrinking lands. From an economic vantage point, Americans believed the land should be exploited for its greatest gain. In addition, in a southern culture dominated by race-based slavery, the southern states were not eager to accept nonwhite Indians as citizens. Since the administration of Thomas Jefferson two conflicting Indian policies had directed the treatment of Native Americans. Assimilation policy encouraged Indians to adopt white customs, culture, and economic practices. Supporters of this policy argued that the only way Indians could flourish in a white-dominated society was to assimilate. To this end, the government financially assisted missionaries to Christianize and educate the Indian tribes and to help them make the transition from tribal life to single-family farms.

Beginning with Thomas Jefferson the government began to urge Indian tribes to sell their lands and move west, viewing removal as the only way to insure the survival of Indian culture. Initially, removal was seen as a voluntary alternative. Indians could of their own volition move to lands farther west where they could live without white interference. Jefferson and other prominent leaders saw relocation of Indians west of the Mississippi as the key to their survival. Most assumed that few whites would ever be interested in these distant lands. One of Jefferson's reasons for purchasing the Louisiana Territory was to acquire lands to be used as Indian country. Assimilationists sided with this policy when they realized that it was the only way to end violence against the Indian cultures.

Under President James Monroe, federal policy began to lean more heavily toward removal after the president suggested that the movement of Native Americans farther west was in the best interests of national security. During the War of 1812 most of the Cherokees and Choctaws resisted siding with the British, aware of their own vulnerability and anxious to prove their loyalty to the United States. Other southern tribes such as the Creeks and Seminoles engaged in protracted warfare against the whites.

The tribes hit hardest by Indian removal were located in the Old Northwest and the South. In 1811 the Shawnee leader Tecumseh (c. 1768–1813) left the Old Northwest (what is now Ohio, Indiana, Illinois, Michigan, and Wisconsin) to visit the southern tribes in an attempt to strengthen bonds of Indian unity. Tecumseh already had earned the enmity of American officials by challenging authorities over federal land grabbing in the Indiana Territory between 1803 and 1809, when the government extorted 33 million acres from several smaller tribes.

Tecumseh's southern visit prompted Creek warriors to resist increasing white encroachments on their lands. Tecumseh would die during the War of 1812 at the Battle of the Thames (1813), but his message stirred the Creeks to wage war for their lands. The subsequent Creek War (1813–1814) ended with the climactic battle of Horseshoe Bend on March 27, 1814, when troops led by Andrew Jackson broke the power of the Creek Confederacy. When the day was over, more than 800 Creek and less than 50 of Jackson's men were dead. Following the battle, the Creeks were forced to cede 20 million acres (more than half their land) and Jackson was promoted to major general, beginning a legendary ascent that would lead to the White House in 1828.

The federal policy of removal can be traced back to at least the mid-1820s, when Secretary of War John C. Calhoun reported to President James Monroe in 1825 what steps should be taken to insure peaceful relations between the two cultures. Beginning in 1826, a series of treaties were forced on the southeastern tribes, requiring tribes first in Georgia, and then Alabama and Mississippi, to relinquish their lands in return for reservations in what is now Oklahoma.

Advocates of removal argued that by removing Indians to the West they would be protected from the debasing influence of whiskey peddlers and other undesirables. West of the Mississippi missionaries and government officials could then be depended on to teach the skills required to make the transition to white ways. Removal also would open vast stretches of territory to land-hungry American settlers and satisfy southern states' insistence on control over their own affairs.

The federal government faced substantial opposition to Indian removal, chiefly from the Northeast and from southern Indians. President John Quincy Adams of Massachusetts, for one, spoke out against removal. In northeastern congregations, missionaries who had worked with Cherokees offered compelling evidence of Cherokee "civilizing" efforts. A series of anti-removal essays, printed under the pseudonym William Penn, was widely published in 1829, leading many northeastern citizens to sign petitions urging their congressmen to oppose removal. These essays found an attentive audience during church sermons and in Congress, where politicians argued over Indian removal policy. But, with few allies in Congress, the Cherokees and other tribes could not stop the removal movement. In 1830 the Indian Removal Act was signed into law.

The government often sent out mixed signals to the southeastern tribes. At the same time it was advocating the move west, the federal government urged the Cherokees and other Indian nations to adopt white agriculture and industry in their current homes. A number of southeastern Indians practiced a culturally accommodationist strategy prior to removal. Believing that they could ensure their survival by becoming "civilized," the Cherokees created a republic in Georgia in 1820, with an elected bicameral legislature, a European-style judicial system, and a police force, and adopted the death penalty for those who sold land without authorization. In 1821 Sequoyah created the Cherokee alphabet, and six years later the Cherokee Nation adopted a written constitution based on the American document. A Cherokee newspaper soon followed. By then they were adopting other aspects of Euro-American culture, including single-family farmsteads and slaveowning.

When Andrew Jackson became president in 1829, 125,000 Native Americans still lived east of the Mississippi River. Some 60,000 Chickasaw, Cherokee, Creek, and Seminoles held millions of acres of land that stretched across Georgia, Alabama, and Mississippi. Jackson initially toed the dual policy of assimilation and removal, but by 1830 clearly advocated removal only. The first westerner (born in Carolina and grown to manhood and prosperity in Tennessee) to be elected president, Jackson seriously considered western issues. He would make it clear in no uncertain terms that America's expansionist needs outweighed the claims of sovereign Indian tribes as he became the leading advocate for Indian removal during his presidency (1829–1837). Indian removal would figure prominently in his 1830 and 1835 State of the Union messages to Congress.

During his first presidential campaign Jackson broached the subject of Indian removal, and almost as soon as he took office requested that Congress create a territory where the Indians could reside outside the boundaries of the states. In 1830 Congress, after a close vote of 102 to 97, approved the Indian Removal Act, after the president implored Congress to create "an ample district west of the Mississippi without limits of any State or Territory to be guaranteed to the Indian tribes as long as they shall occupy it." This act provided for the mandatory resettlement of the southeastern tribes in Indian Territory.

Although Jackson had commanded Cherokee troops during the War of 1812 and had even raised an adopted Creek boy as his son, his sympathies remained with the whites of the Southeast as he made clear his position in favor of the rights of the states and his unwillingness to use federal authority to protect Indian interests. Although Indian affairs were considered a federal responsibility, he let the southern states know that he would not stand in their way when it came to enforcing Indian policy. It was not long before Georgia expanded its jurisdiction over the Indians living within its borders. Meanwhile steps were taken to make it illegal for Indians to testify against whites in court. Mississippi and Alabama soon followed suit.

Although the Cherokee "Trail of Tears" features prominently in any chronicling of the Indian removal saga, other tribes endured similar tragedies. The Choctaws in 1831 became the first to submit. In September 1830, the Choctaws were betrayed by avaricious leaders into signing the Treaty of Dancing Rabbit Creek, which ceded almost 8 million acres of land in Mississippi, necessitating the tribe's removal west of the Mississippi River. The Choctaws were the first Indians to be removed from their homelands under the new policy. Their relocation was handled by the army's Commissary Department, which began gathering nearly 4,000 Choctaws in 1831 in preparation for their move to the Indian Territory. On their way through the forests to the steamboats that would take them part of the way by river, Indians touched the trunks of the trees as they said goodbye to their ancestral lands. Six thousand Choctaws would complete the journey by 1833.

Setting a precedent that would characterize future removals, many would perish from disease, poor food, and natural calamity. In several cases the army gave them food condemned as unfit. The Choctaws refused to eat the repacked, scraped, and rebrined rotten meat that the army provided, preferring to grind up acorns instead. In 1836 more than 3,000 Creeks were removed from Alabama and forced to trek almost barefoot through snow to their Arkansas destination. Over the next decade the Chickasaw were removed from Mississippi and many Seminoles from Florida.

The Cherokee people did not accept their removal without first challenging the policy in court. In 1828 the Georgian Cherokees attempted to secure their lands by adopting a constitution. But the state rejected the document and proclaimed that the Cherokees were subject to state law. Subsequently, Baltimore attorney William Wirt, representing the Cherokee Indian Nation, appealed the case to the U.S. Supreme Court. However, in 1831 the Court ruled in *Cherokee Nation v. Georgia* that it lacked jurisdiction since the Cherokee Nation was not a foreign nation as defined in the U.S. Constitution.

The following year the state of Georgia imprisoned a missionary named Samuel Worcester for living on Cherokee land in violation of state law, which required that he obtain a permit and then swear his allegiance to the state. In the 1832 case of *Worcester v. Georgia*, the Court ruled that the missionary lived in a distinct community where "the laws of Georgia can have no force." The force of this ruling claimed that Georgia had illegally supplanted federal jurisdiction over such matters. It seemed then that this decision effectively demonstrated the power of the federal government over state law. However, in a groundbreaking reversal of precedent, President Jackson refused to intervene, allowing Georgia to ignore the Court decision. Although it has never been verified, Jackson reportedly stated, "John Marshall has made his decision. Now let him enforce it." It was not long before the state of Georgia began distributing Cherokee lands to white farmers.

Without presidential support, it was impossible to protect the tribe, and in the following months Cherokees were evicted from their lands and had much of their livestock stolen. Despite a campaign of harassment, less than one-eighth of the Cherokees had moved after two years.

Although dozens of American Indian tribes were forcibly removed from their ancestral lands in the 1830s and 1840s, the most famous relocation tragedies involved the Cherokees and their Trail of Tears journey from Georgia to what is today Oklahoma. In 1838, after the federal government turned down Cherokee requests for an extension so they would not have to sell their property in a rush, Jackson instructed federal troops to remove the Cherokees. It was a poorly planned operation that took place in the dead of winter and resulted in the deaths of more than 4,000 out of 15,000 who took the trek. Regarding those deaths, General Winfield Scott, who oversaw the Cherokee removal, would later comment that while he had seen thousands of soldiers shot to pieces during the Civil War, "the Cherokee removal was the cruelest work I ever knew."

Some Cherokees were pragmatic in their views on removal. Elias Boudinot was one leader who had been educated in white missionary schools and had at the outset been a firm opponent of Indian removal. But he was also a realist, and when the state began doling out Cherokee lands, he recognized that the only way the Cherokee could stay united as a people was to accept removal. After signing treaties of removal in 1832 and 1835, he was assassinated in 1839 for alienating Cherokee lands.

The events surrounding the removal of the Five Civilized Tribes west in the 1830s laid the groundwork for future Indian policy in the American West. It established the notion that Indians could not live independently with whites and that Indians could only exercise sovereignty outside the borders of American states. Following the 1830s most Indian nations accepted the futility of resistance and were forced to sign over their lands and move west. While the Sauk and Fox tribes were soundly defeated in the short-lived Black War in 1832, the Seminole War would last longer, as Seminoles led by Chief Osceola kept the U.S. Army at bay in the swamps of Florida between 1835 and 1838.

Indian removal demonstrated the worst and best impulses of Americans. On one hand, a growing number of missionaries and humanitarians hoped to protect the besieged southeastern tribes by moving them beyond the threat of white encroachment. But, on the other hand, in an era of limited government there was no precedent for such an enormous undertaking. Without organized social welfare programs and with food, clothing, and transportation for the trek west supplied by the lowest bidders, a tragic denouement was insured. Thousands died from hunger and exposure. Those that survived the trek were forced to subsist on inferior lands most white settlers would not even consider farming. In the end removal demonstrated the deep flaws of federal Indian policy, a process that would be repeated over and over during subsequent decades.

DOCUMENTS

3.1.   The Indian Removal Act

On May 28, 1830, the U.S. Congress authorized the president to exchange lands in the West for Indian lands in any state or territory. This act in effect allowed President Andrew Jackson to proceed with negotiations to remove the southern tribes. Ultimately, the act provided for the mandatory resettlement of the southeastern Indian tribes to the Indian Territory west of the Mississippi River. In September 1830 the Choctaws became the first of the southern tribes to be removed from their homelands. During the following decades dozens of other tribes would be forcibly removed from ancestral lands.

Removal Act

An Act to Provide for an Exchange of Lands with the Indians Residing in any of the States or Territories, and for Their Removal West of the River Mississippi

BE IT ENACTED *by the Senate and House of Representatives of the United States of America, in Congress assembled,* That it shall and may be lawful for the President of the United States to cause so much of any territory belonging to the United States, west of the river Mississippi, not included in any state or organized territory, and to which the Indian title has been extinguished, as he may judge necessary, to be divided into a suitable number of districts, for the reception of such tribes or nations of Indians as may choose to exchange the lands where they now reside, and remove there; and to cause each of said districts to be so described by natural or artificial marks, as to be easily distinguished from every other.

· · ·

Section III

And be it further enacted, That in the making of any such exchange or exchanges, it shall and may be lawful for the President solemnly to assure the tribe or nation with which the exchange is made, that the United States will forever secure and guaranty to them, and their heirs or successors, the country so exchanged with them; and if they prefer it, that the United States will cause a patent or grant to be made and executed to them for the same: *Provided always*, That such lands shall revert to the United States, if the Indians become extinct, or abandon the same.

Source: U.S. Statutes at Large 4 (1830): 411–412.

3.2.   Opposition to Indian Removal (1830)

One of the most steadfast opponents of Indian removal was Senator Theodore Frelinghuysen of New Jersey. In a long speech to the Senate on April 9, 1830, he outlined his case. According to Frelinghuysen, the United States government was overstepping its continental mandate by taking Indian lands. He suggested that at the present rate of land sales, it would take 200 years to sell all of the lands acquired from the native peoples. The following is an excerpt from his speech given less than two weeks after the passage of the Indian Removal Act.

Several years ago, official reports to Congress stated the amount of Indian grants to the United States to exceed 214 millions of acres. Yes, sir, we have acquired, and now own more land as the fruits of their bounty than we shall dispose of at the present rate to actual settlers in two hundred years. For, very recently, it has been ascertained, on this floor, that our public sales average not more than about one million of acres annually. It greatly aggravates the wrong that is now meditated against these tribes, to survey the rich and ample districts of their territories, that either force or persuasion have incorporated into our public domains. As the tide of our population has rolled on, we have added purchase to purchase. The confiding Indian listened to our professions of friendship: we called him brother, and he believed us. Millions after millions he has yielded to our importunity, until we have acquired more than can be cultivated in centuries—and yet we crave more. We have crowded the tribes upon a few miserable acres on our southern frontier: it is all that is left to them of their once boundless forests: and still, like the horse-leech, our insatiated cupidity cries, give! give!

. . . The white men, the authors of all their wrongs, approached them as friends—they extended the olive branch; and, being then a feeble colony and at the mercy of the native tenants of the soil, by presents and professions, propitiated their good will. The Indian yielded a slow, but substantial confidence; granted to the colonists an abiding place; and suffered them to grow up to man's estate beside him. He never raised the claim of elder title: as the white man's wants increased, he opened the hand of his bounty wider and wider. By and by, conditions are changed. His people melt away; his lands are constantly coveted; millions after millions are ceded. The Indian bears it all meekly; he complains, indeed, as well he may; but suffers on: and now he finds that this neighbor, whom his kindness had nourished, has spread an adverse title over the last remains of his patrimony, barely adequate to his wants, and turns upon him, and says, "away! we cannot endure you so near us! These forests and rivers, these groves of your fathers, these firesides and hunting grounds, are ours by the right of power, and the force of numbers." Sir, let every treaty be blotted from our records, and in the judgment of natural and unchangeable truth and justice, I ask, who is the injured, and who is the aggressor? Let conscience answer, and I fear not the result. Sir, let those who please, denounce the public feeling on this subject as the morbid excitement of a false humanity; but I return with the inquiry, whether I have not presented the case truly, with no feature of it overcharged or distorted? And, in view of it, who can help feeling, sir? Do the obligations of justice change with the color of the skin? Is it one of the prerogatives of the white man, that he may disregard the dictates of moral principles, when an Indian shall be concerned? No, sir. In that severe and impartial scrutiny, which futurity will cast over this subject, the righteous award will be, that those very causes which are now pleaded for the relaxed enforcement of the rules of equity, urged upon us not only a rigid execution of the highest justice, to the very letter, but claimed at our hands a generous and magnanimous policy.

Source: Register of Debates in Congress, Washington, D.C., Vol. 6, pp. 311–316, April 9, 1830.

3.3.   Georgian Support for Indian Removal (1830)

The following, from the Senate debate on April 9–15, 1830, is a response to Senator Frelinghuysen of New Jersey by Senator John Forsyth of Georgia, a supporter of Jackson's Indian policy. Forsyth upholds federal Indian removal policy on the grounds that the government has sovereignty over the tribes.

SENATOR FORSYTH.—The Senator from New Jersey no doubt hopes that his zeal and industry in the Indian cause will be crowned with success; that he will be able to persuade the Senate, and his friends in the House of Representatives, to interfere, and compel the President to take new views of the relative power of the State and general governments, and that under these new views the physical force of the country will be used, if necessary, to arrest the progress of Georgia. The expectation the gentleman has expressed, that Georgia will yield, in the event of this desirable change in the executive course, is entirely vain. The gentleman must not indulge it; with a full and fair examination of what is right and proper, Georgia has taken her course and will pursue it. The alternative to which the Senator looks, of coercion, must be the result. While I entertain no fears that the gentleman's hopes will be realized, I consider it a matter of conscience, before entering upon the discussion of the general subject of the bill, to relieve the Senator from any apprehension that it may become necessary to cut white throats in Georgia to preserve inviolate the national faith, and to perform our treaty engagements to the Indians.

I propose, sir, for his relief, to show that, considering this as a treaty question, arising under a fair exercise of the treaty-making power with a foreign government, entirely unconnected with any disputes about the relative power of the State government, and the Government of the United States, Georgia stands perfectly justified, upon his own principles, in the steps she has chosen to take with regard to those Cherokees who reside within her territorial limits. The gentleman asserts that the Creeks and Cherokees are acknowledged to be independent nations, by treaties made, first with Georgia, and lastly with the United States; that the independence of those tribes is guaranteed by the United States; that treaties with the United States are the supreme laws of the land, and must be executed, although in collision with State constitutions and State laws. The independence of the tribes rests on this argument—that the formation of a treaty is, between the parties, an acknowledgment of mutual independence. I will not stop to show the numerous exceptions to this rule; insisting, however, that the gentleman shall admit, what I presume nobody will deny, that the two parties to a treaty, independent when it was made, may, by the terms of that instrument, change their characters, and assume those of sovereign and dependent.

Every professional man who remembers his Blackstone knows that legislation is the highest act of sovereignty. Now, sir, by the ninth article of the treaty of Hopewell, of the 28th November, 1785, a treaty which begins with these words: "The United States give peace to all the Cherokees, and receive them into their favor and protection"—strange words to be used to an unconquered and independent nation!—the Cherokees surrender to Congress the power of legislating for them at discretion.

So much for the independence of the Cherokee nation. It may be asked, however, what has this treaty to do with the question between Georgia and the Cherokee Government! It does not follow that, because the United States have sovereignty over the Cherokees, that the State has it. The compact made by the United States with Georgia, in 1802, furnishes the satisfactory answer to this inquiry. The United States, having acquired, by the ninth article of the treaty of Hopewell, the power of legislation over the Cherokees, had the goodness to transfer it to the State. Gentlemen may amuse themselves with finding fault with this transfer by the United States of a power granted to them, and intended to be used by the United States only. They may prove it, if they choose, an act of injustice to the Cherokees—a violation of faith. We will not take the trouble to interfere with such questions. The United States obtained, by treaty, the power to legislate over the Cherokees, and transferred it to Georgia. The justice and propriety of this transfer must be settled by the United States and the Cherokees. In this settlement Georgia has her burden to bear, as one of the members of the Union; but no more than her fair proportion. If any pecuniary sacrifices are required to do justice to the injured, let them be made: if a sacrifice of blood is demanded as a propitiation for this sin, to avert the judgment of Heaven, let the victim be selected. Justice demands that it be furnished by the whole country, and not by Georgia; and if the honorable Senator from New Jersey will fix upon one between the Delaware and the Hudson, he will escape all imputations of being actuated by any motive but the love of justice—pure justice.

Source: Marion Mills Miller, ed., *Great Debates in American History*, Vol. 8 (New York: Current Literature Publishing Co., 1913), pp. 273–274.

3.4.   *Cherokee Nation v. Georgia* (1831)

After President Andrew Jackson refused to interfere with the state of Georgia's attempts to extend its laws over the Cherokee Nation, the Cherokees took the matter to the U.S. Supreme Court. The Court ruled against the Cherokees, noting that "an Indian tribe or nation within the United States is not a foreign state in the sense of the Constitution, and cannot maintain an action in the United States courts." This decision marked a shift in Indian-white relations by allowing a state to assert its dominance over a formerly sovereign Indian nation.

Is the Cherokee nation a foreign state in the sense in which that term is used in the constitution?

The counsel for the plaintiffs have maintained the affirmative of this proposition with great earnestness and ability. So much of the argument as was intended to prove the character of the Cherokees as a state, as a distinct political society, separated from others, capable of managing its own affairs and governing itself, has, in the opinion of a majority of the judges, been completely successful. They have been uniformly treated as a state from the settlement of our country. The numerous treaties made with them by the United States recognize them as a people capable of maintaining the relations of peace and war, of being responsible in their political character for any violation of their engagements, or for any aggression committed on the citizens of the United States by any individual of their community. Laws have been enacted in the spirit of these treaties. The acts of our government plainly recognize the Cherokee nation as a state, and the courts are bound by those acts.

A question of much more difficulty remains. Do the Cherokees constitute a foreign state in the sense of the constitution?

The counsel have shown conclusively that they are not a state of the union, and have insisted that individually they are aliens, not owing allegiance to the United States. An aggregate of aliens composing a state must, they say, be a foreign state. Each individual being foreign, the whole must be foreign.

This argument is imposing, but we must examine it more closely before we yield to it. The condition of the Indians in relation to the United States is perhaps unlike that of any other two people in existence. In the general, nations not owing a common allegiance are foreign to each other. The term *foreign nation* is, with strict propriety, applicable by either to the other. But the relation of the Indians to the United States is marked by peculiar and cardinal distinctions which exist no where else.

The Indian territory is admitted to compose a part of the United States. In all our maps, geographical treatises, histories, and laws, it is so considered. In all our intercourse with foreign nations, in our commercial regulations, in any attempt at intercourse between Indians and foreign nations, they are considered as within the jurisdictional limits of the United States, subject to many of those restraints which are imposed upon our own citizens. They acknowledge themselves in their treaties to be under the protection of the United States; they admit that the United States shall have the sole and exclusive right of regulating the trade with them, and managing all their affairs as they think proper; and the Cherokees in particular were allowed by the treaty of Hopewell, which preceded the constitution, "to send a deputy of their choice, whenever they think fit, to congress." Treaties were made with some tribes by the state of New York, under a then unsettled construction of the confederation, by which they ceded all their lands to that state, taking back a limited grant to themselves, in which they admit their dependence.

Though the Indians are acknowledged to have an unquestionable, and, heretofore, unquestioned right to the lands they occupy, until that right shall be extinguished by a voluntary cession to our government; yet it may well be doubted whether those tribes which reside within the acknowledged boundaries of the United States can, with strict accuracy, be denominated foreign nations. They may, more correctly, perhaps be denominated domestic dependent nations. They occupy a territory to which we assert a title independent of their will, which must take effect in point of possession when their right of possession ceases. Meanwhile they are in a state of pupilage. Their relation to the United States resembles that of a ward to his guardian.

They look to our government for protection; rely upon its kindness and its power; appeal to it for relief to their wants; and address the president as their great father. They and their country are considered by foreign nations, as well as by ourselves, as being so completely under the sovereignty and dominion of the United States, that any attempt to acquire their lands, or to form a political connexion with them, would be considered by all as an invasion of our territory, and an act of hostility.

These considerations go far to support the opinion, that the framers of our constitution had not the Indian tribes in view, when they opened the courts of the union to controversies between a state or the citizens thereof, and foreign states.

In considering this subject, the habits and usages of the Indians, in their intercourse with their white neighbours, ought not to be entirely disregarded. At the time the constitution was framed, the idea of appealing to an American court of justice for an assertion of right or a redress of wrong had perhaps never entered the mind of an Indian or of his tribe. Their appeal was to the tomahawk, or to the government. This was well understood by the statesmen who framed the constitution of the United States, and might furnish some reason for omitting to enumerate them among the parties who might sue in the courts of the union. Be this as it may, the peculiar relations between the United States and the Indians occupying our territory are such, that we should feel much difficulty in considering them as designated by the term *foreign state*, were there no other part of the constitution which might shed light on the meaning of these words. But we think that in construing them, considerable aid is furnished by that clause in the eighth section of the third article; which empowers congress to "regulate commerce with foreign nations, and among the several states, and with the Indian tribes."

In this clause they are as clearly contradistinguished by a name appropriate to themselves, from foreign nations, as from the several states composing the union. They are designated by a distinct appellation; and as this appellation can be applied to neither of the others, neither can the appellation distinguishing either of the others be in fair construction applied to them. The objects, to which the power of regulating commerce might be directed, are divided into three distinct classes—foreign nations, the several states, and Indian tribes. When forming this article, the convention considered them as entirely distinct. We cannot assume that the distinction was lost in framing a subsequent article, unless there be something in its language to authorize the assumption.

. . .

. . . *Foreign nations* is a general term, the application of which to Indian tribes, when used in the American constitution, is at best extremely questionable. In one article in which a power is given to be exercised in regard to foreign nations generally, and to the Indian tribes particularly, they are mentioned as separate in terms clearly contradistinguishing them from each other. We perceive plainly that the constitution in this article does not comprehend Indian tribes in the general term "foreign nations," not we presume because a tribe may not be a nation, but because it is not foreign to the United States. When, afterwards, the term "foreign state" is introduced, we cannot impute to the convention the intention to desert its former meaning, and to comprehend Indian tribes within it, unless the context force that construction on us. We find nothing in the context, and nothing in the subject of the article, which leads to it.

The court has bestowed its best attention on this question, and, after mature deliberation, the majority is of opinion that an Indian tribe or nation within the United States is not a foreign state in the sense of the constitution, and cannot maintain an action in the courts of the United States.

Source: The Cherokee Nation v. The State of Georgia, 30 U.S. 1 (1831).

3.5.   House Debate on Removal of the Cherokees (1831)

The decision to remove the Cherokees created an intense debate in Congress that lasted for several sessions in February 1831. In the following exchange Edward Everett of Massachusetts argues with Charles Haynes of Georgia over the ethical issues of removal policy. In a most interesting exchange, Everett expresses his outrage at Georgia's actions, while Haynes reminds Everett of the New England Puritan treatment of Indians in the seventeenth century.

MR. EVERETT then rose, and addressed the House as follows:

. . .

I cannot disguise my impression, that it is the greatest question which ever came before Congress, short of the question of peace and war. It concerns not an individual, by [sic] entire communities of men, whose fate is wholly in our hands, and concerns them—not to the extent of affecting their interests, more or less favorably, within narrow limits. As I regard it, it is a question of inflicting the pains of banishment from their native land on seventy or eighty thousand human beings, the greater part of whom are fixed and attached to their homes in the same way that we are. . . .

. . .

But the policy of removal has, I grant, been pursued steadily for thirty years, but never in the same manner as now. It was never thought of, that all the treaties and laws of the United States protecting the Indians could be annulled, and the laws of the States extended over them; laws of such a character that it is admitted, nay urged, that they cannot live under them. The policy of removal has been pursued by treaty, negotiated by persuasion, urgency, if gentlemen please, with importunity. But the compulsion of State legislation, and of the withdrawal of the protection of the United States, was never before heard of. If the President means that the policy of removal under this compulsion is thirty years old, I do not know a fact on which his proposition can stand for a moment. However pursued, the policy of removal had been attended with limited success. Vast tracts of land had indeed been acquired of the Southwestern tribes, but chiefly by bringing their settlements within narrower limits. Between the years of 1809 and 1819, about one-third of the Cherokees went over to Arkansas, and the hardships and sufferings encountered by them were a chief cause why their brethren, the residue of the tribe, resisted every inducement held out to persuade them also to emigrate. The Choctaws, by the treaty of Doak's Stand, acquired a large tract of country between the Red river and the Canadian; but would not, in any considerable numbers, emigrate to it. In 1826, a part of the Creeks were forced, by the convulsions in that tribe, to emigrate, under the treaty of that year. In 1828, the Choctaws and Chickasaws sent a deputation to explore the country west of Arkansas, which returned dissatisfied with its appearance.

While the policy of removal was going on with this limited success, that of civilization, the truly benevolent policy, was much more prosperous. The attempt to settle, to civilize, and to christianize some of these tribes succeeded beyond all example. If the accounts of their previous state of barbarism are not exaggerated, the annals of the world do not, to my knowledge, present another instance of improvement so rapid, within a single generation; unless it be that which has been effected, by a similar agency, in the Sandwich Islands within the last ten years.

During all the time that these two processes were going on, that of removal, (declared last year by the President to be inconsistent with civilizing them,) with partial success; and that of settling and improving their condition, on this side of the Mississippi, in which the success had been rapid and signal, no attempt was made to encroach upon their limited independence. The right of the United States to treat with them was not questioned; the States never attempted to legislate over them; and the possessions and rights guarantied to them by numerous treaties, were considered by them and by us as safe beneath the protection of the national faith. But, at length, under the late administration of the General Government, the Southwestern States, taking advantage of the political weakness of that administration, seemed determined to adventure the experiment, how far they could go, to effect, by a new course of State legislation, a revolution in the Indian policy of the country.

. . .

Such was and is the Cherokee Government which Georgia has avowed her purpose, by one sweeping act of legislation, to put down. That State has enacted a law making it highly penal to exercise any of the functions of this Government. Chiefs, headmen, members of the council, judicial and executive officers, are all subject to four years' imprisonment in the penitentiary, if they presume to exercise any of the functions of Government within their own tribe, and under that constitution which we originally and repeatedly exhorted them to frame.

In this way the greatest confusion is at once introduced into the concerns of this unhappy people. Their own Government is outlawed, and it is made highly penal to execute its functions. The protection of the United States is withdrawn, because Georgia has extended her laws over the Indians; and Georgia herself, although asserting, and in many respects exercising, her jurisdiction, has not yet organized it in such a manner as to keep the peace among this afflicted race. Their system of Government, instead of being regarded as almost all Governments, however defective, are entitled to be, as an institution necessary for the well-being of the people, which ought to be treated with tenderness, and not be destroyed till a substitute is provided, has been abated and broken down as a nuisance.

But among the laws of Georgia, extended over the Cherokees, there are some which, from their nature, must take an immediate effect; and among these I cannot but notice several whose operation must be as injurious to the welfare of the Indians, as the entire system is destructive of their rights. At the late session of the Georgia Legislature, a law was passed, "that no Cherokee Indian should be bound by any contract, hereafter to be entered into, with a white person or persons; nor shall any Indian be liable to be fined in any of the courts of law or equity in this State, on such a contract." I am aware that laws of this kind have been found necessary among the dwindling remnants of tribes, in some of the States, whose members are so degenerate that they are unable to preserve, against the arts of corrupt white men, the little property they possess. But among the Cherokees are men of intelligence and shrewdness, who have acquired and possess large accumulations of property—houses, shops, plantations, stock, mills, ferries, and other valuable possessions; men who understand property and its uses as well as we do, and who need all the laws which property requires for its judicious management. Notwithstanding this, Georgia, at one blow, makes all these people incapable of contracting. Men as competent as ourselves to all business transactions, are reduced by a sweeping law to a state of pupilage.

. . .

CHARLES HAYNES (Dem., Ga.) then rose, and said, when this subject was so elaborately discussed at the last session of Congress, and particularly when so large a share of that discussion was borne by the honorable gentleman from Massachusetts, [Mr. Everett,] and his friends, he had hoped it would never again be agitated in this House. When the proposition of the honorable gentleman was offered, he confessed he felt an excitement which would then have rendered him incapable of discussing it with becoming self-respect, or what was due from him to this House.

In his calmer reflections, he had determined to bring alone to its consideration the dictates of his understanding and his judgment, whatever of passion might heretofore have been mingled with it.

. . .

If this right of discovery does not avail Georgia, it is of as little avail to any other State in this Union. But, to say no more of it, we find ourselves placed under the operation of this principle, and it is too late to talk of changing it. But it might be asked how he arrived at the conclusion that such a principle had been adopted by the discovering European nations which planted colonies on this continent. He would answer, in the history of all. Nor would he shelter himself under the enormities practised by Spain on the aborigines of Mexico, South America, and the West India islands. Great Britain acted on the same principles in granting charters to her North American colonies. From the earliest of those charters to that granted to Georgia in 1732, this principle runs throughout; nor had he observed, upon an examination of a number of them, that any peculiarity existed, except that, by charter, the exclusive right is secured to Rhode Island, "upon just cause, to invade and destroy the native Indians, or other enemies of the said colony." Nor should he complain that Rhode Island chose still to live under that charter, nor inquire why so poor a remnant of the once powerful tribe of Narragansett has escaped from former wars, and the no less destructive vices of civilized life, operating on an inferior and degraded caste.

· · ·

He might have spoken of laws enacted by one, giving a premium for Indian scalps, and for the rearing of dogs to hunt them down, which he believed the honorable gentleman from Massachusetts could not deny had been done by his own State within the period of her colonial existence. He might have spoken of their being transported by another colony beyond seas, and sold for slaves. How another had restrained their liberty, by forbidding their going from home after a certain hour at night, without a pass or permit from a white man, under the penalty of corporal punishment. Of the act passed by Pennsylvania in 1743, adding for criminal jurisdiction all the wild country of that colony to the county of Philadelphia; and how that act, as he had recently understood, on the highest authority, had been enforced upon an Indian the following year, for manslaughter committed in a remote corner of the country thus annexed to that county. He might have adverted to the jurisdiction exercised within a few years past upon an Indian within the limits of New York; but if the facts and principles presented by him be correct, and he did not doubt it, it could not be necessary to go into such particulars. He should not refer to them in this cursory manner for the purpose of inquiring into their propriety or impropriety. He would leave that to be settled by the consciences of those who had presumed to question the conduct of Georgia for the execution of a Cherokee Indian for the murder of another Cherokee Indian. He would not be understood as referring to them for the purpose of examining the comparative cruelty of Georgia and other States, as, among the wise and good, he had too much confidence in the belief that blood will not be considered as sticking to her skirts for the execution of a murderer.

But, since it has suited the convenience of politicians of a certain order to rail against Georgia, we have been stunned by the cry of violations of the treaty-making power. It is, therefore, necessary to inquire what is that power, and wherein has it been violated?

Sources: "House Debate on Removal of the Cherokees," February 14, 21, 1831, *Gales and Seaton's Register*, 21st Congress, 2nd Session, pp. 682–717, 759–775; Wilcomb E. Washburn, ed., *The American Indian and the United States: A Documentary History*, Vol. 2 (New York: Random House, 1973), pp. 1128–1129, 1133–1134, 1141, 1168–1170, 1174–1175.

3.6.   *Worcester v. The State of Georgia* (1832)

This court case arose from the arrest of missionary Samuel A. Worcester for refusing to obey a Georgia state law forbidding whites to live in Cherokee country without taking an oath of allegiance to the state and obtaining a permit. Worcester argued that Georgia had no constitutional power to regulate Cherokee affairs and took the case to the Supreme Court. This time the Court decided in favor of Indian sovereignty, ruling that as the Indians were a distinct community, the laws of Georgia had no force. The state refused to acquiesce, and Worcester remained in jail until the governor pardoned him. President Jackson took no action to enforce the court decision, setting the stage for the removal of the Cherokees from Georgia in 1838.

. . . . Mr. Chief Justice MARSHALL delivered the opinion of the Court.

This cause, in every point of view in which it can be placed, is of the deepest interest.

The defendant is a state, a member of the Union, which has exercised the powers of government over a people who deny its jurisdiction, and are under the protection of the United States.

The plaintiff is a citizen of the state of Vermont, condemned to hard labour for four years in the penitentiary of Georgia; under colour of an act which he alleges to be repugnant to the Constitution, laws, and treaties of the United States.

The legislative power of a state, the controlling power of the Constitution and laws of the United States, the rights, if they have any, the political existence of a once numerous and powerful people, the personal liberty of a citizen, are all involved in the subject now to be considered. . . .

The Indian nations had always been considered as distinct, independent political communities, retaining their original natural rights, as the undisputed possessors of the soil, from time immemorial, with the single exception of that imposed by irresistible power, which excluded them from intercourse with any other European potentate than the first discoverer of the coast of the particular region claimed; and this was a restriction which those European potentates imposed on themselves, as well as on the Indians. The very term "nation," so generally applied to them, means "a people distinct from others." The Constitution, by declaring treaties already made, as well as those to be made, to be the supreme law of the land, has adopted and sanctioned the previous treaties with the Indian nations, and consequently admits their rank among those powers who are capable of making treaties. The words "treaty" and "nation" are words of our own language, selected in our diplomatic and legislative proceedings, by ourselves, having each a definite and well understood meaning. We have applied them to Indians, as we have applied them to the other nations of the earth. They are applied to all in the same sense.

. . .

The Cherokee nation, then, is a distinct community, occupying its own territory, with boundaries accurately described, in which the laws of Georgia can have no force, and which the citizens of Georgia have no right to enter, but with the assent of the Cherokees themselves, or in conformity with treaties, and with the acts of Congress. The whole intercourse between the United States and this nation, is, by our Constitution and laws, vested in the government of the United States.

The act of the state of Georgia, under which the plaintiff in error was prosecuted, is consequently void, and the judgment a nullity. Can this Court revise and reverse it?

If the objection to the system of legislation, lately adopted by the legislature of Georgia, in relation to the Cherokee nation, was confined to its extra-territorial operation, the objection, though complete, so far as respected mere right, would give this Court no power over the subject. But it goes much further. If the review which has been taken be correct, and we think it is, the acts of Georgia are repugnant to the Constitution, laws, and treaties of the United States.

They interfere forcibly with the relations established between the United States and the Cherokee nation, the regulation of which, according to the settled principles of our Constitution, are committed exclusively to the government of the Union.

They are in direct hostility with treaties, repeated in a succession of years, which mark out the boundary that separates the Cherokee country from Georgia; guaranty to them all the land within their boundary; solemnly pledge the faith of the United States to restrain their citizens from trespassing on it; and recognise the pre-existing power of the nation to govern itself.

They are in equal hostility with the acts of Congress for regulating this intercourse, and giving effect to the treaties.

The forcible seizure and abduction of the plaintiff in error, who was residing in the nation with its permission, and by authority of the President of the United States, is also a violation of the acts which authorize the chief magistrate to exercise this authority.

Will these powerful considerations avail the plaintiff in error? We think they will. He was seized, and forcibly carried away, while under guardianship of treaties guarantying the country in which he resided, and taking it under the protection of the United States. He was seized while performing, under the sanction of the chief magistrate of the Union, those duties which the humane policy adopted by Congress had recommended. He was apprehended, tried, and condemned, under colour of a law which has been shown to be repugnant to the Constitution, laws, and treaties of the United States. Had a judgment, liable to the same objections, been rendered for property, none would question the jurisdiction of this Court. It cannot be less clear when the judgment affects personal liberty, and inflicts disgraceful punishment, if punishment could disgrace when inflicted on innocence. The plaintiff in error is not less interested in the operation of this unconstitutional law than if it affected his property. He is not less entitled to the protection of the Constitution, laws, and treaties of his country. . . .

It is the opinion of this Court that the judgment of the Superior Court for the county of Gwinnett, in the state of Georgia, condemning Samuel A. Worcester to hard labour in the penitentiary of the state of Georgia, for four years, was pronounced by that Court under colour of a law which is void, as being repugnant to the Constitution, treaties, and laws of the United States, and ought, therefore, to be reversed and annulled. . . .

Sources: Worcester v. The State of Georgia, 315 U.S. 515 (1832); Richard Peters, Vol. 6, pp. 534–536, 558–563. Reprinted in Francis Paul Procha, ed., *Documents of United States Indian Policy*, 2nd ed. (Lincoln: Univ. of Nebraska, 1993).

ANNOTATED SELECTED BIBLIOGRAPHY

Cotterill, R. S. *The Southern Indians: The Story of the Five Civilized Tribes Before Removal*. Norman: University of Oklahoma Press, 1954. Chronicles events leading to removal.

Debo, Angie. *And Still the Waters Run: The Betrayal of the Five Civilized Tribes*. Princeton: Princeton University Press, 1940. Sensitively written for its time, this is an early appraisal of Indian removal from an Indian perspective.

DeRosier, Arthur H., Jr. *The Removal of the Choctaw Indians*. Knoxville: University of Tennessee Press, 1970. Case study of Choctaw Indian removal.

Foreman, Grant. *Indian Removal: The Emigration of the Five Civilized Tribes of Indians*. Norman: University of Oklahoma Press, 1932. A classic account of southeastern Indian removal.

Satz, Ronald N. *American Indian Policy in the Jacksonian Era*. Lincoln: University of Nebraska Press, 1975. Important examination of Jacksonian Indian policy.

Wallace, Anthony F. C. *The Long, Bitter Trail: Andrew Jackson and the Indians*. New York: Hill and Wang, 1993. Details Jackson's complicated views on Indian-white relations.

Washburn, Wilcomb E., ed. *The American Indian and the United States: A Documentary History*. 4 vols. New York: Random House, 1973. Excellent resource for Indian documents and other primary resources.

4

Manifest Destiny, Texas Annexation, and the War with Mexico: Sowing the Seeds of Sectional Conflict

The American desire to annex Texas can be traced at least as far back as the Louisiana Purchase of 1803, an acquisition that whetted the craving for even more land. In 1819, in a treaty with Spain whereby the United States had acquired Florida, the United States had relinquished claims to Texas arising from the Louisiana Purchase, but Americans persisted in attempts to purchase Texas. In the late 1820s cash offers of $1 million and later $5 million for Texas were rejected by Mexico. Meanwhile, Texas was filling up with American settlers who favored annexation.

The Spanish Empire in America began to fall apart in the early 1800s. In 1821 New Spain, now Mexico, declared its independence from Spain. In subsequent talks between American and Mexican officials, an international boundary line between the two nations left what is now all of Nevada and Utah, as well as parts of Colorado, Kansas, Wyoming, California, Arizona, New Mexico, and Texas, within a newly independent Mexico. In less than thirty years most of these lands would enter the American domain.

It was not until the decade of the 1820s that annexation became a prominent national issue after Stephen Austin led almost 25,000 settlers into Texas, making it virtually an American province within Mexican territory. During the 1820s, Mexico hoped to stimulate its economy by opening up its northern lands to foreign settlers and trade. It also welcomed certain American settlers, viewing them as a buffer to the free-ranging Indian tribes on the northern frontier. Here the American settlers kept their own language, formed schools, and traded with the United

States. Many of the Texas settlers had migrated from the nearby southern states of Alabama and Louisiana, as well as the Arkansas Territory, and brought along their slaves. Although the Mexican constitution of 1824 outlawed slavery, Texans found loopholes in the law until the birth of the republic of Texas formally reestablished the institution. In 1830 Mexico attempted to end immigration from the United States by imposing taxes for the first time and threatening to establish military garrisons.

By the time of the Texas Revolution (1835–1836) Americans outnumbered Mexicans ten to one in Texas outside traditional Mexican strongholds such as San Antonio. At the same time America's population at home had nearly doubled since 1790, while Mexico's population remained relatively static. Accompanying the economic and demographic progress of the United States during the first half of the nineteenth century was a national pride and sense of superiority that found expression in an attitude known as manifest destiny. The phrase was coined by the New York journalist John O'Sullivan, who wrote in 1839 that it was the "manifest destiny" of the United States to spread from sea to sea. Writing in support of Texas annexation, O'Sullivan saw it as an opportunity to prevent foreign interference from "checking the fulfillment of our manifest destiny to overspread the continent allotted by Providence for the free development of our yearly multiplying millions."

More a slogan than a refined idea, manifest destiny is often used to refer to the western expansion of the 1840s, when Texas was annexed, Oregon acquired, and California and the Southwest were purchased from the defeated Mexico. There was no single overriding motive behind the slogan. Some expansionists wanted land for national security, others for farming and lumber, and still others wanted to gain access to Pacific ports to further trade with China. Although expansion has been a recurrent theme throughout the history of the American West, what changed in the 1840s was the rationale for expansion. Formerly predicated on the expansion of farming and national security interests, in the 1840s expansion became entangled with the new vernacular of sectional politics and national predestination.

As with most other major land purchases in American history, there was little unanimity in public opinion. Many Americans feared the impact that the annexation of Texas would have on the expansion of slavery. Secretary of State Henry Clay feared that if the United States purchased Texas, the capital of Mexico would be situated much closer to the center of America.

In 1834 Antonio Lopez de Santa Anna, president of Mexico, proclaimed himself dictator, discarding most of his liberal domestic reforms and then abolishing all state governments. Not only did he declare martial law, but he attempted to expel Anglo-Texans. On October 2, 1835, Texas resisted, and war soon began.

The defeat of the Texans at the Alamo and then the massacre at Goliad only served to steel their resolve. General Sam Houston's army caught up with Santa Anna's forces at San Jacinto on April 21, 1836. His 900 troops surprised the 1,500 Mexican soldiers as they slept, and in less than twenty minutes had vanquished the army, taking Santa Anna prisoner. The Mexican president was forced to sign a treaty recognizing Texas independence and then agreed to withdraw Mexican forces south of the Rio Grande (see map). In 1837 a resolution was introduced to the Senate by a South Carolinian seeking to admit Texas into the Union as a state. Although it was tabled, until the annexation of Texas in 1845, the subject remained one of the preeminent political issues of the day.

What was most disturbing about the prospect of annexation was its ramifications for the slavery question. Southern states obviously supported annexation. Since Texas permitted slavery within its borders, it would greatly increase the slave territory once joining the Union. The main obstacle to the annexation of Texas was the reluctance of the North to accept another slave state. Meanwhile, southern states were convinced on a number of fronts. Using an economic argument that exaggerated British designs on California and Texas, expansionists had an easy time persuading the South that as an independent nation Texas would come under the sway of the British, who were no friends of slavery, but might covet Texas as an alternate source of cotton to the detriment of the rest of the South. In the event the British established hegemony over Texas, the institution of southern slavery could be undermined if Texas became a sanctuary for runaways.

Manipulating northern racism, some expansionists convinced potential expansionists that the future emancipation of slaves would mean the migration of free blacks to the North. However, if Texas was brought into the Union they would probably move there instead, due to the warm climate and proximity to the nonwhite cultures of Latin America. This in effect would create a safety valve for America's African American population. Although most northerners were not swayed by this argument, it did gain currency among northern Democratic congressmen.

In April 1844, the Senate rejected an annexation treaty which, if it had been adopted, would probably have led to immediate war with Mexico. Two years later a similar resolution did precipitate a war with Mexico, because the treaty fixed the southwestern boundary of Texas at the Rio Grande instead of at the Rio Nueces. Mexico still claimed the land between these two rivers. In the intervening years between the two treaties (1844–1846) Texan officials waged a campaign to garner support for annexation that played on the era's expansionist sentiments.

In 1844 James K. Polk was elected president of the United States. Among the major planks on Polk's platform was the "reannexation" of Texas and the "reoccupation" of Oregon. Both national political parties

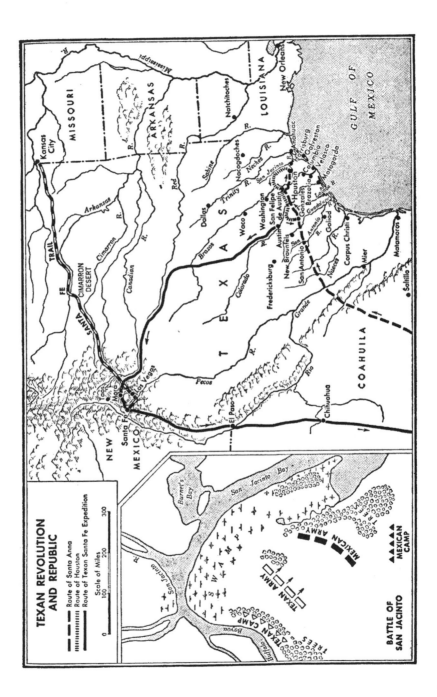

TEXAN REVOLUTION
AND REPUBLIC

Route of Santa Anna
Route of Houston
Route of Texan Santa Fe Expedition

Scale of Miles
0   100   200   300

BATTLE OF
SAN JACINTO

were torn by slavery and antislavery forces. The southern Democrats favored the annexation of Texas, hoping to increase the proslavery bloc of states since slavery was legal in the republic of Texas. But northern Whigs (many of whom would later join the Republican Party) and some northern Democrats were determined not to allow the expansion of slavery. Nonetheless, Polk carried the day in 1844, and three days after his inauguration in 1845 Texas became the twenty-eighth state. The joint resolution of Congress to annex Texas, which required simple majorities in both houses instead of a two-thirds vote in the Senate, was the first use of such a resolution instead of a treaty to accomplish specific results in foreign relations.

The drift toward America's war with Mexico between 1846 and 1848 began years earlier when Mexico threatened that U.S. annexation of Texas would mean war. Following the annexation of Texas, Mexico pointed out the obvious: the United States wanted to steal its far northern frontier, especially California and its ports. America in turn continued to begrudge Mexico's failure to repay its debts and to compensate citizens for losses suffered during the Texas Revolution. Relations between the two countries continued to deteriorate in the 1840s. Insisting that America's southern border extended to the Rio Grande, not the Nueces River, which it arguably did, Polk sent an army under General Zachary Taylor to occupy the land north of the Rio Grande and just across the river from Mexican forces bivouacked in Matamoras. On April 25, 1846, Mexican troops crossed the river and skirmished briefly with U.S. troops. Three weeks later, on May 13, 1846, the United States declared war on Mexico.

Although the war was generally popular, it had its critics, ranging from the Whig Abraham Lincoln of Illinois to conscientious objector Henry David Thoreau of Massachusetts. In one amendment put before Congress, known as the Wilmot Proviso, there was a clause attached that prohibited slavery in any land won from Mexico. However, the amendment was defeated when it went into the Senate, where southerners had the edge. Before the war, the slavery argument was between abolitionists and proslavery southerners. Carried out on the periphery of national politics, the slavery question was mostly a moral and private debate. By 1847 the debate was waged in the national corridors of power. With sides drawn along sectional lines in Congress, outside of Washington poet James Russell Lowell charged the president with wanting "bigger pens to cram with slaves." If the disputes over America's participation in the war were not bad enough, a growing number of "Continental Democrats" favored the seizure of all of Mexico.

During the U.S.-Mexican War, the slavery debate became a dangerous and divisive issue. Supporters of the "peculiar institution" argued that according to the U.S. Constitution, state governments had the right to decide the issue rather than Congress. This would become a different matter in the western territories, which were essentially American possessions not yet accorded self-government. According to the Constitution, Congress made decisions concerning the territories. /Several decisions had already confronted the issue of slavery. The Northwest Ordinance of 1787 forbade slavery north of the Ohio River. The Missouri Compromise of 1820 seemed to have settled the issue once and for all by prohibiting slavery north of 36°30' in the Louisiana Territory. The only western land where slavery was legal was the Indian territory, Oklahoma. The Missouri Compromise adopted the rule that all territories above the Compromise line would be closed to slavery, while all the land below the line would be open to slavery. This formula worked well until the war with Mexico. Most of the land acquired in the subsequent treaty fell below the compromise line, further inflaming the growing sectional crisis.

The war with Mexico, sometimes referred to as "Mr. Polk's War" by his domestic opposition, had far-reaching results as the United States acquired a vast western territory from Texas to the Pacific and north to Oregon. Within a decade, rich mineral strikes were discovered in California and a large Spanish-speaking population buckled to American institutions and society. Soon followed the clamor for transportation development to tie the new region to the East and provide ports to world markets.

Following the U.S.-Mexican War, John Calhoun argued that citizens who immigrated to the western territories had the same rights as they had at home, which meant they should be able to bring their property with them into the former Mexican lands, including their slaves. When President Polk endorsed Calhoun's reasoning, a large number of Democrats bolted the party and formed the Free Soil Party. Although many Free Soilers were antislavery, most cared little about slaves and agreed that the southern states had the constitutional right to preserve slavery at home. But as heirs to the Jeffersonian ideal of a nation of small farmers, the Free Soilers understood that in order to keep slaveowners and their plantation economy from the West, they first had to prevent slaves from going there. One of the party's slogans was "Free soil, free speech, and freemen."

In 1848 Mexican War hero Zachary Taylor was elected president as a Whig, though he had no previous party tie or much political interest. A slaveowning southerner, he nevertheless was dedicated to sectional compromise. Many Americans hoped his election would cool the sectional passions over the Wilmot Proviso and the rise of the Free Soil Party. But the discovery of gold in California soon added to the sectional tensions.

Although western historian Patricia N. Limerick recently noted that the story of the colonization of the Far West in the first half of the nineteenth century has too often been "subordinated to the story of the struggle between the North and South over slavery,"[1] the U.S.-Mexican War and the lands acquired by the Treaty of Guadalupe Hidalgo (1848) did lead to a renewed debate over the extension of slavery and are often credited with hastening the coming of the Civil War. Future Confederate leaders such as Thomas "Stonewall" Jackson, Robert E. Lee, Pierre T. Beauregard, and Jefferson Davis gained battle experience in the conflict that would pay dividends during the Civil War. The Treaty of Guadalupe Hidalgo transferred lands to the United States that would eventually comprise California, Nevada, Utah, parts of Colorado and Wyoming, and most of Arizona and New Mexico. In return, Mexico received $15 million, and American forces were withdrawn from Texas. Besides acquiring these lands, the United States also acquired 80,000 Mexicans, whose citizenship and property were supposedly guaranteed along with their religious freedom. However, that was not to be, as many of the new citizens saw their influence and property dwindle due to the increasing influx of Anglo-American immigrants.

Polk's expansionist goals, which he had set forth in his election platform, succeeded in drawing the United States into war with Mexico. Not only did America gain a more favorable boundary for Texas, but in the process it managed to acquire a large portion of the Southwest. Never of one mind about the war, abolitionists and northern Whigs criticized the U.S.-Mexican War. Following its conclusion it was still to be decided under what terms the new territories should be admitted as states. The Compromise of 1850 would eventually see California admitted as a free state; New Mexico and Utah were organized as territories without restriction on slavery but on the principle of popular sovereignty, by which residents would decide their destiny at the time of their admission to the Union; and for the South a stronger Fugitive Slave Act was passed, balanced by the abolition of the slave trade in the District of Columbia. Antislavery and slavery forces were soon at odds again in the trans-Mississippi West in the Kansas Territory in the 1850s. By upsetting the national balance of power, the U.S.-Mexican War had recast political categories, brought the expansion of the slavery issue into national debate, and contributed to the breakdown of the old party system. The deaths of John Calhoun, Henry Clay, and Daniel Webster would silence the voices of compromise as the nation foundered toward war.

NOTE

1. Patricia N. Limerick, *Something in the Soil* (New York: W. W. Norton, 2000), p. 96.

DOCUMENTS

4.1.   Texas and the Slavery Question (1828)

While slavery was illegal in Mexico, it was never formally banned in Texas. The following passage shows how Texas emigrants were able to sidestep the slavery issue by registering slaves as contract laborers before crossing the border from the United States. This excerpt also demonstrates the attachment of the mostly southern settlers to the institution of slavery.

Anti-slavery sentiment had been strong in Mexico since the liberation from Spain, and the first general colonization law, passed during the short reign of Iturbide, while permitting settlers to bring in their own slaves, forbade the buying and selling of slaves in the empire, and provided that the children of slaves born in Mexico should become free at the age of fourteen. After the downfall of Iturbide, congress took up the matter again and passed a stringent law (July 13, 1824), against the slave trade. "Commerce and traffic in slaves," proceeding from any country were prohibited; and slaves introduced contrary to the tenor of this provision were declared "free in virtue of the mere act of treading Mexican territory." There was some question as to whether the provision of the law did not make illegal the further immigration of slaves with their masters. At the time, however, it was not so interpreted. The federal constitution, which was completed in October, 1824, did not mention slavery, and there were no more federal laws on the subject until the famous decree of April 6, 1830. The state constitution of Coahuila and Texas, however, promulgated March 21, 1827, prohibited the further immigration of slaves after six months, and declared that children of slaves born in the state should be free at birth. A law of September 15 following required each municipality to make a list of the slaves in its jurisdiction, and to keep a register of the children born of slaves after the publication of the constitution, which should be reported to the governor every three months. This, of course, was expected to facilitate the enforcement of the constitutional provision. Shortly afterward (November 24, 1827), a decree was passed giving a slave the right to change his master, provided the new master would indemnify the old one. This was no doubt designed in the interest of the slave, but it can be readily seen that it afforded an easy means of evading the law against buying and selling slaves. We have no evidence concerning its operation, but nothing would have been simpler than for the two masters to come to a satisfactory agreement and then represent that the slave wished to change his master.

The slave question was an intensely practical one in Texas, and settlers already in the province, as well as others who contemplated settling there, were deeply interested. Little free labor was to be had, and slaves were considered indispensable in breaking the wilderness. Austin had bestirred himself from the beginning to prevent the prohibition of slavery, and the recognition of the institution in Iturbide's colonization law was due entirely to his persistent and strenuous efforts. Again, in the state congress, it was the tireless activity of the Texans and of their agent in the capital which prevented the outright liberation by the constitution of the slaves already in the state. By 1828 members of the state congress were brought to see the practical side of the question, and a law of May 5 legalized contracts made in "foreign countries" between emigrants and "the servants or day laborers or working men whom they introduce." The object of this law was palpably to enable colonists to continue to introduce slaves under the device of peonage contracts, and they were not slow to use it. Just before crossing the boundary an emigrant would visit a notary in the United States and have his slaves sign the necessary contract.

Source: Frank Johnson, *A History of Texas and Texans*, Vol. 1 (Chicago: American Historical Society, 1914), pp. 57–58.

4.2.   A Quaker Opposes Annexation (1837)

Born in New Jersey, the Quaker abolitionist Benjamin Lundy was an early opponent of slavery and its expansion. Lundy had visited Texas several times in the 1830s and saw the Texas Revolution against Mexican rule as a slaveholders' conspiracy to promote the slave trade. The arguments Lundy uses in the following passage were popular with antislavery leaders.

It is generally assumed that the war in Texas has assumed a character which must seriously affect both the interests and the honor of this nation. It implicates the conduct of a large number of our citizens, and even the policy and measures of the government are deeply involved in it. The subject, as now presented to our view, is indeed one of vital importance to the people of the United States; and it particularly invites the attention—the most solemn and deliberate consideration—of all who profess to be guided by the true principles of justice and philanthropy. It is not only to be viewed as a matter of interest, at the present day. The great fundamental principles of universal liberty—the perpetuity of our free republican institutions—the prosperity, the welfare, and the happiness of future generations—are measurably connected with the prospective issue of this fierce and bloody conflict.

But the prime cause and the real objects of this war, are not distinctly understood by a large portion of the honest, disinterested, and well-meaning citizens of the United States. Their means of obtaining correct information upon the subject have been necessarily limited; and many of them have been deceived and misled by the misrepresentations of those concerned in it, and especially by hireling writers for the newspaper press. They have been induced to believe that the inhabitants of Texas were engaged in a legitimate contest for the maintenance of the sacred principles of Liberty, and the natural inalienable Rights of Man:—whereas, the motives of the instigators, and their chief incentives of action, have been, from the commencement, of a directly opposite character and tendency. *It is susceptible of the clearest demonstration, that the immediate cause and the leading object of this contest originated in a settled design, among the slaveholders of this country (with land speculators and slave-traders,) to wrest the large and valuable territory of Texas from the Mexican Republic, in order to re-establish the SYSTEM OF SLAVERY; to open a vast and profitable SLAVE-MARKET therein; and, ultimately, to annex it to the United States.* And further, it is evident—nay, it is very generally acknowledged—that the insurrectionists are principally citizens of the United States, who have proceeded thither, *for the purpose* of revolutionizing the country; and that they are dependent upon this nation, for both the physical and pecuniary means, to carry the design into effect. We have a still more important view of the subject. *The Slaveholding Interest is now paramount in the Executive branch of our national government; and its influence operates, indirectly, yet powerfully, through that medium in favor of this Grand Scheme of Oppression and Tyrannical Usurpation.* Whether the national *Legislature* will join hands with the Executive, and lend its aid to this most unwarrantable, aggressive attempt, will depend on the VOICE OF THE PEOPLE, expressed in their primary assemblies, *by their petitions*, and through the ballot boxes.

The writer of this has long viewed, with intense anxiety, the clandestine operations of this unhallowed scheme, and frequently warned the public of the danger to be apprehended, in case of its success. He has carefully noted the preparatory arrangements for its consummation—the combination of influence—the concentration of physical power—the organizations of various means—and, finally, the undissembled prosecution of it, by overt acts of violence and bloodshed:—and he now stands pledged to prove, by the exhibition of well attested facts and documentary evidence, that the original cause, and principal object, and the nature of the contest, are what he has, above, represented them to be.

. . .

In their determination to resist the constituted authorities of the Mexican Republic, the Texas colonists calculated largely on receiving aid from the United States of the North. From the commencement of their settlement in that Province, we must bear in mind, that most of them anticipated its eventual separation from the government of Mexico, and attachment to the Northern Union. This was early resolved on by them, unless indeed other measures could be adopted for the perpetuation of slavery. A full and complete understanding existed between them and the advocates of the system in this country and elsewhere. . . . Their plans were all deeply laid. . . . A vast combination was . . . entered into (though not *formally organized*) the ramifications of which may be traced through a great portion of the United States, and some of the British colonies, as well as the Anglo-American settlements in nearly all the northeastern parts of Mexico. Its immediate object now is the establishment of an "Independent" government in Texas, to promote its grand ulterior designs.

As I have said before, the great land-speculators, in New York and elsewhere . . . have covered with their "grants" almost the whole area of the unsettled parts of Coahuila & Texas, and of the Territory of Santa Fe. The "grants" will nearly all soon be forfeited. . . . The most strenuous exertions are therefore made to throw a population into Texas, that will favor the views of these cormorant speculators; and lands are freely offered as an inducement for the enterprising and daring to emigrate from the United States and other countries. . . .

In case the Independence of Texas shall be established, all grants and claims . . . are legalized, (particularly if the claimants take an active part in the revolution;) the system of slavery is to be re-established upon a firm *Constitutional* basis; and every facility will be given to the introduction of slaves from the United States, Cuba, and Africa. This, it is confidently believed, will afford great opportunities to build up princely fortunes in the *Texian Empire*, by the sale of land, the extended traffic in slaves, &c.

Sources: Benjamin Lundy, *The War in Texas: A Review of Facts . . . Showing that This Contest Is a Crusade . . . to . . . Perpetuate the System of Slavery and the Slave Trade* (Philadelphia: Merrihew and Gunn, 1837), pp. 3–5; Randolph B. Campbell, ed., *Texas History Documents*, Vol. 1 (New York: Worth Publishers, 1997), pp. 35–37.

4.3.   Manifest Destiny (1845)

The New York journalist John L. O'Sullivan is generally credited with having coined the phrase "manifest destiny" in 1839. The term describes America's expansionist tendencies based on the nation's destiny to spread its institutions from coast to coast. In this 1845 article O'Sullivan seeks to influence public opinion in favor of national expansion in light of recent international developments.

It is wholly untrue, and unjust to ourselves, the pretence that the Annexation [of Texas] has been a measure of spoliation, unrightful and unrighteous—of military conquest under forms of peace and law—of territorial aggrandizement at the expense of justice, and justice due by a double sanctity to the weak. This view of the question is wholly unfounded, and has been before so amply refuted in these pages, as well as in a thousand other modes, that we shall not again dwell upon it. The independence of Texas was complete and absolute. It was an independence, not only in fact but of right. No obligation of duty towards Mexico tended in the least degree to restrain our right to effect the desired recovery of the fair province once our own—whatever motives of policy might have prompted a more deferential consideration of her feelings and her pride, as involved in the question. If Texas became peopled with an American population, it was by no contrivance of our government, but on the express invitation of that of Mexico herself; accompanied with such guaranties of State independence, and the maintenance of a federal system analogous to our own, as constituted a compact fully justifying the strongest measures of redress on the part of those afterwards deceived in this guaranty, and sought to be enslaved under the yoke imposed by its violation. She was released, rightfully and absolutely released, from all Mexican allegiance, or duty of cohesion to the Mexican political body, by the acts and fault of Mexico herself, and Mexico alone. There never was a clearer case. It was not revolution; it was resistance to revolution; and resistance under such circumstances as left independence the necessary resulting state, caused by the abandonment of those with whom her former federal association had existed. What then can be more preposterous than all this clamor by Mexico and the Mexican interest, against Annexation, as a violation of any rights of hers, any duties of ours? . . .

    . . . [T]here can be no doubt that the population now fast streaming down upon California will both assert and maintain that independence. Whether they will then attach themselves to our Union or not, is not to be predicted with any certainty. Unless the projected railroad across the continent to the Pacific be carried into effect, perhaps they may not; though even in that case, the day is not distant when the Empires of the Atlantic and Pacific would again flow together into one, as soon as their inland border should approach each other. But that great work, colossal as appears the plan on its first suggestion, cannot remain long unbuilt. Its necessity for this very purpose of binding and holding together in its iron clasp our fast settling Pacific region with that of the Mississippi valley—the natural facility of the route—the ease with which any amount of labor for the construction can be drawn in from the over-crowded populations of Europe, to be paid in the lands made valuable by the progress of the work itself—and its immense utility to the commerce of the world with the whole eastern coast of Asia, alone almost sufficient for the support of such a road—these considerations give assurance that the day cannot be distant which shall witness the conveyance of the representatives from Oregon and California to Washington within less time than a few years ago was devoted to a similar journey by those from Ohio; while the magnetic telegraph will enable the editors of the "San Francisco Union," the "Astoria Evening Post," or the "Nootka Morning News" to set up in type the first half of the President's Inaugural, before the echoes of the latter half shall have died away beneath the lofty porch of the Capitol, as spoken from his lips.

Away, then, with all idle French talk of *balances of power* on the American Continent. There is no growth in Spanish America! Whatever progress of population there may be in the British Canadas, is only for their own early severance of their present colonial relation to the little island three thousand miles across the Atlantic; soon to be followed by Annexation, and destined to swell the still accumulating momentum of our progress.

Source: John L. O'Sullivan, *Democratic Review*, Vol. 17, July–August 1845, pp. 5–6, 9–10.

4.4.   Senators in Support of Polk's War Message (1846)

During the Senate debate over the declaration of war with Mexico on May 12, 1846, Sam Houston and Lewis Cass rose to the defense of the president, charging the Mexican Army with instigating the conflict. Cass (1782–1866) was an expansionist who pressed for the occupation of Mexico and for securing the Oregon Territory. A supporter of popular sovereignty, Cass lost the 1848 presidential election to Zachary Taylor.

GENERAL HOUSTON.—Was not the crossing of the Rio Grande by the Mexican forces of itself an act of war? Was not the entering our territory by an armed force an act of war? However the decision might hereafter be in regard to the precise extent of our territory, the Mexicans knew full well that the river had been assumed as the boundary. Up to the time of annexation it had been so considered, and, more than that, the Mexicans had never once established a military encampment on the east side of the river; it had never been held, even by themselves, to be within the limits of Mexico, otherwise than upon the ridiculous ground of claiming the whole of Texas to be theirs.

They had marched across the river in military array—they had entered upon American soil with hostile design. Was this not war? And now were Senators prepared to temporise and to predicate the action of this Government upon that of the Mexican Government, as if the latter was a systematic, regular, and orderly government? He [Senator John C. Calhoun], for one, was not prepared to do so. How many revolutions had that government undergone within the last three years? Not less than three, with another now in embryo. Perhaps the next arrival might bring us news of another change, and that the American army on the Rio del Norte had been destroyed while awaiting the action of the Mexican Government, in the supposition that it was a regularly constituted government, instead of being a government of brigands and despots, ruling with a rod of iron, and keeping faith with no other nation, and heaping indignities upon the American flag. A state of war now existed as perfect as it could be after a formal declaration or recognition of a state of war by the Congress of the United States. Their action had been continually indicative of a state of war, and the question now was, whether the Government of the United States would respond to that action and visit the aggressors with punishment.

SENATOR CASS.—It is true, sir, that there may be accidental or unauthorized recontres which do not therefore constitute war. But the nature and circumstances of an aggression sufficiently indicate its true character and consequences. A Mexican army invades our territory. How far may the invaders march before we are satisfied that we are at war with Mexico? Why, sir, such a state of things must be judged by moral evidence, by the circumstances attending it. It might be enough to say that the invasion itself throws the responsibility upon the Mexican Government, and is a sufficient justification for us in holding that government accountable. The negative proof is not upon us. The moral presumption is sufficient for our action.

A hostile army is in our country; our frontier has been penetrated; a foreign banner floats over the soil of the Republic; our citizens have been killed while defending their country; a great blow has been aimed at us; and, while we are talking and asking for evidence, it may have been struck and our army been annihilated. And what then? The triumphant Mexicans will march onward till they reach the frontiers of Louisiana, or till we receive such a formal certificate of the intentions of the Mexican Government as will unite us in a determination to recognize the existence of the war, and to take the necessary measures to prosecute it with vigor.

I have no doubt the boundary of Texas goes to the Rio del Norte. But I do not place the justification of our Government upon any question of title. Granting that the Mexicans have a claim to that country as well as we, still the nature of the aggression is not changed. We were in the possession of the country—a possession obtained without conflict. And we could not be divested of this possession but by our own consent or by an act of war. The ultimate claim to the country was a question for diplomatic adjustment. Till that took place the possessive right was in us; and any attempt to dislodge us was a clear act of war.

We have but one safe course before us. Let us put forth our whole strength. Let us organize a force that will leave no doubt as to the result. Let us enter the Mexican territory and conquer a peace at the point of the bayonet. Let us move on till we meet reasonable proposals from the Mexican Government; and if these are not met this side of the capital, let us take possession of the city of Montezuma and dictate our own conditions.

Source: Marion Mills Miller, ed., *Great Debates in American History* Vol. 2, (New York: Current Literature Publishing Co., 1913), pp. 346–348.

4.5.   Opposition to the U.S.-Mexican War (1847)

A steadfast opponent to the war with Mexico, Thomas Corwin was elected to the Senate from Ohio in 1844 as a Whig. In the following speech, Corwin vehemently opposes expenditures to buy territory from Mexico. It is also worth noting his aside on acquiring California's ports. This speech reportedly derailed his future political aspirations.

Mr. President, I . . . beg the indulgence of the Senate to some reflections on the particular bill now under consideration. I voted for a bill somewhat like the present at the last session—our army was then in the neighborhood of our line. I then hoped that the President did sincerely desire a peace. Our army had not then penetrated far into Mexico, and I did hope, that with the two millions then proposed, we might get peace, and avoid the slaughter, the shame, the crime, of an aggressive, unprovoked war. But now you have overrun half of Mexico—you have exasperated and irritated her people—you claim indemnity for all expenses incurred in doing this mischief, and boldly ask her to give up New Mexico and California; and, as a bribe to her patriotism, seizing on her property, you offer three millions to pay the soldiers she has called out to repel your invasion, on condition that she will give up to you at least one-third of her whole territory. . . .

But, sir, let us see what, as the chairman of the Committee on Foreign Relations explains it, we are to get by the combined processes of conquest and treaty.

What is the territory, Mr. President, which you propose to wrest from Mexico? It is consecrated to the heart of the Mexican by many a well-fought battle with his old Castilian master. His Bunker Hills, and Saratogas, and Yorktowns, are there! The Mexican can say, "There I bled for liberty! and shall I surrender that consecrated home of my affections to the Anglo-Saxon invaders? What do they want with it? They have Texas already. They have possessed themselves of the territory between the Nueces and the Rio Grande. What else do they want? To what shall I point my children as memorials of that independence which I bequeath to them when those battle-fields shall have passed from my possession?"

Sir, had one come and demanded Bunker Hill of the people of Massachusetts, had England's Lion ever showed himself there, is there a man over thirteen and under ninety who would not have been ready to meet him? Is there a river on this continent that would not have run red with blood? Is there a field but would have been piled high with the unburied bones of slaughtered Americans before these consecrated battlefields of liberty should have been wrested from us? But this same American goes into a sister republic and says to poor, weak Mexico, "Give up your territory, you are unworthy to possess it; I have got one-half already, and all I ask of you is to give up the other!" England might as well, in the circumstances I have described, have come and demanded of us, "Give up the Atlantic slope—give up this trifling territory from the Alleghany Mountains to the sea; it is only from Maine to St. Mary's—only about one-third of your republic, and the least interesting portion of it." What would be the response? They would say, we must give this up to John Bull. Why? "He wants room." The Senator from Michigan says he must have this. Why, my worthy Christian brother, on what principle of justice? "I want room!"

Sir, look at this pretence of want of room. With twenty millions of people, you have about one thousand millions of acres of land, inviting settlement by every conceivable argument, bringing them down to a quarter of a dollar an acre, and allowing every man to squat where he pleases. But the Senator from Michigan says we will be two hundred millions in a few years, and we want room. If I were a Mexican I would tell you, "Have you not room in your own country to bury your dead men? If you come into mine, we will greet you with bloody hands, and welcome you to hospitable graves."

Why, says the chairman of this Committee on Foreign Relations, it is the most reasonable thing in the world! We ought to have the Bay of San Francisco. Why? Because it is the best harbor on the Pacific! It has been my fortune, Mr. President, to have practised a good deal in criminal courts in the course of my life, but I never yet heard a thief, arraigned for stealing a horse, plead that it was the best horse that he could find in the country! We want California. What for? Why, says the Senator from Michigan, we will have it; and the Senator from South Carolina, with a very mistaken view, I think, of policy, says you can't keep our people from going there. I don't desire to prevent them. Let them go and seek their happiness in whatever country or clime it pleases them.

All I ask of them is, not to require this Government to protect them with that banner consecrated to war waged for principles—eternal, enduring truth. Sir, it is not meet that our old flag should throw its protecting folds over expeditions for lucre or for land. But you still say you want room for your people. This has been the plea of every robber chief from Nimrod to the present hour.

Source: Appendix to the Congressional Globe, 29th Congress, 2nd Session (Washington, DC: Blair and Rives, February 11, 1847), pp. 216–217.

4.6.   Abraham Lincoln's "Spot Resolutions" (1847)

On December 22, 1847, Abraham Lincoln, a freshman Whig congressman from Illinois, questioned whether the "spot" where blood had been shed was actually U.S. soil. While Lincoln relished his public moment, his opponents ridiculed these "spot" resolutions. Lincoln was one of several congressmen to introduce resolutions opposing the war, but many of his constituents turned against him and he did not seek reelection. Lincoln's resolutions were never acted on, and for a time he was known by the derisive nickname "Spotty Lincoln."

First. Whether the spot on which the blood of our citizens was shed, as in his message declared, was or was not within the territory of Spain, at least after the treaty of 1819 until the Mexican revolution.

Second. Whether that spot is or is not within the territory which was wrested from Spain by the revolutionary government of Mexico.

Third. Whether that spot is or is not within a settlement of people, which settlement has existed ever since long before the Texas revolution, and until its inhabitants fled before the approach of the United States army.

Fourth. Whether that settlement is or is not isolated from any and all other settlements by the Gulf and the Rio Grande on the south and west, and by wide uninhabited regions on the north and east.

Fifth. Whether the people of that settlement, or a majority of them, or any of them, have ever submitted themselves to the government or laws of Texas or of the United States, by consent or by compulsion, either by accepting office, or voting at elections, or paying tax, or serving on juries, or having process served upon them, or in any other way.

Sixth. Whether the people of that settlement did or did not flee from the approach of the United States army, leaving unprotected their homes and their growing crops, *before* the blood was shed, as in the message stated; and whether the first blood, so shed, was or was not shed within the inclosure of one of the people who had thus fled from it.

Seventh. Whether our citizens, whose blood was shed, as in his message declared, were or were not, at that time, armed officers and soldiers, sent into that settlement by the military order of the President, through the Secretary of War.

Eighth. Whether the military force of the United States was or was not so sent into that settlement after General Taylor had more than once intimated to the War Department that, in his opinion, no such movement was necessary to the defence or protection of Texas.

Source: Marion Mills Miller, ed., *Great Debates in American History*, Vol. 2 (New York: Current Literature Publishing Co., 1913), p. 374.

ANNOTATED SELECTED BIBLIOGRAPHY

Eisenhower, John D. *So Far from God: The U.S. War with Mexico*. New York: Random House, 1989. Reader-friendly narrative of U.S.-Mexican War.

Fehrenbach, T. R. *Lone Star: A History of Texas and the Texans*. New York: American Legacy Press, 1968. Chronicles the Texas experience from Spanish province to republic to statehood.

Horsman, Reginald. *Race and Manifest Destiny: The Origin of American Racial Anglo-Saxonism*. Cambridge, MA: Harvard University Press, 1981. Examines the origins of American racialism and demonstrates that the belief in white American superiority was firmly rooted in the nation's ideology by 1850.

Merk, Frederick. *Manifest Destiny and Mission in American History*. New York: Alfred A. Knopf, 1963. Reconsiders the role played by manifest destiny in American history.

Weber, David J. *The Mexican Frontier, 1821–1846: The American Southwest under*

Mexico. Albuquerque: University of New Mexico Press, 1982. Leading scholar on Spanish borderlands examines American-Mexican relations in the years leading up to the U.S. war with Mexico.

Weinberg, Albert K. *Manifest Destiny: A Study of Nationalist Expansionism in American History.* Baltimore: Johns Hopkins University Press, 1935. Classic study of the roots of manifest destiny.

5

The Mormon Settlement of the West

People were lured to the West for a variety of reasons in the nineteenth century. While many were seeking to improve their economic prospects or looking for adventure, some, like the Mormons, migrated to escape religious persecution. More than a few historians have compared the Mormon settlement of Utah with the early settling of New England by the Puritans in the seventeenth century, since both communitarian experiments were conducted by highly organized people motivated more by religious ardor than by financial gain.

The Church of Jesus Christ of the Latter-day Saints, better known as the Mormons, was first organized in the "burned over district" of rural New York State by Joseph Smith in 1830. The organization of the church fulfilled a revelation received by Smith nearly a decade earlier. New York in 1820 was the scene of intense proselytizing by a host of religious denominations, as Methodist, Baptist, Universalist, and Presbyterian preachers sought converts. Confused by the convergence of so many beliefs, the teenage Joseph Smith was perplexed over his religious convictions until one day when he experienced a revelation that told him that all current churches were frauds and that the true church of God was about to be reestablished on earth.

Three years later Smith was moved by another spiritual experience in which he claimed to have been visited by God, who informed him of the existence of buried golden plates that contained a lost section from the Bible. He was instructed where to unearth the plates, but because they had been loaned to him by an angel for translation, he was initially prohibited from revealing their existence. Smith went on to translate the plates and publish their messages as the *Book of Mormon* in 1830. Within a year the church had grown from six to several hundred members. His followers saw Smith's revelations as the beginning of a new age that signaled the end of Catholic and Protestant dominance.

With its Puritan emphasis on hard work, many followers of Mormonism were drawn to this generally benevolent theocratic attempt to create an ideal society, where nobody went hungry or without shoes, where the sick and indigent found assistance, and where illiteracy and alcoholism were unknown. Others were attracted by certain communal practices based on the tithe and common storehouse as well as its Old Testament emphasis on patriarchal domination. Throughout much of the nineteenth century, Mormon support for reform movements including temperance and abolitionism incurred widespread hostility.

Almost from the beginning the Mormons were besieged by local resistance. Under Smith's leadership, members of the Mormon Church embarked on a succession of westward migrations that took them first to western Ohio and then near the town of Independence, Missouri, before moving back to Nauvoo, Illinois. In the course of their peregrinations, the Mormons endured countless tribulations before finding their New Zion in the barren wilderness of Utah, where they hoped their remoteness would protect them from the influences of a corrupt and hostile "Gentile" society (see map).

Many of Smith's followers from the New England area exhibited antislavery tendencies, leading the rough-hewn southern sympathizers of the Missouri frontier to view Smith and his church with suspicion. Citing Smith's prophecies of a time when the Mormons would inherit the earth, Missourians saw them as part of a thinly veiled plot to take over the community. By the late 1830s anti-Mormon fervor incited mobs intent on driving out the outsiders. Throughout the winter of 1838 virtual vigilante warfare was waged against the Mormons with the support of the Missouri governor. As a result, they had no choice but to move on. Their time in Missouri was but one episode in a long series of Mormon persecutions in New York, Ohio, Missouri, and Illinois. However, this legacy of persecution would only solidify the beliefs of the Mormons and strengthen their resolve.

Fired by a strong sense of being God's chosen people anointed to create an example of moral purpose, the Mormons became successful town builders. In just a few years Smith and his followers transformed the tiny hamlet of Commerce on the banks of the Mississippi River into Nauvoo, one of Illinois's most populous and economically successful communities. Within five years it would be the second largest city in the state. Mormon missionaries were able to lure thousands of converts from abroad, and by 1844, Smith led a church of 35,000 members. Despite

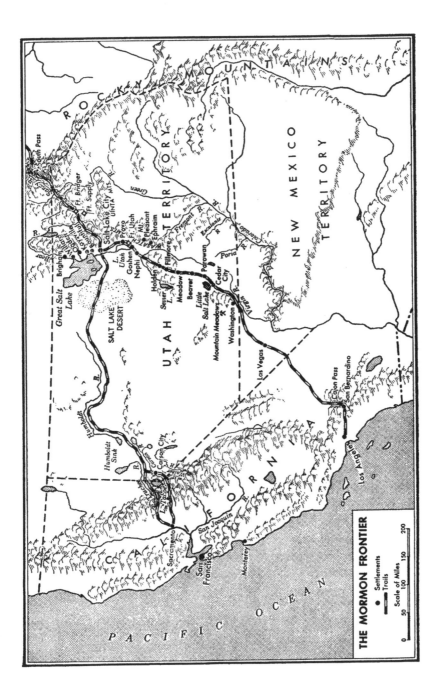

THE MORMON FRONTIER

Settlements •
Trails ▬

Scale of Miles
0   50   100   150   200

efforts to soften the hostility of its neighbors, who envied the growing wealth of the Mormons, the success of Nauvoo and other towns made the Mormons once more the target of outsiders. Together with their growing political and economic clout, rumors of polygamy among the Mormons added to the local clamor against the Mormon community. When Joseph Smith announced his candidacy for the office of president of the United States in 1844, new fears were aroused over a looming Mormon dictatorship.

However, the church was not without its own problems. Some Mormons were opposed to the practice of polygamy. Dissension within Nauvoo had begun over Smith's dictatorial proclivities and rumors of his participation in "plural marriage." Since 1831 Smith had covertly preached the practice of plural marriage or polygamy, where one man has two or more wives at the same time. (The adoption of polygamy was an attempt by Mormon leaders to restore the old gospel and reinstate lost biblical practices. Mormons viewed themselves as the children of Israel, hence their leaders' identification with Old Testament prophets.) When information on this practice reached the East, it only served to stimulate the growing opposition to the Mormons. Some would suggest that it ultimately led to the murder of Joseph Smith. Outraged over criticism from dissidents, Smith ordered their printing press destroyed. In 1844 he and his brother Hyrum were arrested for inciting a riot and locked up in a Carthage, Illinois, jail. It was not long before a mob stormed the jail and executed the brothers.

Several months after the death of Smith, a disciple, Brigham Young, gathered enough support to become the head of the church. Young married eight of Smith's widows, and as the persecution and mob actions increased, Young prepared his congregation for the exodus to the West. Young sensed that in order for the Mormons to survive they would have to move to a remote area to escape Gentile persecution. After considering several destinations, Young settled on the Valley of the Great Salt Lake after reading the explorer John C. Frémont's description of the region, which promised sufficient isolation to build a Mormon kingdom without governmental intrusion or rival claims to the land.

Thousands of Mormons followed Young to the unsettled wilderness where he would achieve what his predecessor had failed to do—establish a permanent sanctuary for the Saints. In 1846 Young led his followers along what came to be called the Mormon Trail in caravans divided into "hundreds" and "fifties," each supervised by a captain. The Mormon exodus to Utah is often regarded as the largest organized migration in the history of the American West.

Part of the reason for pioneering this trail was to avoid the thousands of Missourians who were following the Overland Trail to the West. Close to 16,000 of Young's followers reached the temporary haven at Winter

Quarters, Nebraska, before the hard winter hit. Hundreds would perish before he led the first wagon company into the Great Salt Lake basin in the summer of 1847. They found the isolation they had so long desired in the barren vastness near Utah's Great Salt Lake. In July 1847, the first group of Mormons began laying the rough outline of what would become Salt Lake City. According to the visionary leader Brigham Young, this would be no mere frontier outpost but a city that could rival any west of the Mississippi River.

With the U.S.-Mexican War still under way, the Utah territory had not yet been won from Mexico, but Mormon leaders were confident that they had found their New Zion in the West. Ever the statesman, Young even dispatched a battalion of 500 Mormons to help win the war that would bring Utah within the orbit of the United States government. For the next half century, the history of Utah would be inexorably tied to the Mormon Church.

In early 1848 the U.S.-Mexican War concluded and the signing of the Treaty of Guadalupe Hidalgo extended the United States boundary to the Pacific coast. Utah became American territory. Within days the Mormons formed their own government, creating the state of Deseret, with its own constitution. The Mormons sought to secure their hold on the territory by seeking statehood, which would remove direct federal oversight of the region.

Brigham Young knew that the only way to protect Mormon culture was to declare immediate statehood following the U.S.-Mexican War. However, without the sanction of Congress their efforts at establishing a Mormon state would fail. The petition for statehood led to intense debate in Congress. Mormon leaders were intent on continuing to practice their religion without interference, while congressmen saw the religion as anti-Christian and insisted that the unpopular doctrine of polygamy should be forbidden.

The greatest point of contention between the Mormons of Utah and the federal government would remain the practice of polygamy. The Mormons first became engaged in polygamy while still in Nauvoo in the 1840s. Although some sources indicate that it occurred earlier, in 1841 Joseph Smith started to marry additional wives. While he declared his revelation on plural marriage to his followers in 1843, fearing retaliation from Gentile neighbors, Smith attempted to keep its existence a secret. From the beginning this practice divided church members. Since the religion was originally based on monogamy, the new commandment met with resistance and led to friction among church members. However, its greatest opposition came from the more established communities of the Midwest.

While Brigham Young dominated the theocratic establishment, the Saints created a civil government to supplement its ecclesiastical foundations. During a Mormon convention in Salt Lake City, leaders drafted a constitution creating the provisional state of Deseret. But the very success of the Mormons in their effort to build a separate Zion ironically attracted the interest of outsiders. Flourishing in one of the most inhospitable regions of the country, Deseret demonstrated to the federal government that even the most reviled portion of the "Great American Desert" could be settled and exploited by adopting irrigation and water management.

Once it became clear that there was little hope of influencing statehood, the Mormon committee seeking admission to the Union changed its request to one for territorial organization. With the passage of the Compromise of 1850, Utah, and New Mexico, became territories that would decide the slavery issue for themselves. President Franklin Pierce appointed Brigham Young governor of the Utah Territory, and for the next forty-six years Utah would remain a territory, albeit a Mormon one.

As the 1850s dawned, the Mormons were well entrenched in their desert kingdom. They had survived the "Starving Time" of 1848–1849, and had overcome obstacles of biblical proportions, including famine and swarms of grasshoppers. One of the main goals of the Mormon kingdom was to remain an independent and self-sufficient society. As much as the Mormons wished to remain culturally distinct, unassimilated and untainted by Gentile culture, there is little doubt that the Mormon communities of the 1840s would have had little chance of survival without the economic benefits offered by the largesse of the California Gold Rush trade. As one of the few cities west of the Mississippi River, Salt Lake City became a destination for many miners heading to the goldfields of California. In their rush to reach California, thousands of amateur gold seekers had overequipped themselves, overloading their wagons with tools, clothes, weapons, and countless other commodities. Upon reaching Salt Lake City, they were in a hurry to sell these goods and lighten their loads before venturing into the deserts of the Great Basin. Mormon merchants were only too happy to purchase these precious goods at a huge discount of what they would have paid at wholesale in the East. Overlanders, in turn, had no choice but to pay the usurious prices that the Mormons were asking for flour and other provisions. The California trade continued to contribute to Mormon prosperity over the next several years as the Saints created an economy that would allow them to maintain their political independence.

During the early 1850s western emigrants found a thriving city of over 5,000 inhabitants near the Great Salt Lake. Those that stopped over rested and refitted at a way station superior in comforts and supplies to the army forts and private trading companies that had preceded Salt Lake City. Some emigrants even stayed at Salt Lake City for entire winters, taking advantage of the medical care, cultural and spiritual activities, and outfitting services the Mormon mecca provided. But despite the advantages and hospitality afforded by the Mormons, many emigrants complained about price gouging, anti-swearing statutes, taxes specifically imposed on Gentiles, infringement of personal rights, and religious proselytizing, and these complaints reinforced widespread anti-Mormon sentiments.

Mormon polygamy became a national issue in 1856 when John C. Frémont ran for president on the Republican ticket heralding a platform that called for an end to "the twin relics of barbarism," slavery and polygamy. Frémont lost the election to his Democratic opponent, James Buchanan, but Frémont's platform remained alive and a number of congressional acts were passed with the intention of punishing practitioners. During the next presidential election, in 1860, polygamy was once more a national issue when candidate Abraham Lincoln of the new Republican Party linked the practice to slavery. Reformers and Republicans magnified every anomaly of Mormon culture, making it seem that the plural marriage of Brigham Young and his twenty-seven wives was the norm in the Mormon territory, when in reality only a small minority of the community had more than one wife.

By the mid-1850s dozens of books had been published inveighing against the religion, and in 1857 war broke out between the federal government and the Mormons, although it was essentially bloodless. There is little doubt that the darkest days of this era occurred in September 1857, when more than 120 immigrant men, women, and children on their way to California were massacred by Mormons and Paiute Indians at Mountain Meadows. The motivation for what was the worst massacre of an overland wagon train is still inconclusive. Years after the incident participants offered various reasons for the atrocity. Some blamed the Missouri and Arkansas pioneers for antagonizing Mormons and Indians on their way through Utah or saw it as payback for the 1838 expulsion from Missouri. Others defended their actions, citing fears of invasion or threats of Indian attacks if they did not go along. Perhaps more persuasive was the desire to steal the 1,000 head of cattle belonging to the wagon train.

During his tenure as head of the Mormon Church, Brigham Young supervised the building of 188 Mormon communities in Utah, including Salt Lake City. He also oversaw the construction of cooperative irrigation projects, enhanced the development of church-owned businesses, and with twenty-seven wives himself, publicly supported polygamy in 1852. When Brigham Young died in 1877, 125,000 Mormons lived in Utah.

In 1879 the Supreme Court upheld the constitutionality of federal antipolygamy laws, handing the government the tools for dismantling the power of the Mormon Church. In the late 1880s Congress struck the Mormons socially, economically, politically, and, most important, ecclesiastically, by passing the Edmunds-Tucker Act (1887), which provided for the confiscation of the assets and properties of the Mormon Church and disfranchised Utah's women, who had been voting since 1872. It also dissolved the church fund company which had brought tens of thousands of Mormon converts from Europe to Utah. When the church challenged the act, the Supreme Court upheld its constitutionality in 1890. Later that year the church officially abandoned polygamy. Utah was finally admitted into the Union in 1896, six years after the Mormon Church finally renounced the practice of polygamy.

In the next century the church made great strides in conforming to the norms of U.S. society, and in turn gained acceptance and enhanced the influence of Mormonism. The history of the Mormons is "inseparable from the history of the American frontier and West."[1]

NOTE

1. Leonard J. Arrington, "Latter-Day Saints," *The New Encyclopedia of the American West*, ed. Howard Lamar (New Haven: Yale University Press, 1998), p. 626.

DOCUMENTS

5.1.   Polygamy, a National Reproach (1857)

During the presidential campaign of 1856, the Republican Party coupled the practice of polygamy with slavery, citing it as a "relic of barbarism." In a February 1857 speech before the House of Representatives, Justin S. Morrill of Vermont upheld the constitutional power of the federal government to abolish polygamy.

We are told, because our Constitution declares that "Congress shall make no law respecting an establishment of religion, or prohibiting the free exercise thereof," that we must tamely submit to any burlesque, outrage, or indecency which artful men may seek to hide under the name of religion! But it is impossible to twist the Constitution into the service of polygamy by any fair construction. The fullest latitude of toleration in the exercise of religion could not be understood to license crimes punishable at common law; and, if Congress is prohibited from making an established religion, a Territory must be equally prohibited, for a Territory is the creature of Congress, and Congress cannot authorize a Territory to authorize an incorporated company of priests to do what it may not do itself. The practice under our Constitution has been, and is specially provided for in the organic act of Utah, that territorial laws are annulled and void the moment they are *disapproved* of by Congress. We cannot shirk the responsibility by creating a territorial government to do that which the Constitution inhibits to ourselves. If the laws of Utah are in our judgment such as are "not fit to be made," it is our duty to annul them; and if they create an establishment of religion, then it is clearly an open and palpable violation of the Constitution, and not too sacred to go untouched.

The general assembly of the Territory of Utah has incorporated a church, over which one man presides with an insolent and all-grasping power, with authority to establish the practice of polygamy, and *not be legally questioned* therefor. Now, I submit that we not only have the power, but it is eminently proper that we exercise it by disapproving of and annulling this act.

. . .

I have no desire to make party capital by making any issues touching Utah. It is a subject requiring the deliberate attention of statesmen. It is quite within the power of gentlemen to throw the question into the pool of partisan politics by giving "aid and comfort" to the wildest theories to which any religious imposture ever gave birth. The president and rulers of the Mormon Church have already sought shelter in the bosom of the Democratic party by their proclamation of the 14th August, A.D. 1856. They find fault with the Republican party for including their "sacred institution" in the phrase of "the twin relics of barbarism." ...

There is, I hope, room to doubt whether the Democratic party will allow itself to be used for any such purpose. Their political necessities must be great when they accept of such coadjutors upon the conditions indicated.

It may be very properly asked, supposing it should be shown that a state of things exists in Utah which all would admit to be wrong, what are you going to do about it? The subject is not without its difficulties, but they are not altogether insurmountable. For one, I should greatly prefer that the people of Utah would, upon a calm reconsideration of their own affairs, remove by their own action all just matters of complaint. But, if they choose to refuse, or neglect so to do, we have only to say by our silence and non-action that we will acquiesce, or to constitutionally express our disaproval.

1. We may "disapprove" of all the laws of the Territory that we please, and thereby annul them, and for such reasons as may appear proper.

2. We may circumscribe the boundaries of the Territory, and give the inhabitants much narrower limits.

3. If the second proposition be adopted, we may then abandon them, and leave them to fight out their own independence and salvation, spiritually and temporarily, in their own good time.

4. We may cut up the Territory and annex it to the various adjoining Territories.

5. We may organize a territorial government on the old plan of a Council, consisting of a governor and judges—not Mormons; and with a military force sufficient to maintain it.

Source: Justin S. Morrill, "Polygamy a National Reproach," reprinted in Marion Mills Miller, ed., *Great Debates in American History*, Vol. 8 (New York: Current Literature Publishing Co., 1913), pp. 431–432, 435–436.

5.2.   Polygamy: Crime or Religious Practice? (1870)

On February 17, 1870, a member of the House of Representatives introduced a bill to restrict the legal and constitutional

rights of polygamy practitioners. The proposal also authorized
United States troops to enforce the act if it passed. In this pas-
sage, the architect of the proposal, Shelby M. Cullom of Illinois,
states his argument, using the late Confederacy as an example.
Cullom noted that the Mormons should be held to the same
standards as the defeated South, which meant following the laws
of the land and upholding the Constitution.

As to the qualification to hold any office of trust or profit in the Territory it seems to me that there can be no question that these leading Mormons, openly and defiantly violating law and practicing crime in the face of Federal authority, should be rendered ineligible to hold office; they are criminals, running at large because the Government has not had the courage to arrest them, and are unfit to hold office of honor or trust.

This being shown by the testimony of all who are acquainted with the condition of things existing in that Territory, and, as we have already adopted this principle in regard to certain classes of men lately in rebellion against the Government, I see no good reason why these wicked and vile men should be shielded from the operation of such a law as applied to them. I maintain that men practicing bigamy and polygamy in defiance of law are no better qualified to hold office than those lately in rebellion whom we have deprived of this right by statute and constitutional amendment.

As to the clause in regard to voting, my opinion is that the time has come when stringent, positive, and even severe legislation should be resorted to for the purpose of uprooting and destroying the iniquity that exists everywhere in that Territory; and this enactment, by depriving them of the right to vote and hold office, will take the power out of the hands of these leaders and tend to prevent the election of men sworn to defend the interests of the church at all hazards. This is a matter concerning which there should be no hesitation or timidity; and I contend that these people should neither be entitled to vote, to hold office, nor to have their aliens naturalized so long as they persist in the violation of the laws against bigamy and polygamy. The same as regards the right to preempt lands. Some may say that is too severe a hardship on these people. Sir, it is not a new thing in the history of our Government that persons should be prevented from the right to take possession of the public domain who are living in violation of its laws. It is but a short time since we passed a general law upon this subject as regards the public lands of the South, wherein, while inviting law-abiding men to come forward and partake of the benefits derived under it, we made a proviso that any person so desiring to preempt any portion of the public domain should first swear that he had not taken up nor voluntarily borne arms against the Government of the United States, and that he would support the Constitution. I regard, then, this provision as in entire harmony with the previous legislation of Congress and think it ought to become a part of the law.

. . .

Are we to have any legislation that will effectually crush out this bold and defiant iniquity, or are we to go on as we have been for over thirty years, allowing the practice of bigamy and polygamy to flourish in violation of human and divine laws, cloaked by the title of "Latter-day Saints" and a pretended system of religion? Shall we continue to temporize any longer with it and allow its defenders and abettors to go unpunished?

The great mass of the Mormons are either actively or passively in hostility to the Government of the United States. A great majority of them are of foreign birth, brought from their homes by persons assuming the garb of bishops or apostles of the church, and have never known, and never would know under the present system, anything of the institutions of this country. The power of these priests and presidents and apostles and bishops over them must be destroyed, so that the light of Christianity and civilization may reach their benighted understandings. They know nothing of the glorious principles of our Declaration of Independence. They have no impressions in regard to our people except as they are taught by Mormon teachers. They are led to believe the American people are the most infamous and bloodthirsty people on the face of the earth, and they hear from their pulpits, in their workshops, in their fields, nothing but the denunciations by their leaders against the American people. Under such a system of things it is not to be wondered at that these ignorant and deluded people come finally to regard us as their worst enemies, and become passive or active agents in the hands of their leaders to carry out their infamous designs.

Under almost any other system of religion or ethics we might hope that, in time, they would be divested of their prejudices and partake of the influences of enlightenment and civilization which are spread throughout this great country. And upon this theory the argument is raised that we had better do nothing now, that the system will die out, especially since the completion of the Pacific railroad, which will bring them more and more under the influence of our civilization and our modes of life. I confess that I had some hope that such would be the case upon the completion of the Pacific railroad. But, sir, the testimony shows that, since the completion of that great work, there has been a greater degree of proscription on the part of the leaders of that people than ever before. Within the last few months many men, Gentiles, who had been in business there, and who in years past have been favored with some degree of prosperity, latterly these men have been hunted and persecuted and in every way thwarted in their enterprises until they have been compelled, in order to protect their persons and their property, to leave the Territory and return among people where liberty and freedom prevail.

Source: Marion Mills Miller, ed., *Great Debates in American History*, Vol. 8 (New York: Current Literature Publishing Co., 1913), pp. 440–442.

5.3.   Opposition to the Anti-Polygamy Bill (1870)

During a debate on March 22 and 23, 1870 in the House over the proposed bill to punish polygamists, William H. Hooper, representing the Utah Territory, argued against the bill and its attack on religious freedom, while enumerating some of the contributions made by the Mormons in the preceding decade.

In the midst of this inhospitable waste to-day dwell an agricultural, pastoral, and self-sustaining people, numbering one hundred and twenty thousand souls. Everywhere can be seen the fruits of energetic and persistent industry. The surrounding mining Territories of Colorado, Idaho, Montana, Arizona, and Nevada in their infancy were fed and fostered from the surplus stores of the Mormon people. The development of the resources of these mining Territories was alone rendered possible by the existence at their very doors of an agricultural people who supplied them with the chief necessities of life at a price scarcely above that demanded in the old and populous States. The early emigrants to California paused on their weary journey in the redeemed wastes of Utah to recruit their strength and that of their animals, and California is to-day richer by thousands of lives and millions of treasure for the existence of this halfway house to El Dorado.

This, however, is but a tithe of our contributions to the nation's wealth. By actual experiment we have demonstrated the practicability of redeeming these desert wastes. When the Pacific slope and its boundless resources shall have been developed; when beyond the Rocky Mountains forty million people shall do homage to our flag, the millions of dwellers in Arizona, Nevada, Idaho, Colorado, and Montana, enriched by the products of their redeemed and fertilized deserts, shall point to the valley of Great Salt Lake as their exemplar, and accord to the sturdy toilers of that land due honor, in that they inaugurated the system and demonstrated its possible results. These results are the offering of Utah to the nation.

For the first time in the history of the United States, by the introduction of the bill under consideration, a well-defined and positive effort is made to turn the great law-making power of the nation into a moral channel, and to legislate for the consciences of the people.

Here, for the first time, is a proposition to punish a citizen for his religious belief or unbelief. To restrain criminal acts, and to punish the offender, has heretofore been the province of the law, and in it we have the support of the accused himself. No man comes to the bar for trial with the plea that the charge upon which he is arraigned constitutes no offence. His plea is "Not guilty." He cannot pass beyond and behind the established conclusions of humanity. But this bill reaches beyond that code into the questionable world of morals, the debatable land of religious beliefs; and, first creating the offence, seeks, with the malignant fury of partisan prejudice and sectarian hate, to measure out the punishment.

. . .

The honorable member from Illinois, the father of this bill, informs us that this is a crime abhorred by men, denounced by God, and prohibited and punished by every State in the Union. I have a profound respect for the motives of the honorable member. I believe he is inspired by a sincere hostility to that which he so earnestly denounces. No earthly inducement could make him practice polygamy. Seduction, in the eyes of thousands, is an indiscretion, where all the punishment falls upon the innocent and unoffending. The criminal taint attaches when the seducer attempts to marry his victim. This is horrid. This is not to be endured by man or God, and laws must be promulgated to prevent and punish.

While I have this profound regard for the morals and motives of the honorable member, I must say that I do not respect to the same extent his legal abilities. Polygamy is not denounced by every State and Territory, and the gentleman will search in vain for the statute or criminal code of either defining its existence and punishment. The gentleman confounds a religious belief with a criminal act. He is thinking of bigamy when he denounces polygamy, and, in the confusion that follows, blindly strikes out against an unknown enemy. Will he permit me to call his attention to the distinction? Bigamy means the wrong done a woman by imposing upon her the forms of matrimony while another wife lives, rendering such second marriage null and void. The reputation and happiness of a too confiding woman are thus forever blasted by the fraudulent acts of her supposed husband, and he is deservedly punished for his crime. Polygamy, on the contrary, is the act of marrying more than one woman, under a belief that a man has the right, lawfully and religiously, so to do, and with the knowledge and consent of both the wives.

Source: Marion Mills Miller, ed., *Great Debates in American History*, Vol. 8 (New York: Current Literature Publishing Co., 1913), pp. 443–446.

5.4.   Autobiography of a Mormon Wife (1875)

Mrs. T.B.H. Stenhouse immigrated to Utah from England and eventually became disillusioned with the religion, polygamy, the treatment of women, and its leader, Brigham Young. In 1875 she published a detailed account of life in Mormon Utah. Stenhouse describes her initial reaction to Salt Lake City, her impressions of "pic-nics" and other social customs, and matrimonial complaints of other Mormon wives.

By 1896 the only states in the nation that offered woman suffrage were Utah, Wyoming, Idaho, and Colorado, all in the mountain West. Among the explanations for this phenomenon in Utah was that it may have been an attempt by Mormons to demonstrate to their critics in Congress that their women were not mere slaves but were capable of free choice.

With the eager observation of a woman who has a great personal interest at stake, I took note of everything in Zion which was new to me, and especially all that related to the system of plural marriages, and all my worst fears were abundantly realised.

Although I had looked at the dark side of Mormonism and had pictured with horror the life of women in Polygamy, there were nevertheless some truths which broke upon my mind with painful effect. In England we had heard so frequently from the lips of the Apostles and Elders that not only was Polygamy contrary to the teachings of Joseph Smith, but that it was utterly unknown in Nauvou during the Prophet's lifetime. Directly the Revelation was published, we, of course, knew that if it really proceeded from Joseph he could not have been so innocent of Polygamy as we had been taught; but I was hardly prepared to meet several of his wives out in Utah; and yet almost the first thing that I heard was that there were living in Salt Lake City, ladies well-known and respected, who had been sealed to the Prophet. This I afterwards found was true.

The Mormon Colony in Salt Lake City had at first to contend with all those difficulties and submit to all those privations which beset the path of all new settlers in a strange country. Until very recently the greater number of the dwellings were small and low, like so many little huts, and not infrequently you might see a row of these huts, with one window and a door to each, and, inside, a wife, a bedstead, two chairs and a table—with poverty to crown the whole. But even then might be seen in the laying out of the streets, and in the other arrangements, the germs of a great city. The roadways were broad and the sidewalks convenient, and provision was made—more with an eye to the future than to present necessity—for a great depth in the measurement of the houses and blocks. Down the sides of the streets flowed a sparkling stream—the water of which was brought from the mountains for the purpose of irrigating the gardens in the city; and, as far as they possibly could, the settlers marked out and planned a capital worthy of that name for the Mormon people.

When I arrived in Salt Lake City, a great many improvements had been effected; and expecting, as I did, that this would be our future home for many years, perhaps for life, I was interested in everything that I saw. But even then, in merely taking a walk about the city, I met with evidences of the degrading teachings of Polygamy—I saw that little deference was paid to the women, they were rudely jostled at the crossings, and seemed to be generally uncared for. Since the completion of the railway and the consequent influx of Gentiles, this, of course, has not been noticeable.

. . .

The first Sunday I went to the Tabernacle I was greatly amused at the way in which some of the sisters were dressed. Quite a number wore sun-bonnets, but the majority wore curious and diverse specimens of the milliner's art—relics of former days. Some wore a little tuft of gauze and feathers on the top of the head, while others had helmets of extraordinary size. There were little bonnets, half-grown bonnets, and "grandmother bonnets" with steeple crowns and fronts so large that it was difficult to get a peep at the faces which they concealed. As for the dresses, they were as diversified as the bonnets. Some of them presented a rather curious spectacle. I noticed two young women who sat near me: they were dressed alike in green calico sun-bonnets, green calico skirts, and pink calico sacks. On enquiring who they were, I was told that they were the wives of one man and had both been married to him on the same day, so that neither could claim precedence of the other....

. . .

Often at parties and at pic-nics I met with unhappy wives who unfolded their griefs to me, and some of the things which they related were of a very painful nature. There were instances of downright brutality and cruelty which would not admit of repetition. There were also hundreds of cases in which wives suffered, not so much by any one particular act of wrong, as by innumerable daily and hourly trials, which came upon them at all times, and made existence itself a curse to them.

I remember once, at a pic-nic party, meeting with several first wives whom I had known before I came to Utah, and the stories which they told me were really shocking. At those parties, which, of course, were intended for pleasure and amusement, there was much that was painful in the conversation of the women among themselves, but which would never have been noticed by a stranger. Pic-nics are generally understood to be held in the open air, and in the country; but we used to call the ward-parties which were held in the Social Hall by that name. The Social Hall was built for this and similar purposes, and was provided with a kitchen and other necessary offices, for the preparation of suppers and other refreshments. It was in this building that plays were acted before the theatre was erected.

The pic-nic parties are quite an institution. Rich and poor, young and old, babies and all, assembled at them to have "a good time." They take their own "pic-nic" with them, set their own tables, make their own tea and coffee, and nurse their own babies. On the occasion to which I allude we went rather early, and thus I had an opportunity of watching the arrivals. Some of them presented a very amusing appearance. There was the Bishop of the ward and all his wives. Two of his boys went in front of him, carrying a very large clothes basket full of "pic-nic," as the eatables were called. Then, straggling after him, came four women and a bevy of noisy children. The wives were all dressed in grey linsey skirts, blue muslin sacques, and green sunbonnets. When they took off their bonnets I found that they all wore wreaths of roses or some other flowers. On entering, I found that quite a number had already assembled and were sitting bolt upright along the sides of the hall, as whist as mice— the women on one side, and the men on the other. At the further end of the hall I saw an old lady sitting whom I recognised as one of my neighbors. She struck me as looking so strangely that I went over to see what was the matter with her. She was pleased to see me, asked me how I thought she looked, and said that this was the first party she had attended since she came to the Valley. She had supposed that it was absolutely necessary for her to wear something white, and had therefore arrayed herself in a white night-dress which answered the purpose of a loose sacque. Sacques and skirts were all the rage at that time. She had on also a little white muslin nightcap, and altogether she looked very neat and clean, but certainly not fit for a party. I did not, of course, like to tell her so, but I felt sorry to see her dressed in that style.

. . .

. . . The wives always follow the husband. In fact, everything that is done, whether in word or deed, impresses one with the conviction that the Mormons are determined to make the women feel and fully understand that they are inferior beings. Even in the dance the man takes the lead. In all the *chasses* and promenades he precedes his wives and all other women. In a special council, held in Salt Lake City, Brigham Young once said: "For a man to follow a woman is, in the sight of Heaven, disgraceful to the name of a man." They have a curious kind of dance in Salt Lake City, called a double cotillion, in which one man dances with two women. This is done in order to accommodate those who have many wives. On entering the hall, a number is given to each man, and he is not expected to dance until his number is called. When that is done, they come like a streak across the hall to the ladies' side, to get partners; and when the dance is ended they conduct them back to their seats, and then all retire as they came, with the exception of a few love-sick swains who are reckless enough to break through this rule, in order to enjoy the society of their lady-loves between the dances.

Source: T.B.H. Stenhouse, *"Tell It All": The Story of a Life's Experience in Mormonism* (Hartford: A.D. Worthington, 1875), pp. 246–248, 496–498.

5.5.   A Gentile Visits Salt Lake City (1893)

Curious as to what made the Mormons different from nonbelievers, journalist Julian Ralph visited Salt Lake City in the 1890s on his own fact-finding expedition. What he found were people indistinguishable from their American brethren, except for their religious beliefs. Ralph is especially impressed by the ingenuity of their irrigation methods. Having abandoned polygamy in 1890, the Mormons had entered the American mainstream and were only several years from statehood.

I found Mr. Angus Cannon, and I said all that I had planned to say. Whether he is an apostle or a bishop or a plain saint, I do not know; but he is a brother of George Q. Cannon, the wisest and most forceful man in the Mormon Church, and a counsellor to the head of that body. "I am not out here to open old sores," said I, "nor to stuff any controversial points with straw, and knock them about for the edification of either Gentiles or Mormons. I have seen all the rest of the people between the Mississippi and the Rockies, and now I want to see the Mormons. It is an old story to say that the results reached by your settlers and the changes brought about on your desert land are among the wonders of the West, but it will be a new story, perhaps, to tell what sort of folks you are, and how you live and think and talk. Therefore let me see some thoroughly Mormon community, where Gentiles have nothing to do with the public management, and introduce me so that I can see the home life of the people there."

Any one might have supposed that Mr. Angus Cannon had been approached in precisely that manner three times a day for many years, so entirely at ease was he, and so calmly and readily did he make answer,

"The only difficulty about that," said he, "is to hit upon the best town for the purpose."

Afterwards, when I employed a photographer and asked him if he was a Mormon, the man of the camera said that he was, indeed, and why did I ask? Was it because I did not see his horns? Well, as to his horns, he was sorry to say he had none. He supposed they would begin to grow out when he got older.

"I told a man once," he added, "that I was a Mormon, and he said, 'You don't say so! I thought Mormons were queer-looking people and had horns.'"

Since my reader may wonder what sort of persons they really are, suffice it if it is noted here that they are precisely like the people of the West generally—the Americans being very American indeed, the Germans being more or less German, the Scandinavians being light-haired and industrious as they are at home, and so on to the end. But it is of especial value to say that Mr. Angus Cannon is of old Scotch stock, and that nearly all the leading men to whom he made me known were New-Yorkers or Virginians or Kentuckians or New Jersey born, or perhaps from one or another of the original thirteen colonies. I considered anew that such blood as that is apt to be good, and that this was why they were on top in that Church. Mr. Cannon would have passed for a Mississippi steamboat captain if he had been in St. Louis. He introduced me to his sons—four of them, I think—and one of them was an Ann Arbor graduate and a Democrat. The others were Republicans, and so was he. He introduced me to a Captain Young, a West Point graduate and son of Brigham Young, who looked the American army officer all over, though he has retired from the service. To each one of these persons Mr. Cannon told my story, and of each he asked where I had better go. Nearly every one said I had better go to the Cache (pronounced "cash") Valley, but one or two halted over a place called Provo.

Finally we met Bishop William B. Preston, and in his hands Mr. Cannon left me and went his way. Bishop Preston is a Virginian, and of a fine type of sturdy American manhood—a middle-aged, kindly man, gentle but firm and strong in appearance, speech, and methods. In Virginia he would be set down for a well-to-do man in a large country town—a country banker, for instance. His place in the Church is called "the Presiding Bishopric." He has two counsellors, sits in the counting-room of the great tithing depot in Salt Lake City, and I hazard the guess that he has charge of the property of the Church, and is the man of affairs who cares for the material possessions of the great organization.

. . .

After being introduced to many Mormons it came to be luncheon-time, and I was invited to join the family circle of one of my new-made acquaintances. I must draw the line at the door of a private house, and cannot say a word to indicate whose it was. The husband, as he approached his garden gate, called my attention to the sparkling water coursing down the street gutter, and then to a bit of board beside it. He took up the board, dropped it into a pair of slots in the side of the gutter, and thus dammed the flow, and turned it instantly and full head into his garden. The performance was a familiar one to me, but perhaps the reader does not understand it. The street gutter was an irrigation ditch. The water was that of a mountain stream, tapped high up in the hills. There was the secret of the rich greenery of Salt Lake City, and, for that matter, of the marvellous transformation of Utah from desert to garden. There, too, was seen the only, yet confident, hope of the people of the Dakotas, Wyoming, Idaho, Montana, Colorado, Arizona, New Mexico, Utah, and Nevada—that vast empire of arid land that looks to irrigation to duplicate in the West the imperial wealth of the agriculture of the East. How simple it was! A stream tapped, a rivulet running in the gutter, a block of wood to dam it, and—result, a laughing garden full of grass and flowers and fruit.

Left alone, in-doors, in my first Mormon house, I noticed only one thing, at the outset, that I had never seen in any other house. It was a scroll of Mormon texts hanging in the hall. It displayed on the outer sheet a text from the book called *The Doctrine and Covenants*.

Source: Julian Ralph, *Our Great West* (New York: Harper and Brothers, 1893), pp. 394–396, 401–402.

ANNOTATED SELECTED BIBLIOGRAPHY

Alexander, Thomas G. *Mormonism in Transition: A History of the Latter-Day Saints, 1890–1930*. Urbana: University of Illinois Press, 1986. Chronicles the middle years of the Mormon experience in the West.

Arrington, Leonard J. *Brigham Young: American Moses*. New York: Alfred A. Knopf, 1985. Biography of the famous Mormon leader by a preeminent scholar on Mormon history.

———. *Great Basin Kingdom: An Economic History of the Latter-Day Saints, 1830–1900*. Cambridge, MA: Harvard University Press, 1958. Classic account of the economic development of the Mormons in Utah.

Arrington, Leonard J., and Davis Bitton. *The Mormon Experience: A History of the Latter-Day Saints*. New York: Alfred A. Knopf, 1979. One of the best overviews of Mormon history.

Hafen, LeRoy R., and Ann W. Hafen. *Handcarts to Zion: The Story of a Unique Western Migration, 1856–1860*. Glendale, CA: Arthur Clark Co., 1960. Details the heroic trek made by handcart and foot to Utah.

Shipps, Jan. *Mormonism: The Story of a New Religious Tradition*. Urbana: University of Illinois Press, 1985. This is considered one of the most provocative examinations of the Saints.

Taylor, Samuel W. *Nightfall at Nauvoo*. New York: Macmillan, 1971. The rise and fall of a Mormon frontier city.

6

The Homestead Act: The Dispersal of Western Lands

The tradition of dispersing the public domain to settlers began with the first British colonists in Virginia. According to the headright system established in 1618, any man who paid the transportation costs to America for himself or someone else would be granted fifty acres of land. This system was most fully developed in the southern colonies. Although the system provided a powerful magnet drawing land-hungry immigrants to the colonies, it was undermined by fraud soon after its inception. By the mid-1600s planters in the Chesapeake region were acquiring thousands of acres of "head rights" through subterfuge and deception. Some planters would cross back and forth from England, each time acquiring a new headright grant. During the eighteenth century the headright system was abolished in favor of more controlled land sales.

As the United States expanded west in the years following the American Revolution, the distribution of land became one of the paramount issues for future expansion. Since the birth of the republic, federal land policy hinged on raising revenues by selling public lands. During the nineteenth century, surveying parties were never very far behind the many government expeditions that scouted the West after each new acquisition of land. Historian Richard White has described the transforming of "public lands into private lands" as one of the federal government's main roles in the nineteenth-century American West. Western farmers sought to change existing land policy, seeking free land in exchange for its development. Thomas Jefferson had written in 1776, "The people who will migrate to the Westward will be a people little able to pay taxes. By selling the lands to them you will disgust them. They will settle the lands in spite of everybody." Future architects of American land policy should have heeded these words, as speculators ran roughshod over the land distribution system in the trans-Appalachian West.

Most citizens were under the impression that western expansion would follow the model of eastern growth, as the government turned public domain, lands owned by the government, into private property. In the West new conditions would prevail, leading to different relations between the government and western lands, a relationship in which the government did not relinquish most of the lands.

American land distribution had been remarkably consistent since the 1780s, when the Land Ordinance of 1785 created precedents for future acquisition and distribution. In the process laid out by this legislation, after acquiring lands from various Indian nations, surveyors would march in and divide the land into a patchwork of six-mile squares. These would then be subdivided into one-mile-square sections, which would again be divided into four quarter sections of 160 acres each. According to the ordinance, the smallest amount of land that could be purchased was 640 acres at one dollar per acre. Few settlers could afford these prices, and so a precedent was set early on where the best land went to the better-capitalized speculators. Prospective settlers often opted for un-lawful settlement, squatting on lands and hoping that the government might eventually recognize the legitimacy of their claims.

Land distribution proceeded in an orderly fashion as long as it ad-hered to the Land Ordinance. However, Congress became further in-volved in land policy, trying to satisfy various competing interests seeking access to and control over public lands, and between 1789 and 1834 passed more than 370 different land laws. In reality the original federal land policy worked well to the east of the Appalachian Moun-tains, but once it was applied to the trans-Appalachian region a new set of circumstances blunted much of its impact.

An American tradition, settlers, speculators, and other frontier types often preceded surveyors. Once they found acreage that was to their liking, defying land laws, they settled on a parcel of land that they had no legal title for. Squatters became the bane of western land policy. There was nothing new about this phenomenon. Colonial records are filled with accounts of squatters and conflicts between Scotch-Irish and German settlers on the Pennsylvania frontier. With so many squatters on western lands by the early nineteenth century, politicians had to find a way to deal with the situation. Never of one mind about the squatters, some politicians saw them as lawless land grabbers whose disorderly subversion of land law would destine western expansion to anarchy.

Others, however, saw the squatters as courageous pioneers who would help secure the rapid growth and development of the western country.

Accepting the inevitability of squatters on western lands, Congress sporadically passed special preemption laws. The Preemption Act of 1841 recognized these special conditions, ruling that anyone could move onto public lands that had already been surveyed, and by improving the land by erecting a home or establishing a farm, could then purchase a quarter section, 160 acres of land, at the minimum price of $1.25 an acre. Preemption rights would prevail in one form or another until 1891. One of the unforeseen consequences of preemption was that it soon became difficult to separate the land speculators from the actual homesteaders, as speculators hired legions of squatters to preempt land on their behalf. Meanwhile, money lenders took advantage of preemption requirements to loan money to settlers at usurious interest rates so they could purchase land.

Antislavery advocates favored homestead legislation because it required the public domain to be sold in small units, rather than larger portions that could aid the expansion of the plantation economy farther west. In the 1830s and 1840s homestead legislation entered the political fray as eastern laborers and various reformers began to press the government for a homestead act. Several homestead bills were considered in the 1840s, but none attracted much attention as Congress debated the broader implications of the growing sectional crisis. In 1848 a homestead plank seeking the free distribution of lands to settlers was added to the Free Soil Party platform.

Western settlers would continue to lobby for free lands through the 1800s. From their perspective, it was the intrepid pioneers in the first half of the nineteenth century who created farms on public lands. Having exhausted their own resources in the building of farms and homesteads, roads and fences, the least the government could do was to waive payment. For many settlers any land payment would present one more obstacle in an already difficult situation. Farmers buttressed their argument by citing the worthlessness of the land before their improvements. Why then, they demanded, should they be penalized $1.25 an acre, when the money could be better spent on farm tools, livestock, or household accoutrements? Land payments could force some farmers deeper into debt.

The first vote on a homestead act took place in 1852. While it easily passed the House of Representatives, it was never considered in the Senate. Its greatest adversaries came from the Southeast, the nucleus of the future Confederacy. Here, then, the outlines of the coming sectional crisis were clearly drawn as the Northeast and West sided against the South a decade before the Civil War. The homestead movement would face considerable opposition not just from southern slaveholders who saw homesteaders as antislavery forces, but from eastern employers who did not want their low-paid workers seeking better opportunities farther west.

Western Democrats and Republicans supported the free land movement in 1860. Although Congress passed a watered-down homestead bill that year, it was vetoed by President James Buchanan. Beholden to his proslavery supporters for his election in 1856, Buchanan added his clout to southern attempts to stem free westward settlement. Buchanan's veto and his southern leanings would help split the Democratic Party in 1860 and pave the way to the White House for Abraham Lincoln.

With southern secession in 1861, southern participation in the federal government no longer hindered prospective homestead legislation, and the Republican Party, which had supported the Homestead Act during Abraham Lincoln's 1860 presidential bid, found itself firmly in control. Lincoln signed the Homestead Act into law on May 20, 1862. According to the act, 160 acres of land would be provided free of charge (except for a small filing fee) to any head of family or anyone twenty-one years of age as long as they were American citizens and had lived on and cultivated the land for five years. During the Civil War, Congress rewarded Civil War veterans with land grants or used land as an inducement for enlistment. Fearing that an exodus of labor to the western lands would lead to a labor shortage in the East, Congress authorized the immigration of contract workers from Europe and China. Some of this labor would also add to the diversity of the American West.

While not quite an unmitigated disaster, the 1862 Homestead Act was a mixed success. Contrary to fears that the Homestead Act would play havoc with population demographics, only 2 million out of 32 million new inhabitants between 1862 and 1890 settled on the western lands. Despite the great promise of the act, much of the well-watered Middle West already had been sold or granted to the railroads or states and was not open for settlers. Although millions of acres were still available in the upper Mississippi and Missouri valleys, much of this would also fall into the hands of railroads and land speculators.

While Congress controlled the bulk of western lands, it did not have complete control. When Texas came into the Union, it retained title to its public lands. Also, initially free from federal control were the Indian Territory, and parts of the Southwest and California that had been acquired by private landowners through earlier Mexican and Spanish land grants.

After a generation of agitation for the homestead bill, it was passed only following the outbreak of the Civil War. Among the most glaring inadequacies of the act was the provision of 160-acre homesteads in the arid West. Although this size was adequate for the well-watered Mississippi Valley, the framers of the plan, who lived in the well-watered eastern states, had erred by drafting a strategy that was unworkable in the rain-starved West. On the Great Plains, formerly known as the Great American Desert, it was estimated that a rancher needed 2,000 to 50,000 acres, while farmers would require 360 to 640 acres for any extensive stab at agriculture. Ultimately, beyond the 98th meridian, a spread of 160 acres was not capable of supporting ranching or farming.

Thus, settlers could not acquire enough free land under the Homestead Act to flourish in the West. But matters for homesteaders would get worse in the next decade as speculators plundered the domain and lobbied Congress to adopt amendments that would favor land speculation. The Timber Culture Act of 1873 was actually a rather sincere effort to adapt the Homestead Act to western conditions. According to this amendment, homesteaders could apply for an additional 160 acres if they devoted at least one-quarter to trees within four years. In the fifteen years the Timber Act was in force, 65,292 homesteaders acquired 10 million acres. By most accounts little land went to speculators under this arrangement. By 1888 thousands of homesteaders had successfully seen their lands grow to a sustainable size. At the same time a limited amount of forestation occurred.

Not all measures would benefit legitimate homesteaders. Under pressure from the ranching lobby, in 1877 Congress passed the Desert Land Act. Although theoretically it was supposed to benefit farmers, cattlemen recognized the end of the open range and sought an arrangement by which they could purchase cheap government lands. Prior to the Desert Land Act, the best a rancher could hope for was to purchase 160 acres under the Homestead Act, 160 acres under the Timber Culture Act, and perhaps another 160 under the 1841 Preemption Act. The only other alternative for creating a ranch of suitable size was to have all of the ranch employees serve as dummy ranchers to acquire still more plots of land for the ranch owner. But, even using this ruse, ranchers needed more land on the Great Plains and pressured Congress to pass the Desert Land Act.

According to the terms of the Desert Land Act, individuals could secure a title to 640 acres of land in the Great Plains or the Southwest by making an initial payment of twenty-five cents per acre. If after three years they could prove they had irrigated part of the land and then paid another dollar per acre, the land would become their private property. These claims could later be transferred to others. In reality, the Desert Land Act combined all of the elements necessary for fraudulent land dealings. Cattlemen could demonstrate "irrigation" by convincing several witnesses to swear they saw water on the claim, although in many cases it might only be a bucket of water. But the main problem with the act lay with the original framers, who settled on 640 acres, since it would be nearly impossible to cultivate 640 acres of irrigated soil in the targeted regions. Almost 10 million acres were parceled out under the act, but three-quarters of farmers who staked claims gave up before the three years expired, leaving the land mostly to ranchers.

Timber interests soon learned from other speculators and in 1878 saw their opportunities emerge with the passage of the Timber and Stone Act. This measure targeted lands "unfit for cultivation" and "valuable chiefly for timber" or stone in California, Nevada, Oregon, and Washington. The act allowed citizens to purchase 160 acres at $2.50 per acre, or the price of one good log. Once again fraud was widespread as timber barons hired dummy entrymen to purchase rich forest lands. By the end of the nineteenth century more than 3.5 million acres of forest land were taken out of the public domain.

Countless European immigrants and eastern settlers were lured west by the promise of cheap land. By most accounts the best lands—almost seven-eighths of the public domain—ended up in the hands of nefarious speculators, who purchased strategic lands along rivers and railroads, lands that were destined to be future town sites. Perhaps no figure was more reviled by western settlers than the land speculator, whom they accused of forcing them to settle for lands well off the beaten path unless they were willing to pay exorbitant prices. Since the Homestead Act only applied to surveyed lands, land speculators often moved west ahead of surveyors, taking advantage of preemption rules to squat on the best lands for $1.25 per acre. Speculators mastered subterfuge as they invented methods of circumventing the requirement to build a "suitable habitation." According to some accounts, speculators would build miniature houses, which they then claimed were twelve-by-fourteen dwellings, without explaining they meant inches instead of feet. In other cases, speculators carted portable cabins from site to site, which could be rented for as little as five dollars. So while witnesses could swear that a cabin was on a site on a particular day, by the next day it could be on another plot of land. With land districts almost 20,000 square miles, poorly paid land office agents were unable to keep up with the shenanigans of the speculators or to perform adequate inspections of the public domain.

Although thousands of acres were fraudulently acquired under the auspices of the Homestead and Preemption Acts, the most egregious land grab was performed by the railroad companies. Between 1850 and 1871, Congress awarded the railroads more than 181 million acres of land for railroad construction. More than 131 million of these acres were given directly to railroad corporations in ten to forty alternate sections for every mile of track laid. Another 3 million acres were parceled out to canal and road companies. As the settlement of the Great Plains got under way, the railroad companies were already the country's biggest landowners. When Congress gave land grants to the railroad companies, it expected them to sell the lands quickly and cheaply to expedite settlement. What was unexpected was how long it would take some companies to select their routes, let alone lay their tracks. Until the tracks were laid, settlement and land sales were restricted, and in the process the settlement of millions of acres was delayed. In 1871 Congress put an end to western railroad grants.

Despite the many abuses that took place under the Homestead Act, its passage stimulated the populating of the West in much less time than it took to settle the eastern half of the continent. Between 1870 and 1890 more lands were settled than in the previous 250 years, and in the process the West matured into a powerful sectional force in national politics.

DOCUMENTS

6.1.   The Homestead Law Before the House of Representatives (1852)

In 1849–1850, Andrew Johnson of Tennessee introduced a bill in the House of Representatives that would grant every head of a family a homestead of 160 acres out of the public domain. In 1852 the issue was argued before the House. In the following excerpts, William C. Dawson of Georgia favors homestead legislation, arguing that it would set a good example to the people, increase the tax base, and offer security against hostile forces on the frontier. Thomas J.D. Fuller of Maine responds, suggesting that the bill is unconstitutional because by its terms it would exclude too many citizens and would deed the land to a "select favored few."

House of Representatives, Beginning March 3, 1852

MR. DAWSON.—This Government was founded by the people for the good of the people. Its great basis is popular affection. It possesses an immense property which it cannot sell but by a process equal in time to a period of centuries. Compare the number of acres sold up to this date, and the length of time (sixty-four years) that has been consumed in making the sales, with the number of acres now undisposed of, and it will be seen that it will require, at the same pace, nine hundred years to dispose of the same. The progressive spirit of the age is impatient of the delay, and demands a quickened step. Vast forests and prairies separate our Atlantic and Pacific regions, which every consideration of security and of intercourse require should be settled. Its settlement would place upon a distant frontier a force able and willing to defend us against hostile savages, and thus spare us much of the expense we are now required to defray. It would be justice to the new States in which portions of the public lands are situated, by converting them into private property—subjecting them to taxation—and thus requiring them to bear their legitimate proportion of the burdens of State government.

With all of our unexampled prosperity, Mr. Chairman, in the arts and sciences, in the progress of improvement, in the extent of our commerce, in the growth and success of our manufactures, in wealth and in power, it is nevertheless true that there is great inequality in the condition of life, and that much can be done to ameliorate that condition without doing injustice or violence to the rights of any. There is no government that has so much to spare as ours, and none where the gift would be productive alike of mutual benefit. It would be the exhibition of a union of philanthropy and national interest, consummating a measure by which worthy citizens would be made comfortable, not by wasting the property of the State, not by exactions from the property of others, but by moderate grants of wild land, the cultivation of which would swell the productive property of the country, and thus contribute its proportion to the common necessities, in peace and in war.

. . .

MR. FULLER.—I regard the bill as *unconstitutional, partial*, and *unjust* in its provisions. I deny that this Government holds the public domain by such a *tenure* as that it is susceptible of any such severance and partition as is prayed for by the bill. I ask by what right—by what warrant—by what title deeds—a certain class of persons, aliens and foreigners, or citizens of a limited age—of a particular condition in their domestic relations—of a particular condition in their pecunary affairs—as they chanced to be, on the 1st day of January, 1852, appear here and claim that all, or any portion of the public lands—the common property of the whole people of the United States—shall gratuitously be set off to them, by metes and bounds, and thereafter be held and owned in severalty, to the exclusion of a much greater portion of the people, possessing equal rights and equal privileges.

. . .

Now, sir, this bill proposes to divert these lands from the *general charge and expenditure*, and to bestow them, not upon all the people, but upon a *select favored few*. Is this honestly executing the trust? The seven States from whom the United States derived its title, and all its claim, are now represented upon this floor by eighty-seven Representatives. I ask you if you can sit quietly by and witness so gross and palpable a violation of the objects and purposes for which these grants were made—yea, more—be instrumental in thus violating the sacred compact?

Source: Marion Mills Miller, ed., *Great Debates in American History*, Vol. 10 (New York: Current Literature Publishing Co., 1913), pp. 10–11, 18–20.

6.2.   President James Buchanan Vetoes Homestead Bill (1860)

On June 22, 1860, Congress passed a rather weak homestead bill. President Buchanan vetoed it because of pressure from his southern proslavery constituency, which wanted to slow down

*the settlement of the West. In the presidential election later that
year, Republican Abraham Lincoln defeated a divided Democratic Party. Among his promises was to pass a homestead measure, which was a central plank of the Republican Party platform
and the Republican promise of "free soil" leading to free men.
In this document Buchanan questions the low land prices, noting that the "price is so small that it can scarcely be called a
sale." Buchanan also argues that the Homestead Bill is unjust,
penalizing nonfarmers, such as artisans and laborers.*

Washington, *June 22, 1860.*

To the Senate of the United States:

I return with my objections to the Senate in which it originated, the
bill entitled "An act to secure homesteads to actual settlers on the public
domain, and for other purposes," presented to me on the 20th instant.

This bill gives to every citizen of the United States "who is the head
of a family," and to every person of foreign birth residing in the country
who has declared his intention to become a citizen, though he may not
be the head of a family, the privilege of appropriating to himself 160
acres of Government land, of settling and residing upon it for five years;
and should his residence continue until the end of this period, he shall
then receive a patent on the payment of 25 cents per acre, or one-fifth
of the present Government price. During this period the land is protected
from all the debts of the settler.

This bill also contains a cession to the States of all the public lands
within their respective limits "which have been subject to sale at private
entry, and which remain unsold after the lapse of thirty years." This
provision embraces a present donation to the States of 12,229,731 acres,
and will from time to time transfer to them large bodies of such lands
which from peculiar circumstances may not be absorbed by private purchase and settlement.

To the actual settler this bill does not make an absolute donation, but
the price is so small that it can scarcely be called a sale. It is nominally
25 cents per acre, but considering this is not to be paid until the end of
five years, it is in fact reduced to about 18 cents per acre, or one-seventh
of the present minimum price of the public lands. In regard to the States,
it is an absolute and unqualified gift.

1. This state of the facts raises the question whether Congress, under the
Constitution, has the power to give away the public lands either to States
or individuals. On this question I expressed a decided opinion in my
message to the House of Representatives of the 24th February, 1859, returning the agricultural-college bill. This opinion remains unchanged. . . .

. . .

2. It will prove unequal and unjust in its operation among the actual settlers themselves.

The first settlers of a new country are a most meritorious class. They brave the dangers of savage warfare, suffer the privations of a frontier life, and with the hand of toil bring the wilderness into cultivation. The "old settlers," as they are everywhere called, are public benefactors. This class have all paid for their lands the Government price, or $1.25 per acre. They have constructed roads, established schools, and laid the foundation of prosperous commonwealths. Is it just, is it equal, that after they have accomplished all this by their labor new settlers should come in among them and receive their farms at the price of 25 or 18 cents per acre? Surely the old settlers, as a class, are entitled to at least equal benefits with the new. If you give the new settlers their land for a comparatively nominal price, upon every principle of equality and justice you will be obliged to refund out of the common Treasury the difference which the old have paid above the new settlers for their land.

. . .

4. This bill will prove unequal and unjust in its operation, because from its nature it is confined to one class of our people. It is a boon exclusively conferred upon the cultivators of the soil. Whilst it is cheerfully admitted that these are the most numerous and useful class of our fellow-citizens and eminently deserve all the advantages which our laws have already extended to them, yet there should be no new legislation which would operate to the injury or embarrassment of the large body of respectable artisans and laborers. The mechanic who emigrates to the West and pursues his calling must labor long before he can purchase a quarter section of land, whilst the tiller of the soil who accompanies him obtains a farm at once by the bounty of the Government. The numerous body of mechanics in our large cities can not, even by emigrating to the West, take advantage of the provisions of this bill without entering upon a new occupation for which their habits of life have rendered them unfit.

5. This bill is unjust to the old States of the Union in many respects; and amongst these States, so far as the public lands are concerned, we may enumerate every State east of the Mississippi with the exception of Wisconsin and a portion of Minnesota.

It is a common belief within their limits that the older States of the Confederacy do not derive their proportionate benefit from the public lands. This is not a just opinion. It is doubtful whether they could be rendered more beneficial to these States under any other system than that which at present exists. Their proceeds go into the common Treasury to accomplish the objects of the Government, and in this manner all the States are benefited in just proportion. But to give this common inheritance away would deprive the old States of their just proportion of this revenue without holding out any the least corresponding advantage. Whilst it is our common glory that the new States have become so prosperous and populous, there is no good reason why the old States should offer premiums to their own citizens to emigrate from them to the West. That land of promise presents in itself sufficient allurements to our young and enterprising citizens without any adventitious aid. The offer of free farms would probably have a powerful effect in encouraging emigration, especially from States like Illinois, Tennessee, and Kentucky, to the west of the Mississippi, and could not fail to reduce the price of property within their limits. An individual in States thus situated would not pay its fair value for land when by crossing the Mississippi he could go upon the public lands and obtain a farm almost without money and without price.

6. This bill will open one vast field for speculation. Men will not pay $1.25 for lands when they can purchase them for one-fifth of that price. Large numbers of actual settlers will be carried out by capitalists upon agreements to give them half of the land for the improvement of the other half. This can not be avoided. Secret agreements of this kind will be numerous. In the entry of graduated lands the experience of the Land Office justifies this objection.

. . .

The people of the United States have advanced with steady but rapid strides to their present condition of power and prosperity. They have been guided in their progress by the fixed principle of protecting the equal rights of all, whether they be rich or poor. No agrarian sentiment has ever prevailed among them. The honest poor man, by frugality and industry, can in any part of our country acquire a competence for himself and his family, and in doing this he feels that he eats the bread of independence. He desires no charity, either from the Government or from his neighbors. This bill, which proposes to give him land at an almost nominal price out of the property of the Government, will go far to demoralize the people and repress this noble spirit of independence. It may introduce among us those pernicious social theories which have proved so disastrous in other countries.

Source: James D. Richardson, ed., *A Compilation of the Messages and Papers of the Presidents*, Vol. 5 (New York: Bureau of National Literature, 1910), pp. 3139–3145.

6.3.   The Homestead Act (1862)

There was little difference between the homestead act that was vetoed by Buchanan and the one that was passed in 1862. The

1862 Homestead Act allowed an American citizen to claim 160 acres of public land. If the settler lived on the land for five years and made "a" major improvement on it each year, he was awarded title to the land at the end of five years. The Homestead Act has been amended many times over the years. It was not repealed until October 21, 1976. However, it was extended for ten years in Alaska only, ending on October 21, 1986.

CHAP. LXXV.—*An Act to secure Homesteads to actual Settlers on the Public Domain.*

Be it enacted by the Senate and House of Representatives of the United States of America in Congress assembled, That any person who is the head of a family, or who has arrived at the age of twenty-one years, and is a citizen of the United States, or who shall have filed his declaration of intention to become such, as required by the naturalization laws of the United States, and who has never borne arms against the United States Government or given aid and comfort to its enemies, shall, from and after the first January, eighteen hundred and sixty-three, be entitled to enter one quarter section or a less quantity of unappropriated public lands, upon which said person may have filed a preëmption claim, or which may, at the time the application is made, be subject to preëmption at one dollar and twenty-five cents, or less, per acre; or eighty acres or less of such unappropriated lands, at two dollars and fifty cents per acre, to be located in a body, in conformity to the legal subdivisions of the public lands, and after the same shall have been surveyed: *Provided,* That any person owning and residing on land may, under the provisions of this act, enter other land lying contiguous to his or her said land, which shall not, with the land so already owned and occupied, exceed in the aggregate one hundred and sixty acres.

SEC. 2. *And be it further enacted,* That the person applying for the benefit of this act shall, upon application to the register of the land office in which he or she is about to make such entry, make affidavit before the said register or receiver that he or she is the head of a family, or is twenty-one years or more of age, or shall have performed service in the army or navy of the United States, and that he has never borne arms against the Government of the United States or given aid and comfort to its enemies, and that such application is made for his or her exclusive use and benefit, and that said entry is made for the purpose of actual settlement and cultivation, and not either directly or indirectly for the use or benefit of any other person or persons whomsoever; and upon filing the said affidavit with the register or receiver, and on payment of ten dollars, he or she shall thereupon be permitted to enter the quantity of land specified: *Provided, however,* That no certificate shall be given or patent issued therefor until the expiration of five years from the date of such entry; and if, at the expiration of such time, or at any time within two years thereafter, the person making such entry; or, if he be dead, his widow; or in case of her death, his heirs or devisee; or in case of a widow making such entry, her heirs or devisee, in case of her death; shall prove by two credible witnesses that he, she, or they have resided upon or cultivated the same for the term of five years immediately succeeding the time of filing the affidavit aforesaid, and shall make affidavit that no part of said land has been alienated, and that he has borne true allegiance to the Government of the United States; then, in such case, he, she, or they, if at that time a citizen of the United States, shall be entitled to a patent, as in other cases provided for by law: *And provided, further,* That in case of the death of both father and mother, leaving an infant child, or children, under twenty-one years of age, the right and fee shall enure to the benefit of said infant child or children; and the executor, administrator, or guardian may, at any time within two years after the death of the surviving parent, and in accordance with the laws of the State in which such children for the time being have their domicil, sell said land for the benefit of said infants, but for no other purpose; and the purchaser shall acquire the absolute title by the purchase, and be entitled to a patent from the United States, on payment of the office fees and sum of money herein specified.

SEC. 3. *And be it further enacted,* That the register of the land office shall note all such applications on the tract books and plats of his office, and keep a register of all such entries, and make return thereof to the General Land Office, together with the proof upon which they have been founded.

SEC. 4. *And be it further enacted,* That no lands acquired under the provisions of this act shall in any event become liable to the satisfaction of any debt or debts contracted prior to the issuing of the patent therefor.

SEC. 5. *And be it further enacted,* That if, at any time after the filing of the affidavit, as required in the second section of this act, and before the expiration of the five years aforesaid, it shall be proven, after due notice to the settler, to the satisfaction of the register of the land office, that the person having filed such affidavit shall have actually changed his or her residence, or abandoned the said land for more than six months at any time, then and in that event the land so entered shall revert to the government.

SEC. 6. *And be it further enacted,* That no individual shall be permitted to acquire title to more than one quarter section under the provisions of this act; and that the Commissioner of the General Land Office is hereby required to prepare and issue such rules and regulations, consistent with this act, as shall be necessary and proper to carry its provisions into effect; and that the registers and receivers of the several land offices shall be entitled to receive the same compensation for any lands entered under the provisions of this act that they are now entitled to receive when the same quantity of land is entered with money, one half to be paid by the person making the application at the time of so doing, and the other half on the issue of the certificate by the person to whom it may be issued; but this shall not be construed to enlarge the maximum of compensation now prescribed by law for any register or receiver: *Provided,* That nothing contained in this act shall be so construed as to impair or interfere in any manner whatever with existing preëmption rights: *And provided, further,* That all persons who may have filed their applications for a preëmption right prior to the passage of this act, shall be entitled to all privileges of this act: *Provided, further,* That no person who has served, or may hereafter serve, for a period of not less than fourteen days in the army or navy of the United States, either regular or volunteer, under the laws thereof, during the existence of an actual war, domestic or foreign, shall be deprived of the benefits of this act on account of not having attained the age of twenty-one years.

SEC. 7. *And be it further enacted,* That the fifth section of the act entitled "An act in addition to an act more effectually to provide for the punishment of certain crimes against the United States, and for other purposes," approved the third of March, in the year eighteen hundred and fifty-seven, shall extend to all oaths, affirmations, and affidavits, required or authorized by this act.

SEC. 8. *And be it further enacted,* That nothing in this act shall be so construed as to prevent any person who has availed him or herself of the benefits of the first section of this act, from paying the minimum price, or the price to which the same may have graduated, for the quantity of land so entered at any time before the expiration of the five years, and obtaining a patent therefor from the government, as in other cases provided by law, on making proof of settlement and cultivation as provided by existing laws granting preëmption rights.

APPROVED, May 20, 1862.

VOL. XII. PUB.—50

Source: U.S. Statutes at Large 12 (1862):392–393.

6.4.   Comments on the Homestead Act (1862)

This anonymous editorial was written after the passage of the Homestead Act. The author suggests that it will take great work and expenditures to transform any of the public lands obtained under the act into homesteads. However, the writer predicts the lure of free or cheap land will attract immigration from Europe.

The Homestead Bill having passed both houses of Congress, will probably have received the signature of the President, and become a law before this comes before our readers. It purports to grant to actual settlers, at a nominal price, parcels of public lands. It is called a *homestead* bill, as if a piece of wild land could with any propriety, be considered a homestead for man. A home it may be, to birds, beasts, and reptiles, but how different from a home for a civilized family—who need society, friendship and love. It may pass *land* to the *landless*, but a *home* is to be wrought out by human labor and skill. It is a misnomer to call a parcel of wild land a *farm* and more inappropriate to call it a *homestead*. With much labor and care a farm may be made of it; and with neighbors enough, it may become a homestead. It is no grant of Congress. It *was* and is the property of the people, and Congress could only make needful rules to regulate it. If a free homestead law is valid, it is because it regulates in a needful and proper manner, the public land. The truth cannot be too strongly impressed on the mind of our youth, that *wild land* has no money value except in particular localities, where value has been given to it by labor expended in the neighborhood and reflected on it. Nine-tenths of the farms in the lake States—a region of more merit than any other on the Continent—can now be bought for a sum less than the cost which has been expended in their improvements—leaving nothing for the first cost of the land in a state of nature. The right to appropriate wild land, at a nominal price, accorded by the act of Congress, will in nine cases out of ten, be barren of benefit. If it shall induce additional immigration, especially from Germany, as is not unlikely, it may do good. Western Europe could spare a million a year with little loss there and great gain here. Our rich lands are hungry for tillage. "The poor German in the pleasure which the ownership of land gives him will submit cheerfully to the privations and small returns of a new farm."

Source: Country Gentleman (Albany, New York), May 22, 1862, Vol. 19, p. 337, reprinted in Wayne D. Rasmussen, ed., *Agriculture in the United States: A Documentary History*, Vol. 1 (New York: Random House, 1975), pp. 542–543.

6.5.   A Settler on Behalf of the Homestead Act (1863)

The following is a passage from a widely printed letter describing the benefits of the Homestead Act. It highlights the opportunity for thousands of undercapitalized Americans to start a new life on the farming frontier.

Let those who from untoward circumstances find it impractible or difficult to make their way by other means, find encouragement in the example here shown. The writer says: "I failed up in the mercantile business, had nothing left but a span of horses and some household furniture and a few dollars in money, with which I started for Nebraska to take a homestead under the new law. I arrived here in March with just $5 left, took a claim, put up a log house, and went to work. I have 160 acres of splendid land which will make me a good farm, which only cost me $13; and five years' residence on it secures me the title by paying $2 more at the end of that time. I have got 10 acres of land broken up and a good garden started, and am greatly indebted for the latter to volumes of 20 and 21, of the *Agriculturist*, which I bought on the way out where I stopped over night. I have read them thoroughly, and come to the conclusion that I cannot get along without the paper. I have no experience in farming, and when I want information on any point I refer to the paper and am almost sure to find it—consequently I send the dollar for the present year, which I got by working out by the day, and this is the very best investment I can make. I wish some thousands of the hard-worked clerks and mechanics in the city, that have families to support, could know what a chance there is here for them to secure a home and a sure competency. I have been through the mill, and truly can say that I am happier and better contended here in my log house, with the prospect before me of securing an attractive home for myself and children, than I ever was when in successful pursuit of a mercantile business. Here is ample room for thousands—produce of all kinds is high and commands cash at any time. The soil is light loam with a slight intermixture of sand, the country is healthy, plenty of good water to be had by digging 10 to 20 feet, to say nothing of creeks. My claim is on the great military road from Omaha to the mines, upon which hundreds of teams pass daily, laden with stores of every description. The middle branch of the Pacific Road (when built) will pass near here, and right here in the valley of the Platte River are thousands of acres waiting for somebody to take them in possession—"to tickle with a hoe, that they may laugh a harvest." Do tell the poor hard-working drudges that barely eke out a scanty subsistance, that here they could be lords of the soil and soon gain an independence.

Source: American Agriculturist (New York), July 1863, Vol. 22, no. 7, p. 207, reprinted in Wayne D. Rasmussen, ed., *Agriculture in the United States: A Documentary History*, Vol. 1 (New York: Random House, 1975), pp. 553–554.

6.6.   The Homestead Act After Four Years (1866)

In President Andrew Johnson's second annual message to Congress, on December 3, 1866, he mentions the successes of the

Homestead Act and addresses the "liberal grants of land" to the railroads.

The report of the Secretary of the Interior exhibits the condition of those branches of the public service which are committed to his supervision. During the last fiscal year 4,629,312 acres of public land were disposed of, 1,892,516 acres of which were entered under the homestead act. The policy originally adopted relative to the public lands has undergone essential modifications. Immediate revenue, and not their rapid settlement, was the cardinal feature of our land system. Long experience and earnest discussion have resulted in the conviction that the early development of our agricultural resources and the diffusion of an energetic population over our vast territory are objects of far greater importance to the national growth and prosperity than the proceeds of the sale of the land to the highest bidder in open market. The preemption laws confer upon the pioneer who complies with the terms they impose the privilege of purchasing a limited portion of "unoffered lands" at the minimum price. The homestead enactments relieve the settler from the payment of purchase money, and secure him a permanent home upon the condition of residence for a term of years. This liberal policy invites emigration from the Old and from the more crowded portions of the New World. Its propitious results are undoubted, and will be more signally manifested when time shall have given to it a wider development.

Congress has made liberal grants of public land to corporations in aid of the construction of railroads and other internal improvements. Should this policy hereafter prevail, more stringent provisions will be required to secure a faithful application of the fund. The title to the lands should not pass, by patent or otherwise, but remain in the Government and subject to its control until some portion of the road has been actually built. Portions of them might then from time to time be conveyed to the corporation, but never in a greater ratio to the whole quantity embraced by the grant than the completed parts bear to the entire length of the projected improvement. This restriction would not operate to the prejudice of any undertaking conceived in good faith and executed with reasonable energy, as it is the settled practice to withdraw from market the lands falling within the operation of such grants, and thus to exclude the inception of a subsequent adverse right. A breach of the conditions which Congress may deem proper to impose should work a forfeiture of claim to the lands so withdrawn but unconveyed, and of title to the lands conveyed which remain unsold.

Source: James D. Richardson, ed., *A Compilation of Messages and Papers of the Presidents*, Vol. 5 (New York: Bureau of National Literature, 1910), p. 3651.

6.7.   A Dissident Western Farmer (1892)

*More of the public domain was turned into farms between 1870
and 1900 than in the first 250 years of settlement combined
(1607–1857). Following the passage of the Homestead Act
(1862) and the end of the Civil War (1865), cattle, sheep, wheat,
and corn became staples of farmers in the trans-Mississippi
West. With the introduction of farm machinery and improved
transportation, production grew dramatically. Markets were
flooded with livestock and crops from the West, leading to falling prices. At the same time, the costs of farm machinery, railroad rates, and mortgage rates began to climb. As a result of
declining rural income, in the 1880s and again in the 1890s
many farmers lost their homesteads and were forced to work as
tenant farmers. Angry farmers demanded government regulation
of the railroads and constraints on leaders to keep the robber
barons and monopolists from the East from strangling the West.
In the following passages Populist senator William A. Peffer of
Kansas speaks up for his constituents as he demands government
regulation of the railroads.*

It is said frequently that the farmer himself is to blame for all of these
misfortunes. If that were true it would afford no relief, but it is not true.
The farmer has been the victim of a gigantic scheme of spoliation. Never
before was such a vast aggregation of brains and money brought to bear
to force men into labor for the benefit of a few. The railroad companies,
after obtaining grants of land with which to build their roads, not only
sold the lands to settlers and took mortgages for deferred payments, but,
after beginning the work of building their roads, they issued bonds and
put them upon the market, doubled their capital upon paper, compelling
the people who patronized the roads to pay in enhanced cost of transportation all these additional burdens. The roads were built without any
considerable amount of money upon the part of the original stockhold-
ers, and where any money had been invested in the first place, shrewd
managers soon obtained control of the business and the property. So
large a proportion of the public lands was taken up by these grants to
corporations that there was practically very little land left for the homestead settler. It appears from an examination of the records that from the
time our first land laws went into operation until the present time the
amount of money received from sales of public lands does not exceed
the amount of money received from customs duties on foreign goods
imported into this country during the last year, while the lands granted

to railroad companies directly, and to States for the purpose of building railroads indirectly, if sold at the Government price of $1.25 an acre, would be equal to three times as much as was received from sales of the public lands directly to actual settlers. The farmer was virtually compelled to do just what he has done. The railroad builder took the initiative. Close by his side was the money changer. The first took possession of the land, the other took possession of the farmer. One compelled the settler to pay the price fixed upon the railroad lands by the railroad company; the other compelled the settler on the public lands within the grant to pay the increased price, and to borrow money through him to make the payments on both. This system continued until the farmer, accommodating himself to prevailing conditions, was in the hands of his destroyers. Now we find the railroad companies capitalized for from five to eight times their assessed value, the farmer's home is mortgaged, the city lot is mortgaged, the city itself is mortgaged, the county is mortgaged, the township is mortgaged, and all to satisfy this over-reaching, soulless, merciless, conscienceless, grasping of avarice. In the beginning of our history nearly all the people were farmers, and they made our laws; but as the national wealth increased they gradually dropped out and became hewers of wood and drawers of water to those that own or control large aggregations of wealth. They toiled while others took the increase; they sowed, but others reaped the harvest. It is avarice that despoiled the farmer.

Source: William A. Peffer, *The Farmer's Side* (New York: D. Appleton and Co., 1892), pp. 56–74.

ANNOTATED SELECTED BIBLIOGRAPHY

Carstensen, Vernon, ed. *The Public Lands: Studies in the History of the Public Domain*. Madison: University of Wisconsin Press, 1968. Useful anthology of articles on the public domain.

Gates, Paul Wallace. *History of Public Land Law Development*. Washington, DC: U.S. Government Printing Office, 1968. The standard work on the history of American public lands and the laws dealing with them.

Johnson, David Alan. *Founding the Far West: California, Oregon, and Nevada, 1840–1890*. Berkeley: University of California Press, 1992. A comparative view of the settling of three different regions of the Far West.

Paul, Rodman W. *The Far West and the Great Plains in Transition, 1859–1900*. Norman: University of Oklahoma Press, 1988. Excellent account of trans-Mississippi expansion and its impact on the Great Plains.

Reisner, Marc. *Cadillac Desert: The American West and Its Disappearing Water*. New York: Viking, 1986. A journalist describes the destruction of various western ecosystems and chronicles the story of expansion in the most arid reaches of the Far West.

Stegner, Wallace. *Beyond the Hundredth Meridian*. Boston: Houghton Mifflin, 1954.

The story of John Wesley Powell, irrigation, and settlement in the former "Great American Desert."

White, Richard. *Land Use, Environment, and Social Change: The Shaping of Island County, Washington*. Seattle: University of Washington Press, 1980. Examines major themes of western environmental history.

7

Building the Transcontinental Railroad

Railroads played an integral role in the settling of the American West. Rail lines connected western producers with eastern markets, opened the West to further economic development, even exploitation, and fundamentally transformed the ecological, physical, and social landscape. But the vast distances of the trans-Mississippi West and the lack of navigable river systems like those east of the Mississippi River that might serve as avenues of commerce and settlement proved daunting until the advent of the railroad. Building transcontinental lines was, however, beyond the resources of private interest alone. The effort demanded federal support. Among the most crucial barriers to the construction of a transcontinental railroad were how to finance such a mammoth undertaking, which route the rails would follow to the Pacific coast, and how the railroad would affect the territory designated Indian country in perpetuity.

As early as the 1840s, prescient men such as the merchant trader Asa Whitney (1797–1872) and politician William Gilpin (1815–1894) rhapsodized about the inevitability of a transcontinental railroad linking California to America's vast heartland. But they were almost alone in their optimism. While there was little debate over the goal of building a transcontinental railroad, few imagined that such an enterprise could be completed, let alone paid for, in the immediate future.

In the early 1800s, explorers such as Zebulon Pike and Stephen Long had surveyed much of the country the prospective railroad would need to traverse. Pike compared the Great Plains between the Rocky Mountains and the Mississippi River to the great desert of North Africa. His account was so vivid and so widely read that cartographers labeled the region the Great American Desert. Several years later these details would be embellished by other travelers. According to Santa Fe trader Josiah Gregg (1806–1850), this region was only fit for migratory Indians and the buffalo. By the 1840s, the land that would eventually comprise the states of Kansas, Nebraska, Oklahoma, Montana, Wyoming, Colorado, and the Dakotas had become fixed in the mind of the public as a bare, trackless waste. Initially the heartland of the continent had little lure for politicians and pioneers.

The great temptation lay on the western and southern frontiers. Any plan to build a transcontinental railroad would need the blessing and financial support of the federal government since it owned most of the lands that would be crossed by the proposed railroad. This scheme was not without precedent. The federal government had played an active, though limited, role in transportation projects since the inception of the United States, for example in funding the National Road. In 1850 railroad construction was federally funded for the first time when Congress awarded a grant of 2,595,053 acres to the Illinois Central Railroad to build a railroad connecting the Great Lakes with the Gulf of Mexico. But in considering the trans-Mississippi West, the fact remained that no private syndicate could financially afford to undertake such an enormous project over so vast a landscape, with no prospect of commerce or development along the way, and no railroad construction on public lands could begin without congressional sanction.

With the victory of the United States in the war with Mexico in 1848 and the avalanche of gold seekers pouring into California in 1849 and after, Congress became more predisposed to supporting such a massive undertaking. Another ingredient providing stimulus to the booster campaign for a railroad was the recurrent dream of easy access to trade routes with China. Ever since dreams of a Northwest Passage to Far East trade markets lured late eighteenth-century and early nineteenth-century explorers in the unsuccessful quest for a water route to the Asian trade, there remained a contingent of dreamers keeping the vision alive.

As hundreds of thousands of European immigrants debarked at East Coast ports and gold seekers by the thousands came to California by sea, the United States in 1850 remained a nation divided by an almost insurmountable expanse of physical barriers. None seemed more daunting or hostile to human habitation than what contemporary maps labeled the Great American Desert.

What made the determination of the route so important to all parties concerned was the belief that only one transcontinental railroad route would ever be built, and therefore whichever city was at its eastern terminus would reap the economic rewards in perpetuity.

Beginning in 1853, Congress authorized four transcontinental railroad surveys to determine an appropriate route to the Pacific coast. There was a tremendous rivalry between sections and cities, as each lobbied to be part of the railroad route. However, what was really at stake was whether the terminus would be in the North or in the South. Since the surveys were supervised by a southerner, Secretary of War Jefferson Davis, the prospective routes to be surveyed were construed by some as being politically motivated. Proponents of a southern route envisioned a route to California through the Southwest as a boon to the future economic growth of the South. And there was little doubt that a southern line would be easier to construct and could stay open year round.

In order to separate sectional considerations from the surveying controversy, scientists and engineers were enlisted by the U.S. Army to supervise the surveys in 1853 and 1854. Congress requested a detailed study of various routes before making a decision—in reality an attempt to avoid making a decision that could inflame sectional passions. Of the four routes considered, two were in the north, from roughly Lake Superior to Portland, Oregon, and along the Overland Trail to San Francisco via South Pass. In addition, two surveys were conducted by southern routes, from the Red River west to southern California and from southern Texas to San Diego by way of El Paso and Yuma.

Into the imbroglio stepped the "Little Giant," Stephen A. Douglas (1813–1861), fresh from obtaining territorial status for Kansas and Nebraska. A vigorous supporter of westward expansion and development, Douglas favored the quick organization of territorial governments to expedite their settlement. By favoring western settlement, Douglas, a staunch Unionist, hoped to divert attention from the mounting sectional crisis over the expansion of slavery, viewing the sectional split over slavery as the greatest impediment to westward expansion.

In 1854 Douglas had proposed legislation to organize territorial governments in Kansas and Nebraska. His solution to the expansion of slavery into federal territory was to allow the residents to decide the issue themselves through a process known as popular sovereignty. At the heart of the Kansas-Nebraska Act was Douglas's intention to connect the imminent transcontinental railroad through his home state of Illinois and on to the Pacific coast. In one fell swoop, Kansas-Nebraska repealed the Missouri Compromise, by opening to possible slavery expansion an area north of the line 36°30', where slavery had been prohibited by law since 1820.

Douglas proposed building three transcontinental railroads to placate all sections of the country, but costs for such a project were prohibitive. Ultimately, political considerations won out over scientific ones. The southern route would have been the logical choice, with its lack of geographic barriers, but with the looming sectional crisis Congress became deadlocked over a proposed route. With the outbreak of the Civil War and the secession of the southern states in 1861, the impasse in Congress was broken and congressmen could now discuss the funding of the transcontinental railroad unimpeded by sectional acrimony.

As plans for a transcontinental railroad moved closer to reality, the federal government had to address the impact of a railroad on Indian rights and lands. Since the early years of the century a designated region for Indian peoples had been the foundation of Indian removal. However, following the war with Mexico and the California Gold Rush, "the new geopolitical reality of continentalism invalidated" the premise that a region could be set aside for native peoples "for as long as the grass grows and the waters run."[1] In 1849 Congress had created the Department of the Interior, combining in one department the Bureau of Indian Affairs and the General Land Office. Not long after the Geological Survey and the Territorial Office were added. There was a basic contradiction inherent in this setup that did not bode well for Native Americans, since the same federal department responsible for protecting Indian land rights was also accountable for evaluating, dividing up, and distributing the public domain.

In 1862 a route was approved north of Mexico, along the 42nd parallel. The passage of the first Pacific Railroad Act in 1862 authorized enormous grants of public lands to fund the venture. With the South no longer an obstacle in Congress, Washington was bombarded by lobbyists with a variety of plans for a transcontinental railroad. Among the most intrepid schemers was Theodore Judah (1826–1863). A California railroad pioneer, he was so single-minded about building a transcontinental railroad that his detractors referred to him as "Crazy Judah" behind his back. Obsessed with trains since childhood, he was credited with constructing California's first railway in the hopes that it would become part of the future transcontinental railroad. The plan adopted was for the construction of two railroad lines. Between 1863 and 1869 the western-bound Union Pacific Railroad (starting near Omaha, Nebraska) would race the eastbound Central Pacific (beginning in Sacramento, California) to lay as much track as possible before meeting at a central point, undetermined in the beginning. The formula for success was clear—the more tracklaying, the more government land grants and loan bonds for the railroad company. In the process speed became more important than caution and engineering.

Judah searched high and low for a route for the eastbound line through the forbidding Sierra Nevada range, making several dozen excursions himself before becoming convinced that the Donner and Emigrant passes would be the most likely sites for his mountain route. Next he set up a paper line called the Central Pacific and began canvassing the state for investors. The prospective line would cover over 1,700 miles between Sacramento and Omaha and would require the blasting of fifteen mountain tunnels and the construction of railways across hundreds of miles of waterless desert and prairie. But first he needed money.

After he failed to find backing in the financial center of San Francisco, Judah's prospects seemed bleak until he found four investors in Sacramento. Leland Stanford (1824–1893), Charles Crocker (1822–1888), Mark Hopkins (1813–1878), and Collis P. Huntington (1821–1900) would enter western lore as the "Big Four" for their perspicacious support of Judah's venture. In 1861 Judah arrived at the nation's capital with $100,000 to drum up support among legislators whom he hoped would influence to his benefit the looming passage of the Pacific Railroad Act. On July 1, 1862, the railroad act was signed into law by President Lincoln, and Judah's unrelenting zeal won the Central Pacific the contract to build a railroad line through the Sierras.

In competition with the Central Pacific was the eastern-based Union Pacific, which began construction at the 100th meridian in Missouri. Its most challenging physical barriers included the Great Plains and the Rocky Mountains. With no predesignated meeting point for the two lines, from the start they were in competition with each other to lay the most miles of track. The companies were spurred on by the grant of 6,400 acres of federal lands for each mile of railroad. In addition, both companies were awarded enormous loans for each mile. Both railroads could expect $16,000 for each mile of level track, $32,000 for each mile of track traversing plateaus, and $48,000 for each mile of mountain track.

With such riches at stake both companies resorted to unscrupulous schemes to finance their respective lines. The Central Pacific Railroad awarded the construction contract to none other than Big Four member Charles Crocker, and by the time the project was completed the partners would pay themselves $90 million, nearly triple what the construction should have actually cost. One ruse they employed to insure the highest possible return for the dollar was to have a gullible California geologist proclaim the Sacramento Valley a mountainous region in order to claim the highest rates for railroad construction. Through its holding company, Crédit Mobilier, Union Pacific officers were able to line their own pockets with overinflated building funds and to contribute to influence-peddling pursuits by bribing congressmen. Ironically, Theodore Judah, whose vision had spurred on the great railroad venture, died on his way back east to find investors to buy out the Big Four. While traveling the shortcut from California across the tropical Isthmus of Panama to the Atlantic side, Judah, like so many before him, succumbed to the dreaded yellow fever.

Both railroad companies faced their own distinctive problems. The Union Pacific had to contend with the absence of timber on the vast prairies. In order to obtain the requisite iron and timber for railroad ties, equipment, and supplies for workers, provisions had to be shipped via the Missouri River and then transshipped overland by railroad crews. During the Civil War years there was the additional threat of attack from Cheyenne, Arapaho, and Lakota Indians following the massacre at Sand Creek (see Chapter 8). To protect railroad crews, Union Pacific commander General Grenville Dodge (1831–1916) eventually mustered 5,000 troops to guard the lines and even experimented with using traditional Cheyenne and Lakota enemies such as the Shoshone and Pawnee for protection.

Railroad crews were composed of a cornucopia of cultures, chiefly Irish, but including Germans, Mexicans, Civil War veterans from both sides of the conflict, Englishmen, former slaves, and many others. More than 10,000 workers contributed to building the Union Pacific. With such large numbers of mostly young men earning periodic paychecks, it was only a matter of time before the various denizens from the vice diaspora came flocking to the new communities on the Great Plains. Gamblers and prostitutes, pimps and liquor salesmen made themselves at home in the railroad towns, some permanent, such as Laramie and Rawlins, others ephemeral. Railroad workers referred to these communities, established almost every seventy miles along the rails, as "Hell on wheels," because of the prevalence of saloon gunfights and the proliferation of venereal disease.

As the Union Pacific made great strides across the Plains, its competitor had become mired in the Sierra Nevada range. Undermanned crews slowed the work pace to a crawl. Requiring an army of 10,000 workers, Crocker found that he had less than a thousand ambulatory men at his disposal. Crocker soon came up with the idea of opening employment to the thousands of Chinese men languishing in the played-out goldfields of California. Although his main superintendent strenuously objected, citing the supposed frail physicality of the Chinese, Crocker persuaded him to try out fifty of them for a month, for after all, he observed, who but the Chinese had built China's Great Wall? The experiment was an overwhelming success, and in a short time over 10,000 Chinese workers were staffing the Central Pacific railway. The Chinese proved tireless and efficient, and because of their abstemious tendencies, they missed less work from illness than their non-Chinese counterparts. In addition, they followed a healthier diet, and came to work already divided into crews since they typically found it much easier to work with others from the same province who spoke the same dialect. The end of the Civil War in 1865 stimulated the completion of the railroad, adding thousands of ex-soldiers to the payroll and insuring better access to rails and other equipment.

Following three years of blasting through the Sierras and enduring the most dangerous physical hardships, the Central Pacific had accomplished what many thought was impossible. It had made it out of the mountains and onto the Nevada desert floor and raced across the flats to link up with the Union Pacific.

After having laid a total of 1,776 miles of track, on May 10, 1869, both rail lines met at Promontory Summit, Utah, completing one of the greatest engineering feats in American history. The ceremonial last rails were set down by Irish workers for the Union Pacific and by Chinese employees of the Central Pacific, a fitting testimony to their blood and sweat in bringing the great project to completion. As Leland Stanford drove in the last spike, making two attempts before hitting it, a telegrapher signaled to the rest of the country "Done!"

The completion of the transcontinental railroad proved disastrous for the native cultures in the trans-Mississippi West by increasing the mobility of the Indian-fighting army, giving it the ability to bring an overwhelming force into battle in a shorter time than previously possible. But it was the buffalo hunters that likely had the greatest impact on the lives and folkways of the Plains Indians.

To feed the thousands of railroad workers, the Union Pacific hired skilled marksmen to provide buffalo meat. Between 1870 and 1883 cheap railroad transportation facilitated the slaughter of the buffalo. One hunter stationed upwind from a herd could kill 150 buffalo each day. Other hunters were more interested in buffalo hides that could be sent to commercial tanneries. In just one year, the railroads hauled more than 1,250,000 hides from the Plains. The wanton slaughter of millions of buffalo that began in earnest in the 1870s finally ended by 1900, when buffalo numbers had dwindled to about 1,000.

The rush to complete the transcontinental railroad had a number of negative consequences in the years following its construction. The quality of life in the region traversed by the transcontinental railroad was irrevocably altered. The construction was conducted at such a furious pace that much of it was shoddy, if not dangerous, and would have to be replaced. For the investors and architects of the railroad the land grants that were doled out to pay for the project never came close to paying the bills for either line. Immense tracts of land in Wyoming, Nevada, and Utah were worthless unless minerals were discovered. A great deal of this land is still owned by the federal government.

The development of the transcontinental railroad was part of a much larger transformation taking place as industrialization profoundly changed the economic realities of American life. The great transcontinental railroads made the settlement of the interior frontier a reality by linking the most remote regions with markets on both coasts. While Americans could rejoice in technological accomplishment and the promise of prosperity associated with railroad building, few could have predicted how soon the railroad would become a symbol of corporate industrialism, greed, and labor unrest.

NOTE

1. Robert V. Hine and John Mack Faragher, *The American West: A New Interpretive History* (New Haven: Yale University Press, 2000), p. 217.

DOCUMENTS

7.1.   Franklin Pierce's First Annual Message to Congress (1853)

In President Pierce's first annual message to Congress, he al-
luded to the inherent problems of constructing a transcontinental
railroad, but also recognized its necessity if the nation was to
protect its western territories in time of war.

There is one subject of a domestic nature which, from its intrinsic importance and the many interesting questions of future policy which it involves, can not fail to receive your early attention. I allude to the means of communication by which different parts of the wide expanse of our country are to be placed in closer connection for purposes both of defense and commercial intercourse, and more especially such as appertain to the communication of those great divisions of the Union which lie on the opposite sides of the Rocky Mountains.

That the Government has not been unmindful of this heretofore is apparent from the aid it has afforded through appropriations for mail facilities and other purposes. But the general subject will now present itself under aspects more imposing and more purely national by reason of the surveys ordered by Congress, and now in the process of completion, for communication by railway across the continent, and wholly within the limits of the United States.

The power to declare war, to raise and support armies, to provide and maintain a navy, and to call forth the militia to execute the laws, suppress insurrections, and repel invasions was conferred upon Congress as means to provide for the common defense and to protect a territory and a population now widespread and vastly multiplied. As incidental to and indispensable for the exercise of this power, it must sometimes be necessary to construct military roads and protect harbors of refuge. To appropriations by Congress for such objects no sound objection can be raised. Happily for our country, its peaceful policy and rapidly increasing population impose upon us no urgent necessity for preparation, and leave but few trackless deserts between assailable points and a patriotic people ever ready and generally able to protect them. These necessary links the enterprise and energy of our people are steadily and boldly struggling to supply. All experience affirms that wherever private enterprise will avail it is most wise for the General Government to leave to that and individual watchfulness the location and execution of all means of communication.

The surveys before alluded to were designed to ascertain the most practicable and economical route for a railroad from the river Mississippi to the Pacific Ocean. Parties are now in the field making explorations, where previous examinations had not supplied sufficient data and where there was the best reason to hope the object sought might be found. The means and time being both limited, it is not to be expected that all the accurate knowledge desired will be obtained, but it is hoped that much and important information will be added to the stock previously possessed, and that partial, if not full, reports of the surveys ordered will be received in time for transmission to the two Houses of Congress on or before the first Monday in February next, as required by the act of appropriation. The magnitude of the enterprise contemplated has aroused and will doubtless continue to excite a very general interest throughout the country. In its political, its commercial, and its military bearings it has varied, great, and increasing claims to consideration. The heavy expense, the great delay, and, at times, fatality attending travel by either of the Isthmus routes have demonstrated the advantage which would result from interterritorial communication by such safe and rapid means as a railroad would supply.

These difficulties, which have been encountered in a period of peace, would be magnified and still further increased in time of war. But whilst the embarrassments already encountered and others under new contingencies to be anticipated may serve strikingly to exhibit the importance of such a work, neither these nor all considerations combined can have an appreciable value when weighed against the obligation strictly to adhere to the Constitution and faithfully to execute the powers it confers.

Within this limit and to the extent of the interest of the Government involved it would seem both expedient and proper if an economical and practicable route shall be found to aid by all constitutional means in the construction of a road which will unite by speedy transit the populations of the Pacific and Atlantic States. To guard against misconception, it should be remarked that although the power to construct or aid in the construction of a road within the limits of a Territory is not embarrassed by that question of jurisdiction which would arise within the limits of a State, it is, nevertheless, held to be of doubtful power and more than doubtful propriety, even within the limits of a Territory, for the General Government to undertake to administer the affairs of a railroad, a canal, or other similar construction, and therefore that its connection with a work of this character should be incidental rather than primary.

Source: James D. Richardson, ed., *Messages and Papers of the Presidents*, Vol. 4 (New York: Bureau of National Literature, 1910), pp. 2753–2754.

7.2.   Debate over National Aid to the Railroads (1853)

The debate over the financing of the transcontinental railroad from December 22, 1852 to February 22, 1853, centered on sectional issues and was discussed in highly partisan language. Beginning in 1850 a system was introduced for granting public lands to encourage railroad construction. Much of the impetus for this legislation came from the rapid growth of the Pacific states following the Gold Rush. The costs for such a construction project were so prohibitive that there were few alternative suggestions for financing the railroad outside of the combination of private enterprise and public capital. The following excerpts from the debate in Congress reflect the opinions of politicians from various sections of the country, including Stephen A. Douglas, architect of the Kansas-Nebraska Act. Opponents of a federal plan to donate public lands to the railroads saw it as an unconstitutional attempt to expand the power of the federal government and to create a powerful undemocratic corporation.

[Senator Robert F. Stockton (N.J.)]: I am opposed to this whole scheme of a great national road. I go against it from the beginning to the end, from first to last; therefore it cannot be expected that I will yield any of the common and usual forms of legislation to facilitate its progress. I have no idea that such a bill as the one contemplated can pass the Congress of the United States at the present day. Sir, those who are endeavoring to extend the powers of this Government with the expectation and hope of making a splendid and magnificent empire of ours may well approve of this scheme, but I think the day has not yet arrived when the Congress of the United States will lend itself to such a project or proceed to make a railroad from the Atlantic to the Pacific. I am for a simple and frugal government, and against the proposed bill, and intend from the very start to oppose it.

. . .

[Senator Thomas J. Rusk (Tex.)]: If gentlemen say there is a violation of the Constitution, let them point it out. Let them take up the bill, and point out where it conflicts with the Constitution. Let them prove that you cannot carry a mail to California. Let them prove that it is not your duty to protect that defenceless frontier. Let them take up the Constitution and prove that you cannot adopt the means necessary to defend all your possessions; and then prove that it is not your duty to do it. Let them select from the bill, and not from the workings of imagination, its objectionable features. Let us have no more of this raw-head and bloody-bones business of allusions to the United States Bank, and talk about Democracy. Why, sir, the chief apostle of Democracy, General Jackson, said that he would vote money out of the treasury, or that he would sanction the voting of money out of the treasury, for internal improvements of a general and national character. Then, to keep within the pale of Democracy, let gentlemen take up and prove that the Pacific Railroad, without which you cannot defend California in case an attack should be made upon her, is a matter of local, and not of general, importance, then I will submit.

· · ·

[Senator John B. Weller (California)]: The Senator from Indiana [Jesse D. Bright], who also says here is an incorporation which is going to eat out the liberties of the country, contended that this work was not within the constitutional powers of the Government. I desire to know whether there is no power in Congress to construct a military road? Is there no power in Congress to establish a post route? Is there not an obligation resting upon this great and powerful Government to protect the people who stand upon its frontier? Sir, the man who stands upon the remotest portion of the Republic is as much entitled to the protection of this Government as he who stands in its center. If you desire the confidence and support of the people, you must take care to protect them.

I had supposed that it was long since settled that Congress had a constitutional power to appropriate the public money for works of internal improvement of a national character. The Cumberland or National road, which was designed to connect the East with what was then the far West, was first sanctioned by Mr. Jefferson. It was approved by all our Democratic Presidents down to Mr. Polk. Yet, sir, a new light has sprung up here in the State of Indiana, discovering that there is no constitutional power to do that which all those apostles of Democracy have sanctioned. I am inclined to think that they were right and the Senator wrong.

SENATOR BAYARD.—By the bill the contractors are made a body politic and corporate, a great corporation, extending throughout the whole line of the road, and created for the express purpose of constructing the road. Then the last section refers to the existence of a company for the purpose of working this road. It secures the rights of that company, but provides that, at the lapse of thirty years, the Government may purchase the road from them, paying them their capital, with ten percent interest.

Now, if, after looking at all these sections, anyone can say that this bill does not create a corporation, that it does not contemplate the construction of this road by means of a great corporation, which is only to a very limited extent to be within the control of the Congress of the

United States, I confess that I cannot understand the meaning of language and the objects of the bill.

. . .

[Senator Stephen A. Douglas (Ill.)]: I apprehend that gentlemen travel beyond the terms of the bill, and make arguments which are negatived by its provisions. They argue in defiance of it, when they pretend to show that the Government of the United States is about to go into an unknown expenditure, and to create a boundless public debt. One great merit of this bill is that it fixes precisely and exactly the liability of the Government; and it not only does that, but it contains such guards that by no possibility, under its terms, can there be a loss to the United States. By no possibility can the contractors get one dollar of public money, until they have expended on the road five times that amount, and given us a priority of lien on that fivefold amount as security for our advance. We do not part with our security even when the road is completed. I think, therefore, that an examination of the provisions of the bill will put an end entirely to any apprehensions upon that score.

The Senator from Georgia says he would like to see this road made, provided it can be done consistently with the Constitution. I did not understand distinctly from him that it violated the Constitution.

. . .

I undertake to predict to the honorable Senator from Georgia that, although the country through which this road is to be constructed is now a wilderness, before it is finished the line of the road and the country for a wide extent on either side will be more densely populated than the State of which he is the able representative on this floor. I undertake to say to the Senator that I am willing to put myself on the record as predicting that, when you get this road half done, the local travel along the finished portion of it will be beyond the capacity of a single track to perform. Each one hundred miles that you penetrate the wilderness, you shorten the distance for hauling supplies, and a greater number of teams will be required to concentrate upon it, and population will be swelling in upon each side to raise provisions to sell to the men engaged in the work.

. . .

The Senator from Georgia says that no individual, no nation, no State, ever undertook a work of this magnitude without a survey. They never did, either with or without a survey; for never has a road of this magnitude been proposed, much less executed, anywhere.

Source: Marion Mills Miller, ed., *Great Debates in American History*, Vol. 10 (New York: Current Literature Publishing Co., 1913), pp. 160–174.

7.3.   Overland from New York to San Francisco (1859)

*Ever the booster for westward expansion, in 1859 the noted jour-
nalist Horace Greeley persuasively argued for a transcontinental
route to the Pacific from Missouri. In the following excerpts,
Greeley notes the various benefits of such an endeavor.*

I can have no doubt that a railroad from the Missouri to the Pacific
would earn seventeen millions of dollars the year after its completion,
and that its income would increase thenceforth at the rate of at least one
million per annum for ten or fifteen years.

Let us now consider the political or national necessity and use for a
railroad from the Missouri to the Pacific:

1. The Federal government is now paying some twenty-five millions
per annum for military service, mainly west of the Mississippi. Nearly
half of this heavy sum is paid for transportation in its various shapes—
for the conveyance of provisions, munitions, etc., to the army in Utah,
and to the various posts scattered through the Indian country; for horses,
mules, and wagons, required to facilitate the conveyance of soldiers,
arms, munitions, and baggage from post to post, etc., etc. Every regiment
employed in the Indian country, or on the Pacific, costs the treasury at
least one thousand dollars per man per annum, of which I estimate that
nearly half would be saved by a Pacific railroad. Certainly, the saving
from this source could not fall short of five millions per annum.

2. But the efficacy, the power of an armed force, in the defense and
protection of a vast empire, depend less on its numbers than on its mobility—on the facility with which it can be conveyed to the point at
which it may at any time be wanted. For instance, our government has
now some six to eight thousand regulars scattered over Nebraska, Kansas, New Mexico, Northern Texas, Utah, California, Oregon, and Washington. These six or eight thousand are not as efficient as two thousand
would be, if it were in the power of the government instantly to transfer
those two thousand, by a mere order, to the point at which they might
at any time be wanted. A Pacific railroad would not, indeed, fully effect
this; but it would go far toward it.

3. Suppose our little army, now largely concentrated in Utah, were
urgently needed to repel some sudden danger, whether on the Pacific or
the Atlantic coast: It would be a good three month's work to provide
the needful animals, and remove that force to either seaboard. But with
a Pacific railroad, the whole might be in New York, Charleston, New
Orleans, or San Francisco, within a fortnight after the order was dis-

patched by telegraph from the War department, at Washington. The value of this facility of movement can hardly be over-estimated.

4. At present, the regiments employed on the Pacific are almost or quite wholly raised and recruited in the Atlantic States. Their removal thence to their destination costs largely, heavily, in direct expense, and in that time which is money. Suppose a regiment to cost half a million per annum, and that six months are now consumed in sending it from Baltimore to Puget's Sound, while one month would suffice with a Pacific railroad. In addition to the saving on the present cost of its transportation, the saving in the time of that regiment would be two hundred thousand dollars directly, and practically much more; as a part of the cost of recruiting, drilling, etc., now lost in the tedious transportation, would be saved by the accelerated movement.

5. In case of war with any great maritime power, in the absence of a Pacific railroad, we should be compelled either to surrender the Pacific states to subjugation and spoliation, or maintain a double armament at enormous cost. Our army on this side of the Rocky Mountains would be utterly ineffective as against an expedition launched against the Pacific coast, and *vice versa*. But, with a Pacific railroad, and the telegraph which would inevitably accompany it, it would be morally impossible that an expedition directed against either seaboard, should not be anticipated in its arrival by the concentration, to oppose its landing, of our soldiers, drawn from every part of the country. Our government, in aiding the construction of such road, would inevitably stipulate for its use—exclusive, if required—in times of public peril; and would thus be enabled to transfer fifty thousand men from either coast to the other in the course of twenty or thirty days.

6. We have already expended some scores of millions of dollars on fortifications, and are urgently required to expend as many more. Especially on the Pacific is their construction pressingly demanded. I do not decide how fast nor how far this demand may or should be responded to; but I do say that a Pacific railroad, whereby the riflemen of the mountains could be brought to the Pacific within three days, and those of the Missouri within ten, would afford more security to San Francisco than ever so many gigantic and costly fortifications.

But enough on this head.

The social, moral, and intellectual blessings of a Pacific railroad can hardly be glanced at within the limits of an article. Suffice it for the present that I merely suggest them.

1. Our mails are now carried to and from California by steamships, via Panama, in twenty to thirty days, starting once a fortnight. The average time of transit from writers throughout the Atlantic states to their correspondents on the Pacific exceeds thirty days. With a Pacific railroad,

this would be reduced to ten; for the letters written in Illinois or Michigan would reach their destinations in the mining counties of California quicker than letters sent from New York or Philadelphia would reach San Francisco. With a daily mail by railroad from each of our Atlantic cities to and from California, it is hardly possible that the amount of both letters and printed matter transmitted, and consequently of postage, should not be speedily quadrupled.

2. The first need of California to-day is a large influx of intelligent, capable, virtuous women. With a railroad to the Pacific, avoiding the miseries and perils of six thousand miles of ocean transportation, and making the transit a pleasant and interesting overland journey of ten days, at a reduced cost, the migration of this class would be immensely accelerated and increased. With wages for all kinds of women's work at least thrice as high on the Pacific as in this quarter, and with larger opportunities for honorable and fit settlement in life, I cannot doubt that tens of thousands would annually cross the Plains, to the signal benefit of California and of the whole country, as well as the improvement of their own fortunes and the profit of the railroad.

3. Thousands now staying in California, expecting to "go home" so soon as they shall have somewhat improved their circumstances, would send or come for their families and settle on the Pacific for life, if a railroad were opened. Tens of thousands who have been to California and come back, unwilling either to live away from their families or to expose them to the present hardships of migration thither, would return with all they have, prepared to spend their remaining days in the land of gold, if there were a Pacific railroad.

4. Education is the vital want of California, second to its need of true women. School-books, and all the material of education, are now scarce and dear there. Almost all books sell there twice as high as here, and many of the best are scarcely attainable at any rate. With the Pacific railroad, all this would be changed for the better. The proportion of school-houses to grog-shops would rapidly increase. All the elements of moral and religious melioration would be multiplied. Tens of thousands of our best citizens would visit the Pacific coast, receiving novel ideas and impressions, to their own profit and that of the people thus visited. Civilization, intelligence, refinement, on both sides of the mountain—still more, in the Great Basin inclosed by them—would receive a new and immense impulse, and the Union would acquire a greater accession of strength, power, endurance, and true glory, than it would from the acquisition of the whole continent down to Cape Horn.

Source: Horace Greeley, *An Overland Journey from New York to San Francisco in the Summer of 1859* (New York: Saxton Barker, 1860), pp. 374–379.

7.4.   The Union and Central Pacific Railroads (1869)

The following passage offers a summary of the construction of the two railroad lines. Grace Raymond Hebard (1861–1936), a political scientist and historian who wrote several books on the American West, like most critics of the transcontinental railroad project seems most concerned with its creative financing and the depredations endured by the workers. This excerpt is from Hebard's history of the "Great West," originally published in 1911.

In order to make possible the building of the first transcontinental railroad, our government appropriated vast sums of money and gave extensive tracts of land to the Union Pacific and Central Pacific railways, the combination of the two roads making a continuous line of transportation from the Missouri to the Pacific coast. In money and land the Union Pacific received $450,000,000, the Central Pacific $380,000,000. Yet with this stupendous gift it was difficult, almost impossible, to get men of means interested enough in the enterprise to risk their money in the venture. Oakes Ames and Sidney Dillon, whose names can never be separated from that of the Union Pacific, searched the money markets and pleaded with millionaires for capital to build the great road. President Lincoln, too, worked night and day trying to get capitalists to furnish money for the construction of the road, which he considered of vast importance. It was a heartbreaking task. The man of business did not believe the scheme was practicable. He had no money to invest in two thousand miles of railway, declaring that the Indians would tear up the track and make bonfires of the flag stations along the line. In all the 650 miles between Reno, Nevada, and Corinne, Utah, there was only one white man living. How could a railroad pay across such deserts? All honor to Ames and Dillon for their perseverance. Had it not been for those two men and the generous aid of Congress this splendid undertaking must have failed.

The first sod of the new road was turned at Omaha on the 5th of November, 1865, and with that act one of the greatest engineering feat[s] of all times was commenced. At the very outstart the company encountered enormous expense. All the machinery, men, cars and material had to be brought up from St. Louis by boats. Wages were high, for each man realized that he was to encounter known and unknown dangers. Then there was no fuel along the right of way. The deserts were treeless, and as a result ties had to be hauled a great distance. Often there was no stone or rock for ballast. In fact, as Warman says, "They found absolutely nothing; only the great right of way and the west wind sighing over the dry, wide waste of a waveless sea."

"For three long winters engineers living in tents and dugouts watched every summit, slope, and valley along the entire fifteen hundred miles of road, to learn from the currents where the snow would drift deep and where the ground would be blown bare. In summer they watched the washouts that came when the hills were denuded by what, in the West, they called cloud-bursts. These were the only experts competent to say whether a draw should be bridged or filled, and only after years of residence in the hills."

The story of the Indian depredations committed along this road while it was being built would fill many books. Loss of life and property was a daily occurrence. These trail-makers were as brave and fearless as those who had gone over the path years before. At some points along the line they never knew when night came if they or some one else would be wearing their scalps in the morning. A large number of the men employed in the construction of the road had been soldiers in the South and easily adapted themselves to camp life and the dangers of the plains. These unemployed men who had experienced battles in the ranks of war found civilization too tame for them, and longed for some excitement. The freedom of the West offered alluring attractions, and the railroad construction benefited by this restlessness. Thus, at a moment's warning, a thousand men could be put into the field thoroughly trained for a battle, able to subdue three times their number of untrained and undisciplined red men. In the ranks of these railroad employees might be found those soldiers of other battles who had ranked from generals to privates.

Source: Grace Raymond Hebard, *The Pathbreakers from River to Ocean* (Chicago: Lakeside Press, 1913), pp. 233–235, 237.

7.5. The Completion of the Pacific Railroad (1869)

In the following passage, Henry Varnum Poor, railroad authority and founder of Poor's Manual of Railroads, revels in the recently completed transcontinental railroad and predicts an economic windfall for the federal government if it is able to convince the public of the necessity of granting more money and lands for more railroad projects.

The present year witnesses the completion of the most important enterprise of the kind ever executed in any country—a line of railroad from the Missouri River across the Continent, and with connecting lines, from the Atlantic to Pacific Ocean, a distance of 3,250 miles. This great undertaking was commenced in the latter part of 1863, but no considerable amount of work was made till 1865, in which year only about 100 miles were constructed; in 1866, about 300 miles were opened; in 1867, about the same number; in 1868, about 800 miles; and in the present year, about 300: the whole distance from the Missouri to Sacramento being 1,800 miles. . . . Toward the construction of these roads the Government has, or will, issue its 6 per cent, *currency* bonds, to the amount of about $63,616,000, viz: upon 300 miles at the rate of $48,000 per mile; upon 976 miles at the rate of $32,000 per mile; and upon 1,124 miles at the rate of $16,000 per mile. The annual interest upon the above sum will equal $3,816,960. These bonds are a second mortgage upon the respective lines, the several Companies being authorized to issue their own bonds to an amount equal to the Government subsidy, and to make them a first mortgage upon their roads.

The influence of these works . . . upon the commerce and welfare of the country, must be immense. A vast commerce, yet in its infancy, already exists between the two shores of the Continent. With the advantage and stimulus of the railroad this commerce must soon assume colossal proportions. Fronting the Pacific slope are hundreds of millions of people in Eastern Asia, who are rapidly taking part in the commerce of the world, and who will have the most intimate relations with our own Continent, which produces the gold and silver which at present forms one of the chief staples of commerce with them. It is hardly possible to estimate the magnitude of the commerce which will eventually exist between the Pacific coast and China and Japan. It is a commerce in which the world is to engage, and in which the Pacific Railroad is to be one of the most important instruments.

This road, too, will open up to settlement vast tracts of hitherto inaccessible territory, either fertile in soil, or rich in the more valuable minerals which are likely amply to compensate for the want of agricultural wealth. The main line will serve as the trunk from which lateral roads, constructed by private enterprise, will branch off in every direction. Already several important branches are in progress—one to Denver, Colorado; one to Salt Lake City; and one to connect it with the Columbia River. These branches will open up wide sections and add largely to the traffic of the trunk line.

The construction of this, and of similar works, by the aid of the Federal Government, has excited great interest, and although at present public opinion seems to be against any further grants of money, there can be no doubt that Government has been largely the gainer by the aid it has extended to the Pacific Railroad and its branches. The public taxes equal, at the present time, ten dollars per head of our population. These works have been instrumental in adding more than 500,000 to our population, whose contributions to the National treasury have far exceeded the interest on the bonds issued to them. They have certainly been instrumental in securing the construction of an equal extent of line which, but for them, would not have been built. Assuming the tonnage of these roads to equal 2,000 tons to the mile of road, the aggregate will be 9,800,000 tons, having a value of $490,000,000. The gain to the Federal Government from the creation of such an immense tonnage and value far exceeds the sums it has paid in aid of their construction, while the gain will, in a very short time, more than equal the principal sum of the bonds issued. Equally beneficent results will follow the construction of similar works. The people of the United States cannot afford to have extensive portions of their wide domain remain without means of access. In cases where such means have not been supplied by navigable water-courses they must be by a railway, or vast territories must remain, what they now are, deserts. The argument in favor of Government aid is as conclusive as it is simple. . . .

There can be no doubt, if the railroads of the United States could have been secured in no other way, it would have been the soundest policy for Government to have assumed their construction, even without the expectation of realizing a dollar of direct income from them. The actual cost of these works have been about $1,200,000,000. The interest on this sum is $72,000,000. They have created a commerce worth $10,000,000,000 annually. Such a commerce has enabled the people to pay $400,000,000 into the public treasury with far greater ease than they could have paid $100,000,000 without them. No line of ordinary importance was ever constructed that did not, from the wealth it created, speedily repay its cost, although it may never have returned a dollar to its share or bond-holders. If this be true of local and unimportant works, how much more so must it be of great lines, which will open vast sections of our public domain, now a desert, but abounding in all the elements of wealth.

While, therefore, there are but few cases which would justify the Government in extending aid to railroads, there are some in which its interposition becomes an imperative duty. In addition to the Central line now constructed, nothing could be more promotive of the general welfare than the opening, by its aid, both the Northern and Southern routes. Upon each of these are immense extents of territory, full of natural wealth, but which, without a railroad, are utterly beyond the reach of settlement or commerce. Aid extended to both lines, instead of weakening the public credit, would greatly strengthen it.

Source: Henry V. Poor, *Manual of the Railroads of the United States, 1869–1870* (New York, 1869), pp. xlvi–xlviii.

ANNOTATED SELECTED BIBLIOGRAPHY

Ambrose, Stephen E. *Nothing Like It in the World: The Men Who Built the Transcontinental Railroad, 1863–1869*. New York: Simon and Schuster, 2000. Very readable study of the construction of the transcontinental railroad, which Abraham Lincoln said was second in importance only to the abolition of slavery.

Bain, David Haward. *Empire Express: Building the First Transcontinental Railroad*. New York: Viking, 1999. Monumental study of the railroad project.

Gordon, Sarah H. *Passage to Union: How the Railroads Transformed American Life, 1829–1929*. Chicago: Ivan R. Dee, 1997. Gordon examines how various railroad projects throughout America stimulated the transition to the modern era.

Lewis, Oscar. *The Big Four: The Story of Huntington, Stanford, Hopkins, and Crocker, and of the Building of the Central Pacific*. New York: Alfred A. Knopf, 1938. Biographical portrait of the businessmen who financed the building of the Central Pacific.

Williams, John Hoyt. *A Great and Shining Road: The Epic Story of the Transcontinental Railroad*. New York: Times Books, 1988. Hoyt tells the whole story of the iron road in scholarly detail, discussing not only its historical significance, but also its influence on the American industrial revolution and on American politics.

8

The Sand Creek Massacre

The discovery of gold in Colorado in 1859 lured thousands of fortune seekers to the region near Pike's Peak. Perhaps as many as 100,000 miners crossed Cheyenne and Arapaho territory to reach the gold fields. The outbreak of the Civil War hardly slowed the westward migration. The flood of miners soon included prospective ranchers, land speculators, and even Civil War draft dodgers. In a short time, the region's buffalo herds had been depleted after thousands of livestock animals were introduced onto the Plains. But despite the encroachment of the mining frontier in the months preceding the Civil War, local Indians offered little resistance.

Some Indian leaders saw the handwriting on the wall. They heard tales from railroad surveyors of how the transcontinental railroad would soon cleave their territory, bringing even more settlers through their ancestral lands. Meanwhile, prospectors followed the beaver streams into the Rocky Mountains in the persistent search for mineral riches. Anti-Indian panic together with the punitive Indian policy currently in favor persuaded Plains Indian leaders either to resist or to conduct peace overtures.

Agents for the federal government tried to avert warfare by creating a barrier between whites and the Indians. In February 1861, government officials met with the Arapaho and Cheyenne chiefs at Fort Lyon. The forceful officials induced some of the Indians to give up their claims for lands promised to them by the 1851 Fort Laramie Treaty in exchange for a small reservation in eastern Colorado between the Arkansas River and

Sand Creek. Not all of the Indians followed the agreement, with many choosing the warpath and their nomadic way of life.

In 1861 Colorado became a territory. Comprised of parts of Nebraska, Wyoming, Utah, and New Mexico, much of the land still was in the hands of the Indians. But the following year Congress passed legislation that made it easier for settlers to claim quarter sections of unsurveyed land. As prospectors and settlers descended on Colorado, crowding in on Indian lands, bottled up tensions finally burst into warfare.

Over the next three years Arapaho and Cheyenne warriors ambushed mail coaches and attacked mining camps as Colorado's territorial governor unsuccessfully lobbied for federal troops. But during the Civil War soldiers for Indian wars were in short supply, and the governor was forced to create the Third Colorado Regiment, comprised of volunteers from the mining camps and Denver's saloons.

In 1864 a ranch family was brutally massacred and mutilated, apparently by Indian raiders near Denver, although it was unknown for certain who the actual perpetrators were. Later that year, in an effort to control the Indian population, the governor ordered all Indians not on the reservation to move to Fort Lyon or face extermination. This proclamation only led to more resistance as the warriors proceeded to raid homesteads from the North Platte River to the Arkansas, killing settlers and travelers, burning homes, and destroying overland mail stations. Most settlers left the region, and with the countryside in smoldering ruins and the major road to the east shut down by marauding Indians, Denver became a secluded community.

As fall turned to winter, tribal leaders enforced the traditional cessation of hostilities during the cold months. This interlude allowed Chief Black Kettle to pursue a peace initiative with the federal commander at Fort Lyon. The commander responded by claiming he did not have the authority to end the war. Black Kettle was told that he must surrender to the territorial governor. But the governor was unreceptive to ending the war, which he thought was clearly provoked by the Indians. During the Civil War era there were few supporters of compromise, and Governor John Evans was not ready to negotiate, knowing that it was only a matter of time before federal troops would be free to stamp out Indian resistance on the Great Plains.

Like most Americans during the 1860s, President Lincoln was absorbed by the Civil War. This left Congress to conduct Indian policy. Most of the congressional committees related to Indian affairs were dominated by westerners, who in the best interests of their constituents relied on military solutions to any Indian problems they encountered.

The Colorado governor was solidly supported by his militia commander, the "Fighting Parson," Colonel John M. Chivington, who had risen to prominence for his role in the Union victory at Glorietta Pass in the 1862 New Mexico campaign. Chivington was a well-known advocate of Indian extermination, including the killing of children, noting that "nits breed lice."[1] He brooked no resistance from Black Kettle in 1862, telling him, "My rule for fighting white men or Indians, is to fight them until they lay down their arms and submit to military authority."[2]

Black Kettle was resolute in his craving for peace. Hearing that the commander at Fort Lyon had been replaced, he once more proceeded to the fort, hoping that the new officer would accept their surrender. Unused to the vagaries of a frontier command, the new commander vacillated. First he offered protection, but he quickly withdrew his offer and forced the Indians to leave the fort.

Black Kettle thought that hostilities were over and that his eviction from the fort was just a formality. The Cheyenne chief and his 600 followers camped along Sand Creek, figuring that federal troops would protect them. Not long after, 700 militiamen under Colonel Chivington arrived at Fort Lyon. Although Chivington mentioned that he was preparing a campaign against hostile villages in eastern Colorado, it was readily apparent that he planned to strike the Indian encampments on Sand Creek. At this juncture an argument broke out between some of the officers at Fort Lyon, some of them objecting to the attack on the grounds that the Indians were under a pledge of protection. Nonetheless, the new commander told Chivington that he had not guaranteed the Indians protection and that he should attack them as soon as possible. Chivington left the fort on the night of November 28, 1864, and in the cold dawn hush of the following morning led his volunteers in an attack on Chief Black Kettle's encampment along Sand Creek in the Colorado Territory.

According to one of Chivington's scouts, only 60 of the 600 Indians in camp were men; the rest were women and children. Other reports indicated that only a small number of men would be required to take the camp, since most of the men were away hunting and those who were there had voluntarily given up most of their weapons to demonstrate their peaceful intentions. Chivington made clear his hostile intentions, reportedly commenting in response to this report, "Well, I long to be wading in gore."

The Indians were asleep when the militia made their assault. They were so convinced of their safety that they did not even post a night watch, except to guard the small pony herd. As the militia moved into the camp firing their weapons, Black Kettle raised an American flag and then a white flag, but it was too late. Hundreds of women and children flocked to Black Kettle's flag for sanctuary. The soldiers had come too far to leave without a fight. After surrounding the village, the militia attacked, killing without distinction. Without offering resistance and while attempting to surrender, women, children, old men, and warriors perished in the furious onslaught. Cannons were fired into groups of Indians as mounted militiamen ran roughshod through the encampment. As the seventy-year-old Cheyenne chief White Antelope saw his imminent death, he began singing the traditional death chant, "Nothing lives long, Only the Earth and the Mountains."

Before the massacre was over, virtually all of the dead had been scalped and mutilated. Some of the militiamen made grotesque souvenirs of body parts cut from their victims. One of the militiamen reportedly made a tobacco pouch out of White Antelope's scrotum. Having killed between 100 and 200 women and children and several old men, Chivington led his men back to Denver, claiming to have killed "five hundred warriors." Among the many survivors was Black Kettle, who would die later in another massacre.

During the Sand Creek Massacre the Colorado militia reportedly suffered nine deaths and thirty-eight wounded. Many of the casualties were no doubt caused by friendly fire as a result of heavy drinking on the nighttime ride and by an almost total absence of discipline during the attack. To the credit of the overmatched Indians, some of the younger warriors were able to dig rifle pits and hold out until dark.

Chivington's exploits were initially supported by many Coloradans, who agreed with the Methodist minister and militia officer that all Indians were "vermin deserving of extinction." Most had bought into Chivington's account in which he had just participated in one of the greatest victories of the Indian wars. Newspapers heralded his victory, and during the intermission at a performance at the Denver Opera House a hundred scalps taken in the massacre were displayed to the warm applause of an appreciative community. But having allowed Black Kettle and others to escape to tell their tale of the massacre and mutilations, Chivington had aroused the wrath of Sioux, Arapaho, and Cheyenne Indians and now had a war on his hands.

The actions of the Colorado volunteers undermined the peaceful overtures of Black Kettle and other moderate leaders as survivors flocked to war chiefs. Following Sand Creek, war parties wreaked havoc on ranches, overland mail stations, and telegraph wires. The Cheyenne took considerable revenge against the community of Julesburg, Colorado, which they sacked on several occasions. With the end of the Civil War, federal troops were rushed into the territory and after several battles convinced the Indians to seek peace. In late 1865, Indian leaders gave up their reservation on Sand Creek, and in 1867 federal troops relocated them to western Oklahoma.

The Sand Creek Massacre was one of the bloodiest events of the Indian wars of the 1860s. Little was accomplished by the carnage except to make Indian resistance more resolute in the future. The tragedy stimulated a review of the punitive Indian policy and provided a symbol of military brutality in the years that followed. While reformers used the incident as a rallying cry against the military establishment, western newspaper editors cited it as a model that should be followed in future campaigns. As the facts of the massacre became public, many people sided with the Indians and an enormous political controversy ensued that resulted in pressure for a more humane Indian policy. Slowly the truth came out, generating a wave of revulsion. According to one critic, the lowly volunteers had concocted the "Indian war" in an attempt to avoid conscription in the Civil War, while even the noted Indian fighter Kit Carson regarded the instigators of the massacre as cowards. During congressional fact-finding missions, investigators found shocking evidence that depicted a massacre rather than a noble military victory. On one visit to the site, a senator found infant skulls, replete with "milk-teeth [that] had not yet been shed,"[3] mute testimony to the atrocities committed at Sand Creek.

In 1867 Congress initiated a special investigation into the Sand Creek Massacre that uncovered gross mismanagement in the handling of Indian affairs, leading Evans to resign as Colorado governor. According to some authorities, the outrage over the Sand Creek Massacre delayed Colorado's admission into the Union for another twelve years. Chivington was saved from court-martial only by the timely expiration of his militia term in 1865.

In the wake of the tragedy, Congress also created the Indian Peace Commission. Eschewing the martial traditions of previous administrations, this federal agency strove to pursue peaceful negotiations with Indian tribes over the following years. If anything positive came out of this dark episode in American history, it was President Ulysses Grant's transition to a peace policy in the decade following the Civil War. Under this short-lived policy, the federal government entered into new treaties with Plains Indian tribes that emphasized smaller reservations but preserved the traditional right to hunt on lands that were not part of the reservation.

Initially proclaimed a major victory, the Sand Creek Massacre soon became the subject of a military investigation, precipitating a tremendous political controversy in the United States. Large numbers of people sided with the Indians, and political pressure mounted for a more humane approach to Indian affairs. The massacre became a symbol of the failure of American Indian policy to the nation at large and an emblem of frontier justice to westerners. Following the attack and extensive congressional investigation, the government condemned the "gross and wanton outrages" committed at Sand Creek and granted a quarter section of land to any tribal members who lost family members in the massacre. Among the reparations received by the accommodationist Cheyenne and Arapahos were a reservation and thirty years of annuities as long as peace prevailed. However, members of the vaunted Cheyenne warrior society known as the Dog Soldiers continued to challenge the forts and stagecoach lines for years to come.

NOTES

1. Quoted in David E. Stannard, *American Holocaust: The Conquest of the New World* (New York: Oxford University Press, 1993), p. 131.

2. Quoted in Elliott West, *The Contested Plains: Indians, Goldseekers, and the Rush to Colorado* (Lawrence: University Press of Kansas, 1998), p. 295.

3. Quoted in Stannard, *American Holocaust*, p. 134.

DOCUMENTS

8.1.   Colonel J. M. Chivington's Testimony (1865)

In April 1865, Colonel Chivington, the architect of the Sand Creek Massacre of November 1864, gave his account of the event to the Joint Committee on the Conduct of the War. Chivington placed his actions in the context of wartime conditions on the Colorado frontier. Earlier in 1864 there had been a number of Indian attacks in the region. The soldiers saw this as a chance to get even. When asked his reason for attacking the camp, Chivington responded that he "believed the Indians in camp were hostile to the whites." As proof, he noted that the soldiers found more than a dozen scalps of white people in camp.

. . .

3d question. Did you, as colonel in command of Colorado troops, about the 29th of November, 1864, make an attack on an Indian village or camp at a place known as Sand creek? If so, state particularly the number of men under your command; how armed and equipped; whether mounted or not; and if you had any artillery, state the number of guns, and the batteries to which they belonged.

Answer. On the 29th day of November, 1864, the troops under my command attacked a camp of Cheyenne and Arapaho Indians at a place known as Big Bend of Sandy, about forty miles north of Fort Lyon, Colorado Territory. There were in my command at that time about (500) five hundred men of the 3d regiment Colorado cavalry, under the immediate command of Colonel George L. Shoup, of said 3d regiment, and about (250) two hundred and fifty men of the 1st Colorado cavalry; Major Scott J. Anthony commanded one battalion of said 1st regiment, and Lieutenant Luther Wilson commanded another battalion of said 1st regiment. The 3d regiment was armed with rifled muskets, and Star's and Sharp's carbines. A few of the men of that regiment had revolvers. The men of the 1st regiment were armed with Star's and Sharp's carbines and revolvers. The men of the 3d regiment were poorly equipped; the supply of blankets, boots, hats, and caps was deficient. The men of the 1st regiment were well equipped; all these troops were mounted. I had four 12-pound mountain howitzers, manned by detachments from cavalry companies; they did not belong to any battery company.

4th question. State as nearly as you can the number of Indians that were in the village or camp at the time the attack was made; how many of them were warriors; how many of them were old men, how many of them were women, and how many of them were children?

Answer. From the best and most reliable information I could obtain, there were in the Indian camp, at the time of the attack, about eleven (11) or twelve (12) hundred Indians; of these about seven hundred were warriors, and the remainder were women and children. I am not aware that there were any old men among them. There was an unusual number of males among them, for the reason that the war chiefs of both nations were assembled there evidently for some special purpose.

5th question. At what time of the day or night was the attack made? Was it a surprise to the Indians? What preparation, if any, had they made for defence or offence?

Answer. The attack was made about sunrise. In my opinion the Indians were surprised; they began, as soon as the attack was made, to oppose my troops, however, and were soon fighting desperately. Many of the Indians were armed with rifles and many with revolvers; I think all had bows and arrows. They had excavated trenches under the bank of Sand creek, which in the vicinity of the Indian camp is high, and in many places precipitous. These trenches were two to three feet deep, and, in connexion with the banks, were evidently designed to protect the occupants from the fire of an enemy. They were found at various points extending along the banks of the creek for several miles from the camp; there were marks of the pick and shovel used in excavating them; and the fact that snow was seen in the bottoms of some of the trenches, while all snow had disappeared from the surface of the country generally, sufficiently proved that they had been constructed some time previously. The Indians took shelter in these trenches as soon as the attack was made, and from thence resisted the advance of my troops.

6th question. What number did you lose in killed, what number in wounded, and what number in missing?

Answer. There were seven men killed, forty-seven wounded, and one was missing.

7th question. What number of Indians were killed; and what number of the killed were women, and what number were children?

Answer. From the best information I could obtain, I judge there were five hundred or six hundred Indians killed; I cannot state positively the number killed, nor can I state positively the number of women and children killed. Officers who passed over the field, by my orders, after the battle, for the purpose of ascertaining the number of Indians killed, report that they saw but few woman or children dead, no more than would certainly fall in an attack upon a camp in which they were. I myself passed over some portions of the field after the fight, and I saw but one woman who had been killed, and one who had hanged herself; I saw no dead children. From all I could learn, I arrived at the conclusion that but few women or children had been slain. I am of the opinion that when the attack was made on the Indian camp the greater number of squaws and children made their escape, while the warriors remained to fight my troops.

8th question. State, as nearly as you can, the number of Indians that were wounded, giving the number of women and the number of children among the wounded.

Answer. I do not know that any Indians were wounded that were not killed; if there were any wounded, I do not think they could have been made prisoners without endangering the lives of soldiers; Indians usually fight as long as they have strength to resist. Eight Indians fell into the hands of the troops alive, to my knowledge; these, with one exception, were sent to Fort Lyon and properly cared for.

. . .

10th question. What reason had you for making the attack? What reasons, if any, had you to believe that Black Kettle or any other Indian or Indians in the camp entertained feelings of hostility towards the whites? Give in detail the names of all Indians so believed to be hostile, with the dates and places of their hostile acts, so far as you may be able to do so.

Answer. My reason for making the attack on the Indian camp was, that I believed the Indians in the camp were hostile to the whites. That they were of the same tribes with those who had murdered many persons and destroyed much valuable property on the Platte and Arkansas rivers during the previous spring, summer and fall was beyond a doubt. When a tribe of Indians is at war with the whites it is impossible to determine what party or band of the tribe or the name of the Indian or Indians belonging to the tribe so at war are guilty of the acts of hostility. The most that can be ascertained is that Indians of the tribe have performed the acts. During the spring, summer and fall of the year 1864, the Arapaho and Cheyenne Indians, in some instances assisted or led on by Sioux, Kiowas, Comanches and Apaches, had committed many acts of hostility in the country lying between the Little Blue and the Rocky mountains and the Platte and Arkansas rivers. They had murdered many of the whites and taken others prisoners, and had destroyed valuable property, probably amounting to $200,000 or $300,000. Their rendezvous was on the headwaters of the Republican, probably one hundred miles from where the Indian camp was located. I had every reason to believe that these Indians were either directly or indirectly concerned in the outrages which had been committed upon the whites. I had no means of ascertaining what were the names of the Indians who had committed these outrages other than the declarations of the Indians themselves; and the character of Indians in the western country for truth and veracity, like their respect for the chastity of women who may become prisoners in their hands, is not of that order which is calculated to inspire confidence in what they may say. In this view I was supported by Major Anthony, 1st Colorado cavalry, commanding at Fort Lyon, and Samuel G. Colby, United States Indian agent, who, as they had been in communication with these Indians, were more competent to judge of their disposition towards the whites than myself. Previous to the battle they expressed to me the opinion that the Indians should be punished. We found in the camp the scalps of nineteen (19) white persons. One of the surgeons informed me that one of these scalps had been taken from the victim's head not more than four days previously. I can furnish a child captured at the camp ornamented with six white women's scalps; these scalps must have been taken by these Indians or furnished to them for their gratification and amusement by some of their brethren, who, like themselves, were in amity with the whites.

Source: U.S. Congress, House of Representatives, 38th Congress, 2nd Session, "Massacre of the Cheyenne Indians" (Washington, DC: GPO, 1865), pp. 101–104. Hereafter cited as "Massacre of Cheyenne Indians."

8.2.   A Great Victory (1865)

The following editorial from the December 18, 1864, issue of the Rocky Mountain News *portrays the events at Sand Creek as a "battle," in which Colorado soldiers defeated Indian warriors in one of the greatest victories of the Indian wars. This excerpt was reprinted in the 1865 government report. In it, the author defends the attack, detailing stolen government property and scalps found in the Indian encampment after the massacre.*

THE BATTLE OF SAND CREEK.

Among the brilliant feats of arms in Indian warfare, the recent campaign of our Colorado volunteers will stand in history with few rivals, and none to exceed it in final results. We are not prepared to write its history, which can only be done by some one who accompanied the expedition, but we have gathered from those who participated in it, and from others who were in that part of the country, some facts which will doubtless interest many of our readers.

The people of Colorado are well aware of the situation occupied by the third regiment during the great snow-storm which set in the last of October. Their rendezvous was in Bijou Basin, about eighty miles southeast of this city, and close up under the foot of the Divide. That point had been selected as the base for an Indian campaign. Many of the companies reached it after the storm set in; marching for days through the driving, blinding clouds of snow and deep drifts. Once there, they were exposed for weeks to an Arctic climate, surrounded by a treeless plain covered three feet deep with snow. Their animals suffered for food and with cold, and the men fared but little better. They were insufficiently supplied with tents and blankets, and their sufferings were intense. At the end of a month the snow had settled to the depth of two feet, and the command set out upon its long contemplated march. The rear guard left the Basin on the 23d of November. Their course was southeast, crossing the Divide and thence heading for Fort Lyon. For one hundred miles the snow was quite two feet in depth, and for the next hundred it ranged from six to twelve inches. Beyond that the ground was almost bare and the snow no longer impeded their march.

On the afternoon of the 28th the entire command reached Fort Lyon, a distance of *two hundred and sixty miles, in less than six days*, and so quietly and expeditiously had the march been made that the command at the fort was taken entirely by surprise. When the vanguard appeared in sight it was reported that a body of Indians were approaching, and precautions were taken for their reception. No one upon the route was permitted to go in advance of the column, and persons who it was suspected would spread the news of the advance were kept under surveillance until all danger from that source was past.

At Fort Lyon the force was strengthened by about two hundred and fifty men of the first regiment, and at nine o'clock in the evening the command set out for the Indian village. The course was due north, and their guide was the Polar star. As daylight dawned they came in sight of the Indian camp, after a forced midnight march of forty-two miles, in eight hours, across the rough, unbroken plain. But little time was required for preparation. The forces had been divided and arranged for battle on the march, and just as the sun rose they dashed upon the enemy with yells that would put a Comanche army to blush. Although utterly surprised, the savages were not unprepared, and for a time their defence told terribly against our ranks. Their main force rallied and formed in line of battle on the bluffs beyond the creek, where they were protected by rudely constructed rifle-pits, from which they maintained a steady fire until the shells from company C's (third regiment) howitzers began dropping among them, when they scattered and fought each for himself in genuine Indian fashion. As the battle progressed the field of carnage widened until it extended over not less than twelve miles of territory. The Indians who could, escaped or secreted themselves, and by three o'clock in the afternoon the carnage had ceased. It was estimated that between three and four hundred of the savages got away with their lives. Of the balance there were neither wound nor prisoners. Their strength at the beginning of the action was estimated at nine hundred.

Their village consisted of one hundred and thirty Cheyenne and eight Arapahoe lodges. These, with their contents, were totally destroyed. Among their effects were large supplies of flour, sugar, coffee, tea, &c. Women's and children's clothing were found; also books and many other articles which must have been taken from captured trains or houses. One white man's scalp was found which had evidently been taken but a few days before. The chiefs fought with unparalleled bravery, falling in front of their men. One of them charged alone against a force of two or three hundred, and fell pierced with balls far in advance of his braves.

Our attack was made by five battalions. The first regiment, Colonel Chivington, part of companies C, D, E, G, H and K, numbering altogether about two hundred and fifty men, was divided into two battalions; the first under command of Major Anthony, and the second under Lieutenant Wilson, until the latter was disabled, when the command devolved upon Lieutenant Dunn. The three battalions of the third, Colonel Shoup, were led, respectively, by Lieutenant Colonel Bowen, Major Sayr, and Captain Cree. The action was begun by the battalion of Lieutenant Wilson, who occupied the right, and by a quick and bold movement cut off the enemy from their herd of stock. From this circumstance we gained our great advantage. A few Indians secured horses, but the great majority of them had to fight or fly on foot. Major Anthony was on the left, and the third in the centre.

Among the killed were *all* the Cheyenne chiefs, Black Kettle, White Antelope, Little Robe, Left Hand, Knock Knee, One Eye, and another, name unknown. Not a single prominent man of the tribe remains, and the tribe itself is almost annihilated. The Arapahoes probably suffered but little. It has been reported that the chief Left Hand, of that tribe, was killed, but Colonel Chivington is of the opinion that he was not. Among the stock captured were a number of government horses and mules, including the twenty or thirty stolen from the command of Lieutenant Chase at Jimmy's camp last summer.

The Indian camp was well supplied with defensive works. For half a mile along the creek there was an almost continuous chain of rifle-pits, and another similar line of works crowned the adjacent bluff. Pits had been dug at all the salient points for miles. After the battle twenty-three dead Indians were taken from one of these pits and twenty-seven from another.

Whether viewed as a march or as a battle, the exploit has few, if any, parallels. A march of 260 miles in but a fraction more than five days, with deep snow, scanty forage, and no road, is a remarkable feat, whilst the utter surprise of a large Indian village is unprecedented. In no single battle in North America, we believe, have so many Indians been slain.

It is said that a short time before the command reached the scene of battle an old squaw partially alarmed the village by reporting that a great heard of buffalo were coming. She heard the rumbling of the artillery and tramp of the moving squadrons, but her people doubted. In a little time the doubt was dispelled, but not by buffaloes.

A thousand incidents of individual daring and the passing events of the day might be told, but space forbids. We leave the task for eye-witnesses to chronicle. All acquitted themselves well, and Colorado soldiers have again covered themselves with glory.

THE FORT LYON AFFAIR.

The issue of yesterday's News, containing the following despatch, created considerable of a sensation in this city, particularly among the Thirdsters and others who participated in the recent campaign and the battle on Sand creek:

WASHINGTON, *December* 20, 1864.

"The affair at Fort Lyon, Colorado, in which Colonel Chivington destroyed a large Indian village, and all its inhabitants, is to be made the subject of congressional investigation. Letters received from high officials in Colorado say that the Indians were killed after surrendering, and that a large proportion of them were women and children."

Indignation was loudly and unequivocally expressed, and some less considerate of the boys were very persistent in their inquiries as to who those "high officials" were, with a mild intimation that they had half a mind to "go for them." This talk about "friendly Indians" and a "surrendered" village will do to "tell to marines," but to us out here it is all bosh.

The *confessed* murderers of the Hungate family—a man and wife and their two little babes, whose scalped and mutilated remains were seen by all our citizens—were "friendly Indians," we suppose, in the eyes of these "high officials." *They* fell in the Sand creek battle.

The confessed participants in a score of other murders of peaceful settlers and inoffensive travellers upon our borders and along our roads in the past six months must have been *friendly*, or else the "high officials" wouldn't say so.

The band of marauders in whose possession were found scores of horses and mules stolen from government and from individuals; wagon loads of flour, coffee, sugar and tea, and rolls of broad cloth, calico, books, &c, robbed from freighters and emigrants on the plains; under-clothes of white women and children, stripped from their murdered victims, were probably peaceably disposed toward *some* of those "high officials," but the mass of our people "can't see it."

Probably those scalps of white men, women and children, *one of them fresh not three days taken*, found drying in their lodges, were taken in a *friendly* playful manner; or possibly those Indian saddle-blankets trimmed with the scalps of white women, and with braids and fringes of their hair, were kept simply as mementoes of their owners' high affection for the pale face. At any rate, these delicate and tasteful ornaments could not have been taken from the heads of the wives, sisters or daughters of these "high officials."

That "surrendering" must have been the happy thought of an exceedingly vivid imagination, for we can hear of nothing of the kind from any of those who were engaged in the battle. On the contrary, the savages fought like devils to the end, and one of our pickets was killed and scalped by them the next day after the battle, and a number of others were fired upon. In one instance a party of the vidette pickets were compelled to beat a hasty retreat to save their lives, full twenty-four hours after the battle closed. This does not look much like the Indians had surrendered.

But we are not sure that an investigation may not be a good thing. It should go back of the "affair at Fort Lyon," as they are pleased to term it down east, however, and let the world know who were making money by keeping those Indians under the sheltering protection of Fort Lyon; learn who was interested in systematically representing that the Indians were friendly and wanted peace. It is unquestioned and undenied that the site of the Sand creek battle was the rendezvous of the thieving and marauding bands of savages who roamed over this country last summer and fall, and it is shrewdly suspected that somebody was all the time making a very good thing out of it. By all means let there be an investigation, but we advise the honorable congressional committee, who may be appointed to conduct it, to get their scalps insured before they pass Plum creek on their way out.

Source: "Massacre of Cheyenne Indians," pp. 56–58.

8.3.   The Testimony of Lieutenant James D. Cannan

Lieutenant James D. Cannan's testimony during the investigation into the Sand Creek Massacre lends credence to reports of atrocities committed against the Indians by members of Chivington's command.

FORT LYON, COLORADO TERRITORY,
January 16, 1865.

Personally appeared before me Lieutenant James D. Cannan, 1st New Mexico volunteer infantry, who, after being duly sworn, says:

That on the 28th day of November, 1864, I was ordered by Major Scott J. Anthony to accompany him on an Indian expedition as his battalion adjutant. The object of that expedition was to be a thorough campaign against hostile Indians, as I was led to understand. I referred to the fact of there being a friendly camp of Indians in the immediate neighborhood, and remonstrated against simply attacking that camp, as I was aware that they were resting there in fancied security, under promises held out to them of safety from Major G. W. Wynkoop, from commander of the post of Fort Lyon, as well as by Major S. J. Anthony, then in command. Our battalion was attached to the command of Colonel J. M. Chivington, and left Fort Lyon on the night of the 28th of November, 1864. About daybreak on the morning of the 29th of November we came in sight of the camp of the friendly Indians aforementioned, and was ordered by Colonel Chivington to attack the same, which was accordingly done. The command of Colonel Chivington was composed of about one thousand men. The village of the Indians consisted of from one hundred to one hundred and thirty lodges, and, as far as I am able to judge, of from five hundred to six hundred souls, the majority of whom were women and children.

In going over the battle-ground the next day, I did not see a body of man, woman, or child but was scalped; and in many instances their bodies were mutilated in the most horrible manner, men, women, and children—privates cut out, &c. I heard one man say that he had cut a woman's private parts out, and had them for exhibition on a stick; I heard another man say that he had cut the fingers off of an Indian to get the rings on the hand. According to the best of my knowledge and belief, these atrocities that were committed were with the knowledge of J. M. Chivington, and I do not know of his taking any measures to prevent them. I heard of one instance of a child a few months old being thrown in the feed-box of a wagon, and after being carried some distance, left on the ground to perish. I also heard of numerous instances, in which men had cut out the private parts of females, and stretched them over the saddle-bows, and worn them over their hair, while riding in the ranks. All these matters were a subject of general conversation, and could not help being known by Colonel J. M. Chivington.

JAMES D. CANNAN,
First Lieutenant 1st Infantry, New Mexico Volunteers.

Source: "Massacre of Cheyenne Indians," pp. 88–89.

8.4.   Medicine Calf Beckwourth's Account

Chivington conscripted the sixty-nine-year-old mulatto James Beckwourth to accompany his regiment as a guide and scout. Beckwourth had lived with the Indians for most of his life and tried to avoid going, but Chivington threatened him with hanging unless he joined the expedition. In the following account Beckwourth describes his peace mission to the Cheyennes following the massacre and records the sense of betrayal the Cheyenne felt toward the white men who ravaged the land and did not honor their word.

I went into the lodge of Leg-in-the-Water. When I went in he raised up and he said, "Medicine Calf, what have you come here for; have you fetched the white man to finish killing our families again?" I told him I had come to talk to him; call in your council. They came in a short time afterwards, and wanted to know what I had come for. I told them I had come to persuade them to make peace with the whites, as there was not enough of them to fight the whites, as they were as numerous as the leaves of the trees. "We know it," was the general response of the council. "But what do we want to live for? The white man has taken our country, killed all of our game; was not satisfied with that, but killed our wives and children. Now no peace. We want to go and meet our families in the spirit land. We loved the whites until we found out they lied to us, and robbed us of what we had. We have raised the battle ax until death."

Source: "Report of the Secretary of war communicating . . . a copy of the evidence taken at Denver and Ft. Lyon, Colorado Territory, by a military commission, ordered to inquire into the Sand Creek Massacre, November 1864," U.S. Senate Executive Document 26, 39th Congress, 2nd Session, February 14, 1867.

8.5.   The Testimony of Robert Bent (1867)

When guide James Beckwourth's age proved to be an impediment, Chivington forced the half-Cheyenne Robert Bent (1816–1841) to lead his men to Sand Creek. In his testimony to Congress, Bent chronicles the events of that fateful morning.

ROBERT BENT: I am twenty-four years old; was born on the Arkansas River. I am pretty well acquainted with the Indians of the plains, having

spent most of my life among them. I am employed as guide and inter-
preter at Fort Lyon by Major Anthony. Colonel Chivington ordered me
to accompany him on his way to Sand Creek. The command consisted
of from nine hundred to one thousand men, principally Colorado volunteers. We left Fort Lyon at eight o'clock in the evening, and came on
to the Indian camp at daylight the next morning. Colonel Chivington
surrounded the village with his troops. When we came in sight of camp
I saw the American flag waving and heard Black Kettle tell the Indians
to stand around the flag, and there they were huddled—men, women,
and children. This was when we were within fifty yards of the Indians.
I also saw a white flag raised. These flags were in so conspicuous a
position that they must have been seen. When the troops fired, the Indians ran, some of the men into their lodges, probably to get their arms.
They had time to get away if they had wanted to. I remained on the
field five hours, and when I left there were shots being fired up the creek.
I think there were six hundred Indians in all. I think there were thirty-
five braves and some old men, about sixty in all. All fought well. At the
time the rest of the men were away from the camp, hunting. I visited
the battleground one month afterwards; saw the remains of a great
many; counted sixty-nine, but a number had been eaten by the wolves
and dogs. After the firing the warriors put the squaws and children
together, and surrounded them to protect them. I saw five squaws under
a bank for shelter. When the troops came up to them they ran out and
showed their person to let the soldiers know they were squaws and
begged for mercy, but the soldiers shot them all. I saw one squaw lying
on the bank whose leg had been broken by a shell; a soldier came up to
her with a drawn saber; she raised her arm to protect herself, when he
struck, breaking her arm; she rolled over and raised her other arm, when
he struck, breaking it, and then left her without killing her. There seemed
to be indiscriminate slaughter of men, women, and children. There were
some thirty or forty squaws collected in a hole for protection; they sent
out a little girl about six years old with a white flag on a stick; she had
not proceeded but a few steps when she was shot and killed. All the
squaws in that hole were afterwards killed, and four or five bucks outside. The squaws offered no resistance. Every one I saw dead was
scalped. I saw one squaw cut open with an unborn child, as I thought,
lying by her side. Captain Soule afterwards told me that such was the
fact. I saw the body of White Antelope with the privates cut off, and I
heard a soldier say he was going to make a tobacco pouch out of them.
I saw one squaw whose privates had been cut out. I heard Colonel Chivington say to the soldiers as they charged past him, "Remember our
wives and children murdered on the Platte and Arkansas." He occupied
a position where he could not have failed to have seen the American
flag, which I think was a garrison flag, 6 × 12. He was within fifty yards

when he planted his battery. I saw a little girl about five years of age who had been hid in the sand; two soldiers discovered her, drew their pistols and shot her, and then pulled her out of the sand by the arm. I saw quite a number of infants in arms killed with their mothers.

Source: U.S. Congress, "Condition of the Indian Tribes. Report of the Joint Special Committee, U.S. Senate Document 156, 39th Congress, 2nd Session, Washington, D.C.: U.S. Government Printing Office, 1867).

8.6.   Helen Hunt Jackson's Apologia for the Cheyenne (1880)

In the aftermath of Sand Creek there was little time for Indian sympathizers to rally support. With the nation's attention focused on the Civil War and its aftermath, outside of an 1865 congressional investigation, there was little public outcry. Over the next decade, as the protracted Indian wars came to an end, the particulars of this tragic episode became more widely known. Fifteen years after the Sand Creek Massacre a letter was sent to the New York Tribune *vilifying the behavior of the Colorado regiment years earlier. Helen Hunt Jackson drew on such outrages, and testimony from congressional and other investigations, to write her widely read condemnation of American Indian policy,* A Century of Dishonor.

In June, 1864, Governor Evans, of Colorado, sent out a circular to the Indians of the Plains, inviting all friendly Indians to come into the neighborhood of the forts, and be protected by the United States troops. Hostilities and depredations had been committed by some bands of Indians, and the Government was about to make war upon them. This circular says:

"In some instances they (the Indians) have attacked and killed soldiers, and murdered peaceable citizens. For this the Great Father is angry, and will certainly hunt them out and punish them; but he does not want to injure those who remain friendly to the whites. He desires to protect and take care of them. For this purpose I direct that all friendly Indians keep away from those who are at war, and go to places of safety. Friendly Arapahoes and Cheyennes belonging to the Arkansas River will go to Major Colby, United States Agent at Fort Lyon, who will give them provisions and show them a place of safety."

In consequence of this proclamation of the governor, a band of Cheyennes, several hundred in number, came in and settled down near Fort Lyon. After a time they were requested to move to Sand Creek, about forty miles from Fort Lyon, where they were still guaranteed "perfect safety" and the protection of the Government. Rations of food were issued to them from time to time. On the 27th of November, Colonel J. M. Chivington, a member of the Methodist Episcopal Church in Denver, and Colonel of the First Colorado Cavalry, led his regiment by a forced march to Fort Lyon, induced some of the United States troops to join him, and fell upon this camp of friendly Indians at daybreak. The chief, White Antelope, always known as friendly to the whites, came running toward the soldiers, holding up his hands and crying "Stop! stop!" in English. When he saw that there was no mistake, that it was a deliberate attack, he folded his arms and waited till he was shot down. The United States flag was floating over the lodge of Black Kettle, the head chief of the tribe; below it was tied also a small white flag as additional security—a precaution Black Kettle had been advised by United States officers to take if he met troops on the Plains. In Major Wynkoop's testimony, given before the committee appointed by Congress to investigate this massacre, is the following passage:

"Women and children were killed and scalped, children shot at their mothers' breasts, and all the bodies mutilated in the most horrible manner. *** The dead bodies of females profaned in such a manner that the recital is sickening, Colonel J. M. Chivington all the time inciting his troops to their diabolical outrages."

Another man testified as to what he saw on the 30th of November, three days after the battle, as follows:

"I saw a man dismount from his horse and cut the ear from the body of an Indian, and the scalp from the head of another. I saw a number of children killed; they had bullet-holes in them; one child had been cut with some sharp instrument across its side. I saw another that both ears had been cut off. *** I saw several of the Third Regiment cut off fingers to get the rings off them. I saw Major Sayre scalp a dead Indian. The scalp had a long tail of silver hanging to it."

Robert Bent testified:

"I saw one squaw lying on the bank, whose leg had been broken. A soldier came up to her with a drawn sabre. She raised her arm to protect herself; he struck, breaking her arm. She rolled over, and raised her other arm; he struck, breaking that, and then left her without killing her. I saw one squaw cut open, with an unborn child lying by her side."

Major Anthony testified:

"There was one little child, probably three years old, just big enough to walk through the sand. The Indians had gone ahead, and this little child was behind, following after them. The little fellow was perfectly naked, travelling in the sand. I saw one man get off his horse at a distance of about seventy-five yards and draw up his rifle and fire. He missed the child. Another man came up and said, 'Let me try the son of a b——. I can hit him.' He got down off his horse, kneeled down, and fired at the little child, but he missed him. A third man came up, and made a similar remark, and fired, and the little fellow dropped."

The Indians were not able to make much resistance, as only a part of them were armed, the United States officers having required them to give up their guns. Luckily they had kept a few.

When this Colorado regiment of demons returned to Denver they were greeted with an ovation. *The Denver News* said: "All acquitted themselves well. Colorado soldiers have again covered themselves with glory;" and at a theatrical performance given in the city, these scalps taken from Indians were held up and exhibited to the audience, which applauded rapturously.

After listening, day after day, to such testimonies as these I have quoted, and others so much worse that I may not write and *The Tribune* could not print the words needful to tell them, the committee reported: "It is difficult to believe that beings in the form of men, and disgracing the uniform of United States soldiers and officers, could commit or countenance the commission of such acts of cruelty and barbarity;" and of Colonel Chivington: "He deliberately planned and executed a foul and dastardly massacre, which would have disgraced the veriest savage among those who were the victims of his cruelty."

This was just fifteen years ago, no more. Shall we apply the same rule of judgment to the white men of Colorado that the Government is now applying to the Utes? There are 130,000 inhabitants of Colorado; hundreds of them had a hand in this massacre, and thousands in cool blood applauded it when it was done. There are 4000 Utes in Colorado. Twelve of them, desperate, guilty men, have committed murder and rape, and three or four hundred of them did, in the convenient phrase of our diplomacy, "go to war against the Government;" *i.e.*, they attempted, by force of arms, to restrain the entrance upon their own lands—lands bought, owned and paid for—of soldiers that the Government had sent there, to be ready to make war upon them, in case the agent thought it best to do so! This is the plain English of it. This is the plain, naked truth of it.

And now the Secretary of the Interior has stopped the issue of rations to 1000 of these helpless creatures; rations, be it understood, which are not, and never were, a charity, but are the Utes' rightful dues, on account of lands by them sold; dues which the Government promised to pay "annually forever." Will the American people justify this? There is such a thing as the conscience of a nation—as a nation's sense of justice. Can it not be roused to speak now? Shall we sit still, warm and well fed, in our homes, while five hundred women and little children are being slowly starved in the bleak, barren wildernesses of Colorado? Starved, not because storm, or blight, or drouth has visited their country and cut off their crops; not because pestilence has laid its hand on them and slain the hunters who brought them meat, but because it lies within the promise of one man, by one word, to deprive them of one-half their necessary food for as long a term of years as he may please; and "the Secretary of the Interior cannot consistently feed a tribe that has gone to war against the Government."

We read in the statutes of the United States that certain things may be done by "executive order" of the President. Is it not time for a President to interfere when hundreds of women and children are being starved in his Republic by the order of one man? Colonel J. M. Chivington's method was less inhuman by far. To be shot dead is a mercy, and a grace for which we would all sue, if to be starved to death were our only other alternative.

New York, Jan. 31st, 1880.   H. H.

Source: New York Tribune, January 31, 1880, article reprinted in Helen H. Jackson, A Century of Dishonor (Boston, 1917), pp. 343–346.

8.7.   A Chivington Supporter

In the following letter published on February 6, 1880, William N. Byers, the former editor of Denver's Rocky Mountain News, *responds to the charges by the* New York Tribune *letter writer, by defending the actions of Chivington's men at Sand Creek. He claims that the government investigation that followed was biased and represented only one side of the story. Byers offers several examples of Indian atrocities and evidence found at Sand Creek to support his claims.*

To the Editor of the Tribune:

Sir,—In your edition of yesterday appears an article, under the above caption, which arraigns the people of Colorado as a community of barbarous murderers, and finally elevates them above the present Secretary of the Interior, thereby placing the latter gentleman in a most unenviable light if the charges averred be true. "The Sand Creek Massacre" of 1864 is made the text and burden of the article; its application is to the present condition of the White River band of Utes in Colorado. Quotations are given from the testimony gathered, and the report made thereon by a committee of Congress charged with a so-called investigation of the Sand Creek affair. That investigation was made for a certain selfish purpose. It was to break down and ruin certain men. Evidence was taken upon one side only. It was largely false, and infamously partial. There was no answer for the defence.

The Cheyenne and Arapahoe Indians assembled at Sand Creek were not under the protection of a United States fort. A few of them had been encamped about Fort Lyon and drawing supplies therefrom, but they had gradually disappeared and joined the main camp on Dry Sandy, forty miles from the fort, separated from it by a waterless desert, and entirely beyond the limit of its control or observation. While some of the occupants were still, no doubt, occasional visitors at the fort, and applicants for supplies and ammunition, most of the warriors were engaged in raiding the great Platte River Road, seventy-five miles farther north, robbing and burning trains, stealing cattle and horses, robbing and destroying the United States mails, and killing white people. During the summer and fall they had murdered over fifty of the citizens of Colorado. They had stolen and destroyed provisions and merchandise, and driven away stock worth hundreds of thousands of dollars. They had interrupted the mails, and for thirty-two consecutive days none were allowed to pass their lines. When satiated with murder and arson, and loaded with plunder, they would retire to their sacred refuge on Sand Creek to rest and refresh themselves, recruit their wasted supplies of ammunition from Fort Lyon—begged under the garb of gentle, peaceful savages—and then return to the road to relieve their tired comrades, and riot again in carnage and robbery. These are facts; and when the "robbers' roost" was cleaned out, on that sad but glorious 27th day of November, 1864, they were sufficiently proven. Scalps of white men not yet dried; letters and photographs stolen from the mails; bills of lading and invoices of goods; bales and bolts of the goods themselves, addressed to merchants in Denver; half-worn clothing of white women and children, and many other articles of like character, were found in that poetical Indian camp, and recovered by the Colorado soldiers. They were brought to Denver, and those were the scalps exhibited in the theatre of that city. There was also an Indian saddle-blanket entirely fringed around the edges with white women's scalps, with the long, fair hair attached. There was an Indian saddle over the pommel of which was stretched skin stripped from the body of a white woman. Is it any wonder that soldiers flushed with victory, after one of the hardest campaigns ever endured by men, should indulge—some of them—in unwarranted atrocities after finding such evidence of barbarism, and while more than forty of their comrades were weltering in their own blood upon the field?

If "H. H." had been in Denver in the early part of that summer, when the bloated, festering bodies of the Hungate family—father, mother, and two babes—were drawn through the streets naked in an ox-wagon, cut, mutilated, and scalped—the work of those same red fiends who were so justly punished at Sand Creek; if, later, "H. H." had seen an upright and most estimable business man go crazy over the news of his son's being tortured to death a hundred miles down the Platte, as I did; if "H. H." had seen one-half the Colorado homes made desolate that fateful season, and a tithe of the tears that were caused to flow, I think there would have been one little word of excuse for the people of Colorado—more than a doubtful comparison with an inefficient and culpable Indian policy. Bear in mind that Colorado had no railroads then. Her supplies reached her by only one road—along the Platte—in wagons drawn by oxen, mules, or horses. That line was in full possession of the enemy. Starvation stared us in the face. Hardly a party went or came without some persons being killed. In some instances whole trains were cut off and destroyed. Sand Creek saved Colorado, and taught the Indians the most salutary lesson they had ever learned. And now, after fifteen years, and here in the shadow of the Nation's Capitol, with the spectre of "H. H.'s" condemnation staring me in the face, I am neither afraid nor ashamed to repeat the language then used by *The Denver News*: "All acquitted themselves well. Colorado soldiers have again covered themselves with glory."

Source: Reprinted in Helen H. Jackson, *A Century of Dishonor* (Boston: Little, Brown, 1917), pp. 346–350.

ANNOTATED SELECTED BIBLIOGRAPHY

Calloway, Colin G. *Our Hearts Fell to the Ground: Plains Indian Views of How the West Was Lost*. Boston: Bedford Books, 1996. Excellent short volume of documents and history recording Native American perspectives of the winning/losing of the West.

Hoig, Stan. *The Sand Creek Massacre*. Norman: University of Oklahoma Press, 1961. Hoig traces activities and events surrounding the Sand Creek Massacre.

Osborn, William M. *The Wild Frontier: Atrocities During the American-Indian War from Jamestown Colony to Wounded Knee*. New York: Random House, 2000. Osborn draws from thousands of eyewitness accounts to chronicle the bloodletting on both sides during almost 300 years of Indian conflict.

Schultz, Duane. *Month of the Freezing Moon: The Sand Creek Massacre, November 1864*. New York: St. Martin's Press, 1990. Straightforward and most recent account of the massacre and the investigation that followed.

Utley, Robert M. *Frontiersmen in Blue: The United States Army and the Indian, 1848–1865*. New York: Macmillan, 1967. Excellent one-volume account of mid-nineteenth-century conflict between the U.S. Army and Indians in the trans-Mississippi West.

West, Elliott. *The Contested Plains: Indians, Goldseekers, and the Rush to Colorado*. Lawrence: University Press of Kansas, 1998. The first book to examine the Colorado gold rush as the key event in the modern transformation of the central Great Plains.

9

The Battle of the Little Big Horn: The End of the Plains Indian Wars and a Way of Life

The most famous Native American victory of the Indian wars of the second half of the nineteenth century, the Battle of the Little Big Horn, also signaled the beginning of the end for America's free-ranging Plains Indian cultures. The Plains Indians celebrated the confrontation as the Battle of the Greasy Grass, while Anglo Americans memorialized it as Custer's Last Stand. The intrigue surrounding the defeat of Lieutenant Colonel George Armstrong Custer and his Seventh Cavalry is one of the most enduring legends of the American West. Although Custer finished at the bottom of his West Point class, he went on to serve with distinction in the Civil War. Following the war, he participated in several Indian campaigns, including the controversial Battle of the Washita.

On June 25, 1876, Custer led his regiment of almost 655 men against Sioux and Cheyenne forces camped near the Rosebud River. However, Custer fatefully divided his troops into three forces after locating a large Indian camp along the Little Big Horn River. Majors Marcus Reno and Frederick Benteen were ordered to lead their troops toward the village from different directions as Custer led the remaining members of the Seventh Cavalry toward the lower village. Custer and his command were never seen alive again, and the Battle of the Little Big Horn entered the American consciousness as Custer's Last Stand, joining the battles of the Alamo in Texas and Thermopylae in Greece as symbolic heroic last stands against overwhelming odds, in which only the victors survived to chronicle the event. In reality, the Battle of the Little Big Horn was the last gasp of the Plains Indians.

The arid lands of the Great Plains cover a huge expanse of America. Reaching from the Missouri River to the Rocky Mountains and from Saskatchewan, Canada, to Texas, this land has been home to Indian cultures for thousands of years. The Indian tribes of the Great Plains come closest to matching the stereotypical Hollywood image of mounted warriors with plumed headdresses, chasing buffalo and counting coup in battle. This incarnation of the Great Plains Indians was a result of relatively recent adaptations, following the introduction of the horse by the Spanish in the late sixteenth century.

Prior to Spanish contact, Plains Indians hunted buffalo and other animals on foot, but with the introduction of the horse most tribes made the transition to a mounted, more mobile existence. The horse transformed the lives of the warrior-hunters, who by the early 1700s were capable of traveling great distances and exploiting their environment to the fullest.

Relations between whites and Indians were considerably less acrimonious than relations between the various Indian cultures before the 1850s. The Sioux, who were once located in what is now Minnesota, were forced out of their homelands by the movement of other tribes into the area. To escape these pressures, they migrated to the Great Plains region in the late eighteenth century. Among the Sioux peoples that made this shift were the Lakota or Teton Sioux, which included members of the Oglala, Hunkpapa, Blackfeet, and other tribes, which together comprised a huge Indian nation. As they moved west, they came into conflict with smaller tribes such as the Pawnee and the Crow. The Indian Removal of eastern tribes during the 1830s added to the continuing collision of cultures on the Plains. As Indians acquired firearms, warfare became more protracted, leading to heavier casualties and worsening competition between the tribes. White settlers joined the mix during the 1840s and 1850s, and the Great Plains became a battleground for a way of life threatened by a rapidly changing landscape.

The buffalo played a central role in Plains culture, providing food, clothing, shelter, and weapons. However, as these cultures became increasingly tied to the existence of the seemingly inexhaustible buffalo herds, so too did their dark destiny. The virtual extinction of the buffalo herds in the last decades of the nineteenth century ended a golden era in Plains culture as once proud mounted warriors were reduced to wards of the government, living a meager existence on the reservation.

When American settlers moved onto the Great Plains in the nineteenth century, they came into contact with a variety of nomadic Indian cultures, such as the Lakotas, Arapaho, and Cheyenne, who were at the apogee of their power, controlling most of the northern plains, like the Comanche on the southern plains. Initial contacts between whites and the Sioux were peaceful. But as the western migration gathered steam in the years surrounding the California Gold Rush, driving off the buffalo herds and carrying cholera into Sioux territory, tensions heightened. One can view the subsequent clash of cultures from several vantage points. How could a warrior hunting society adapt to American expansion? Was this truly the "advance of civilization," as the Anglo culture viewed it, or was it the invasion and dispossession of Indian cultures? Several parallels with American expansion into Mexican lands can be discerned here.

Like other Plains Indian tribes, the Sioux were not united under a central leader, but were a loose confederation of tribes linked by intermarriage and a common culture that revolved around the buffalo. The Sioux were often at war with Indian adversaries as they sought to expand their hunting grounds and raided for horses. Smaller tribes such as the Pawnee and the Crows were only too happy to help the Americans wage war against their traditional and more powerful Sioux foes.

Despite popular mythology, which pictures wagon trains being attacked by Indian raiders on the overland trails to Oregon and California, there was little hostility between the overlanders and the Indians in the 1840s. But as the overland traffic heated up in the 1850s, bringing contagious disease to Indian villages and destroying scarce game and timber resources, relations worsened. Initially, the Treaty of Fort Laramie in 1851 kept conflict to a minimum as the major Plains tribes accepted certain tribal boundaries in order to prevent violent confrontations. In 1854 Lieutenant John Grattan and his entire command were wiped out by Brule Sioux. This was followed by army retaliation against an Indian village at Ash Hollow in 1855, setting the stage for a quarter century of conflict between the Sioux and the U.S. Army.

Compared to the more peaceful removal of the eastern tribes in the 1820s and 1830s, the relocation of the Plains Indians to the reservation led to several decades of fierce conflict. Except for the Black Hawk War (1832), the Creek War (1836), and the Seminole War (1835–1842), the majority of Indian-white violence in the nineteenth century took place in the trans-Mississippi West. Between 1865 and 1891 the army fought in twelve major campaigns that were officially recognized by the armed forces. These wars make up a distinct category of Indian conflict in that they resulted from the federal government's attempt to clear the Great Plains of Indian cultures, who considered this a permanent home.

The Civil War between 1861 and 1865 drew troops from the frontier and slowed down western migration, but Indian conflicts continued on the Plains. In 1862 the Sioux rose up against white settlers in Minnesota, leading to the hanging of thirty-eight Indians for murder, the largest mass hanging in American history. Following the end of the Civil War, an industrializing America looked to expand farther west. In order to create an environment suitable for homesteaders and cattle ranching, the federal government launched a campaign to remove the nomadic Plains tribes to reservations where they could be assimilated to white ways.

The years following the Civil War saw almost constant conflict on the Great Plains as the U.S. Army fought to clear the Indians from what was supposed to be their permanent homeland. Bound by traditional methods of waging war, the army was ill-prepared to fight the well-armed and mobile Plains Indians. But the onslaught of the buffalo hunters soon hastened the demise of the animals on which the Plains Indian culture was based and helped bring an end to this theater of the Indian wars.

Nothing was more important to young Plains Indian males than acquiring prestige and status in warfare. With this option dissolving before their very eyes, most initially chose resistance, initiating a series of Indian wars as the U.S. Army waged war on Indian villages, pony herds, and the diminished buffalo herds. In 1866, during the "winter of one hundred slain," the Oglala under Chief Red Cloud waged a successful campaign to halt the building of the Bozeman Trail from Fort Laramie to Montana. Among his greatest victories was the annihilation of Captain William Fetterman's command, which, according to the 1868 Treaty of Fort Laramie, led the army to abandon its string of forts on the Bozeman Trail and guaranteed Sioux territory, which included the Black Hills. However, before the final version of the treaty was hammered out, a final clause was added which would grant the Black Hills hunting lands to the United States once the buffalo were gone. While Red Cloud counseled for a peaceful transition to the reservation, other Indian leaders such as Sitting Bull and Crazy Horse continued to resist and refused to sign the treaty or even acknowledge its provisions.

In 1874–1875 the discovery of gold in the Black Hills region of the Dakotas led the federal government to try to remove the Sioux and Cheyenne Indians to reservations. Sacred to the Sioux, the Black Hills were also inviolable Indian lands according to the 1868 Treaty of Fort Laramie. In the early 1870s George A. Custer led an expedition into the Black Hills to verify the discovery of gold. At that time the United States was deep into a recession and could do little to keep fortune seekers off the sacred lands. When the federal government attempted to purchase the Black Hills, Sitting Bull reportedly responded that they were not for sale.

The opening of the Black Hills to settlers and gold seekers violated the 1868 Treaty of Fort Laramie, in which the United States had guaranteed the boundaries of the Sioux territory, which included the Black Hills. Demonstrating the ineptness of federal Indian policy during the Grant administration, the government had two choices. On one hand, it could attempt to eject the white gold seekers who had flooded the Black Hills. On the other, it could violate earlier commitments and enter into hostilities with the Indian tribes that legally lived on the lands and then seize the land. For the federal government the latter choice ruled the day.

The government issued an ultimatum for all Sioux to report to the reservation by January 31, 1876. By the time the relocation date came and passed, a number of Indians ignored the proclamation and had soon flocked to Chief Sitting Bull's encampment along the Little Big Horn River in what is now southern Montana. In response, the U.S. Army began a campaign against those who refused to surrender, and in the subsequent campaign against the Northern Cheyenne and Sioux in 1876–1877 would destroy the concentrated power of the Northern Plains Indians. Precipitating this action were government attempts to clear the Wyoming-Montana and Black Hills regions of Sioux and Cheyenne. When few complied with the ultimatum, the army began a three-pronged offensive.

Under the direction of General Philip Sheridan, troops led by Brigadier General Alfred Terry, Colonel John Gibbon, and George C. Crook converged on the Bighorn-Yellowstone region in May and June 1876. While Indian agents estimated their adversaries to be not much more than 500 warriors, in reality the soldiers were approaching the largest concentration of Plains Indians ever recorded. More than 2,000 Indians were prepared to contest the field against the 1,000-troop commands under Crook and Terry. After the Battle of the Rosebud, in which Crook engaged warriors under Chief Crazy Horse, both sides withdrew before any conclusive victory. While Crook waited for reinforcements, Terry advanced into the same region. Among his forces was the Seventh Cavalry under George Custer. On June 25, 1876, Custer's fateful mission would take him and his force to the Little Big Horn River.

The death of Custer and his troops would come back to haunt the Plains Indians. There would be little time for the Sioux to celebrate. In 1877 Crazy Horse and his band surrendered to military authorities. Sitting Bull and some of his followers fled to Canada before giving up and returning to the reservation in 1881. Meanwhile, in the East, politicians waved the bloody shirt, calling for a military campaign to push the remaining western tribes onto reservations once and for all.

The world of the Plains Indians had begun to unravel even before the 1870s. The completion of the transcontinental railroad in 1869 and other railroads soon thereafter helped facilitate the movement of immigrants, army troops, and supplies into the West. Paralleling this development was the rapid depletion of the buffalo herds, which were systematically destroyed between 1867 and 1883, declining from millions to only a handful by the turn of the new century. With the end of their food supply, and with their buffalo hunting culture in shambles, Indians could choose either starvation on the Plains or a meager existence in the reservation system. In 1890 and 1891 the Indian wars came to an end with the death of Sitting Bull and the Wounded Knee Massacre.

During the past thirty years Custer's Last Stand has resonated as an important cultural issue for the Indian civil rights movement. Most recently, the federal government in 1993 changed the name of the monument commemorating the battle from Custer Battlefield National Monument to Little Big Horn National Battlefield Monument, after Cheyenne activists protested the glorification of Custer, whom most Indians considered a nefarious frontier presence and a symbol of white aggression and perfidy.

DOCUMENTS

9.1.   Fort Laramie Treaty (1868)

According to the terms of this 1868 treaty, the United States acknowledged Red Cloud's victory against the U.S. Army in the war of 1866–1867. The United States agreed to abandon its string of forts along the Bozeman Trail, which ran from Fort Laramie to the gold fields of Montana, and recognized the boundaries of Sioux territory, which included the Black Hills. However, the final terms of the agreement included ceding the Black Hills back to the United States once the buffalo were gone.

Article XI

In consideration of the advantages and benefits conferred by this treaty, and the many pledges of friendship by the United States, the tribes who are parties to this agreement hereby stipulate that they will relinquish all right to occupy permanently the territory outside their reservation [as] herein defined, but yet reserve the right to hunt on any lands north of North Platte, and on the Republican Fork of the Smoky Hill River, so long as the buffalo may range thereon in such numbers as to justify the chase. And they, the said Indians, further expressly agree:

1st. That they will withdraw all opposition to the construction of the railroads now being built on the plains.

2d. That they will permit the peaceful construction of any railroad not passing over their reservation as herein defined.

3d. That they will not attack any persons at home, or travelling, nor molest or disturb any wagon-trains, coaches, mules, or cattle belonging to the people of the United States, or to persons friendly therewith.

4th. They will never capture, or carry off from the settlements, white women or children.

5th. They will never kill or scalp white men, nor attempt to do them harm.

6th. They withdraw all pretence of opposition to the construction of the railroad now being built along the Platte River and westward to the Pacific Ocean, and they will not in future object to the construction of railroads, wagon-roads, mail-stations, or other works of utility or necessity, which may be ordered or permitted by the laws of the United States.

But should such roads or other works be constructed on the lands of their reservation, the Government will pay the tribe whatever amount of damage may be assessed by three disinterested commissioners to be appointed by the President for that purpose, one of said commissioners to be a chief or head-man of the tribe.

7th. They agree to withdraw all opposition to the military posts or roads now established south of the North Platte River, or that may be established, not in violation of treaties heretofore made or hereafter to be made with any of the Indian Tribes.

Source: Charles J. Kappler, ed., *Indian Affairs: Laws and Treaties*, Vol. 2 (Washington, DC: U.S. Government Printing Office, 1904), pp. 998–1003.

9.2.   Congressional Debate on Peace with the Indians (1867)

> *The rush of settlers in western territories following the Civil War led to increased tension and hostilities with various Indian tribes. Despite treaties and agreements, current Indian policy had to be reassessed. Having promised the Indians certain lands in perpetuity, how could the promise be kept? In the following debate Representative William Windom of Massachusetts blames the post–Civil War Indian conflict on the Plains on the Sand Creek Massacre and provocative comments by General William Tecumseh Sherman.*

MR. WINDOM: We passed a bill during the last session of the Thirty-Ninth Congress declaring that nobody should have any power to make peace with the Indian tribes. I want merely to remove that obstruction, so that if a condition of affairs shall transpire whereby peace can be made we shall have power in somebody's hands to make it. I have not to-day any definite plan of peace prepared, because I suppose the House would not act upon any such measure at this time. But I do desire to place in the hands of somebody the power to make peace, if it is possible, without expending money after this fashion.

Sir, I firmly believe this whole Indian war might have been avoided in the first place. I will not now go into that question, though I would like to do so. I will only say I think its origin was in the massacre of the Cheyennes at Sand Creek by Colonel Chivington. There the war commenced, and from that most atrocious act it has grown to its present proportions. The Indians were further aroused during the last session of Congress when General Sherman issued an order that any Indian found within certain boundaries, between the Platte and Missouri rivers, without a written pass from a military officer should be summarily dealt with; that is to say, shot.

Now, the Indians who occupied that territory had a right, by treaty stipulation with this Government, to hunt on that very territory; but your military commander issued a proclamation that if any of them were found hunting there they should be shot. Delegations from all these tribes were here in this city and in these galleries last winter, and remained here for a month. They heard this military order of General Sherman, and considered it a proclamation of war against every Indian on the Plains, and they are now uniting against us to resist this declaration of war.

Another thing: General Sherman at the same time issued an order to which I once before called the attention of the House, and which, on account of its unequaled atrocity, I desire again to repeat. It was in these words:

> We must act with vindictive earnestness against the Sioux, even to their extermination, men, women, and children. Nothing else will reach the root of the case.

The Indians know that the commanding general of your Army in the West coolly proposes to murder their wives and little children, and they are in open resistance to that order. Are they not justifiable in resisting it?

Source: Congressional Globe, 40th Congress, 1st Session, 1867, pp. 667–670, reprinted in Wilcomb E. Washburn, ed., The American Indian and the United States, Vol. 3 (New York: Random House, 1973), pp. 1496–1497.

9.3.   Report of Commissioner of Indian Affairs (1875)

In the following passage, Commissioner of Indian Affairs Edward P. Smith reports on the reversal of federal Indian policy after white miners flooded the gold fields in the Black Hills, violating the Fort Laramie Treaty of 1868. This influx of miners into Indian country severely strained an already tense situation. Commissioner Smith offers a number of arguments why the Indians should be given a fair equivalent for their land.

The occupation and possession of the Black Hills by white men seems now inevitable, but no reason exists for making this inevitability an occasion of wrong or lasting injury to the Sioux. If an Indian can be possessed of rights of country, either natural or required, this country belongs for occupation to the Soux; and if they were an independent, self-supporting people, able to claim that hereafter the United States Government should leave them entirely alone, in yearly receipt of such annuities only as the treaty of 1868 guarantees, they would be in a position to demand to be left in undisturbed possession of their country, and the moral sense of mankind would sustain the demand; but unfortunately the facts are otherwise. They are not now capable of self-support; they are absolute pensioners of the Government in the sum of a million and a quarter of dollars annually above all amounts specified in treaty-stipulations. A failure to receive Government rations for a single season would reduce them to starvation. They cannot, therefore, demand to be left alone, and the Government, granting the large help which the Sioux are obliged to ask, is entitled to ask something of them in return. On this basis of mutual benefit the purchase of the Black Hills should proceed. If, therefore, all attempts at negotiation have failed on the plan of going first to the Indians, I would respectfully recommend that legislation be now sought from Congress, offering a fair and full equivalent for the country lying between the North and South Forks of the Cheyenne River, in Dakota, a portion of which equivalent should be made to take the place of the free rations now granted.

Survey of the Black Hills—Their Value to the Indians

In order to provide for the question of a fair equivalent for this country, by direction of the President, a topographical and geological survey of the Black Hills was ordered, the preliminary report of which, by Walter P. Jenney, mining engineer in charge, will be found herewith. It furnishes many interesting and important facts respecting a region hitherto almost unknown. Professor Jenney and his assistants are entitled to large credit for the conscientious diligence and thoroughness, which are apparent at every point in their work. The aid rendered by the War Department, by the courtesy of the General of the Army, and by Col. R. I. Dodge, commanding the escort, has been invaluable to the success of the survey. Without such aid, no satisfactory results could have been obtained, on account of the limited funds available for this purpose. The report confirms, in a large degree, the statements of travelers and explorers and the reports of General Custer's military expedition of last year, and shows a gold-field with an area of eight hundred square miles, and around this gold region, principally to the north, an additional area within the Black Hills country of three thousand square miles of arable lands, and this latter embracing along its streams an area equal to two hundred square miles finely adapted to agriculture, while the hill-sides and elevations continguous thereto are equally adapted to purposes of grazing, making the whole area of three thousand square miles of timber, grazing, and arable land of great value for agricultural purposes.

According to the findings of this report, if there were no gold in this country to attract the white man, and the Indians could be left to undisturbed occupation of the Black Hills, this region, naturally suited to agriculture and herding, is the one of all others within the boundaries of the Sioux reservation best adapted to their immediate and paramount necessities. I doubt whether any land not remaining in the possession of the General Government offers equal advantages; but it will be found impracticable to utilize the country for the Sioux. So long as gold exists in the same region, the agricultural country surrounding the gold-fields will be largely required to support the miners, and to attempt to bring the wild Sioux into proximity to the settlers and miners would be to invite provocations and bloody hostility.

These facts respecting the country which the Sioux seem about to be compelled to surrender, for the sake of promoting the mining and agricultural interests of white men, have an important bearing upon the question of compensation which shall be allowed for their lands; for it must be borne in mind that unless the Sioux Nation becomes extinct, of which there is no probability, the time is close upon them when they must have just such an opportunity for self-support as that which is now known to be offered in the Black Hills; and if, for the want of another such country, they are obliged to begin civilization under increased disabilities, humanity as well as equity demands that such disability shall be compensated by increased aid from the Government; and to avoid the perils of future legislation, or want of legislation, the compensation should be provided for and fixed at the time when we are taking away their valuable lands.

The fact that these Indians are making but little if any use of the Black Hills has no bearing upon the question of what is a fair equivalent for the surrender of these rare facilities for farming and grazing. They are children, utterly unable to comprehend their own great necessities just ahead; they cannot, therefore, see that the country which now only furnishes them lodge-poles and a few antelope has abundant resources for their future wants, when they shall cease to be barbarous pensioners upon the Government and begin to provide for their own living. Their ignorance of themselves and of true values makes the stronger appeal to our sense of what is right and fair.

The true equivalent to be offered the Sioux, as helpless wards of the Government, for the Black Hills will be found by estimating what eight hundred square miles of gold-fields are worth to us, and what three thousand square miles of timber, agricultural, and grazing lands are worth to them.

Source: Report of Commissioner of Indian Affairs, Edward P. Smith, *Report for 1875*, November 1, 1875, pp. 506–514.

9.4.   *Harper's Weekly* Covers the Battle of the Little Big Horn

---

> *The most popular weekly magazine of the post–Civil War era,* Harper's Weekly *carried the guidon for Custer's Seventh Cavalry after their defeat at the Little Big Horn. The first passage describes the battle and eulogizes Custer. The second piece criticizes the current Indian policy. The final passage is a poetic homage to Custer's defeat.*

THE MONTANA SLAUGHTER

CLOSE upon the intelligence of the check to General Crook's command on Rosebud River comes the news of a disaster on the Little Horn River so terrible and ghastly in its details that at the first announcement it was considered incredible or grossly exaggerated. Later dispatches, however, confirmed the dreadful story in all its shocking particulars.

The map on this page gives the scene of the disaster, and the sketches on page 592, engraved from drawings sent us by officers in the field, show the character of the country where our troops are operating against the Indian forces under the command of Sitting Bull, the famous Sioux chief. It is admirably adapted by its rough, broken character, its precipitous, craggy hills and deep, narrow defiles, for a defensive war on the part of the Indians; and Sitting Bull, a chief of great natural sagacity and intelligence, sharpened by fifteen years of fighting, knows how to avail himself of every advantage offered by the *terrain*. The region where the recent battles have taken place lies, as a reference to the map will show, between the Big Horn spur of the Rocky Mountains and the Yellowstone River, and through it flow the Big and Little Horn and the Rosebud rivers. Early last spring a campaign was planned against the Indians located in this region to compel them to remove to the reservation set apart for them by the government, which they had refused to do. Three columns, under command of Generals Gibbon, Terry, and Crook, were equipped and placed under marching orders, their objective point being Sitting Bull's camp, in the Big Horn country. These columns were to meet on the Powder or the Tongue river, and combine their forces in the heart of the hostile territory. General Crook, at Fort Reno, was to strike north; General Terry, with General Custer's cavalry, at Fort Lincoln, was to march west; and General Gibbon, at Fort Buford, was to descend the Yellowstone Valley and join General Terry.

General Crook set out from Fort Fetterman, of which we give an illustration on page 592, on the 29th of May, and after a short halt at Fort Reno advanced to the head waters of the Tongue River. On the 9th of June the Indians attacked his camp, and were gallantly repulsed. On the 16th of June the march was resumed, in the direction of the Rosebud Valley. The next day the Sioux surprised the troops while on the march. The attack was made with great vigor, the Indians having all the advantages of position and superior numbers. Ten of the troops were killed and nineteen wounded, and General Crook deemed it necessary to order a retreat to Goose Creek.

Meanwhile General Terry, with 1500 men, had left Fort Lincoln, striking for the Powder River and the Yellowstone, where he was to meet General Gibbon, with 500 men, coming from Fort Ellis. At the Rosebud, General Custer, with twelve companies of cavalry, left Terry to make a detour around by the Little Horn. This was on the 22d of June. On the 25th he struck what was probably the main camp of Sitting Bull. He had pushed forward with greater rapidity than his orders directed, and arrived at the point where a junction of the forces was intended, a day or two in advance of the infantry. Without waiting for the rest of the troops to come up, General Custer decided upon an immediate attack. The Indians were posted in a narrow ravine, about twenty miles above the mouth of the river. At the head of five companies of cavalry he charged into the ravine, while Colonel Reno, with four companies, made an attack on the other side, three companies being held in reserve. According to the story of the scout who brought the intelligence of the disaster, Custer led his brave men into a fearful slaughter-pen. The Indians poured a murderous fire upon them from all sides, and not one of the detachment escaped alive. General Custer himself, his two brothers, his brother-in-law, and his nephew were all killed. The Indians surrounded Colonel Reno's command, and held the troops on the hills, cut off from water, for a whole day, when the force under General Gibbon, for which Custer should have waited before going into the fight, arrived on the ground. The Indians then broke up and retired under cover of darkness.

A survey of the disastrous battle-ground disclosed a dreadful slaughter. Two hundred and seven men were buried in one place, and the total number of killed is estimated at three hundred and fifteen, including seventeen commissioned officers. The bodies of the dead were terribly mutilated. The Indians are supposed to have numbered from 2500 to 4000, and all the courage and skill displayed by our troops was of no avail against such overwhelming odds. The Indian loss can not be ascertained, as they carried off both killed and wounded. They stripped our killed of arms and ammunition.

General George A. Custer, of whom we give a portrait on page 601, was a native of Ohio. He graduated at West Point in 1861, with the grade

of Second Lieutenant of Cavalry. He was attached to the Army of the
Potomac, and distinguished himself at Williamsburg in the Peninsular
campaign, for which he was made a First Lieutenant. Promotion now
came to him rapidly, as a reward for gallant services. He was soon made
Captain, and displayed so much ability while acting as a brigade commander of mounted cavalry that in 1863 he was appointed a Brigadier-
General of Volunteers. General Custer participated in many important
engagements, and won great honor for dash and gallantry during the
terrible campaign in the Wilderness and in Sheridan's brilliant operations
in the Shenandoah Valley, for which he received the commission of
Major-General of Volunteers. He participated with distinguished ability
in the grand movements which decided the fate of Lee's army and of
the rebellion in 1865, and was breveted Colonel and Brigadier-General
in the regular army for his eminent services. Since the close of the war
General Custer has been chiefly engaged in the Indian country. At the
time of his death he was acting simply as commander of his regiment,
the Seventh Cavalry.

Source: Harper's Weekly, July 22, 1876.

A NATIONAL DISGRACE

THE fate of the brave and gallant Custer has deeply touched the public
heart, which sees only a fearless soldier leading a charge against an ambushed foe, and falling at the head of his men and in the thick of the
fray. A monument is proposed, and subscriptions have been made. But
a truer monument, more enduring than brass or marble, would be an
Indian policy intelligent, moral, and efficient. Custer would not have
fallen in vain if such a policy should be the result of his death. It is a
permanent accusation of our humanity and ability that over the Canadian line the relations between Indians and whites are so tranquil, while
upon our side they are summed up in perpetual treachery, waste, and
war. When he was a young lieutenant on the frontier, General Grant saw
this, and, watching attentively, he came to the conclusion that the reason
of the difference was that the English respected the rights of the Indians
and kept faith with them, while we make solemn treaties with them as
if they were civilized and powerful nations, and then practically regard
them as vermin to be exterminated. The folly of making treaties with the
Indian tribes may be as great as treating with a herd of buffaloes. But
the infamy of violating treaties when we have made them is undeniable,
and we are guilty both of the folly and the infamy.

We make treaties—that is, we pledge our faith—and then leave swin-
dlers and knaves of all kinds to execute them. We maintain and breed
pauper colonies. The savages, who know us, and who will neither be
pauperized nor trust our word, we pursue, and slay if we can, at an

incredible expense. The flower of our young officers is lost in inglorious forays, and one of the intelligent students of the whole subject rises in Congress and says, "The fact is that these Indians, with whom we have made a solemn treaty that their territory should not be invaded, and that they should receive supplies upon their reservations, have seen from one thousand to fifteen hundred miners during the present season entering and occupying their territory, while the Indians, owing to the failure of this and the last Congress to make adequate appropriations for their subsistence, instead of being fattened, as the gentleman says, by the support of this government, have simply been starved." The Red Cloud investigation of last year, however inadequate, sufficed to show the practice under our Indian policy, and we regretted then that ex-Governor Bullock, of Massachusetts, declined the appointment upon the commission, because there was evidently the opportunity of an exhaustive report upon the whole subject, which would have commanded the attention of the country, and would sooner or later have led to some decisive action.

It is plain that so long as we undertake to support the Indians as paupers, and then fail to supply the food; to respect their rights to reservations, and then permit the reservations to be overrun; to give them the best weapons and ammunition, and then furnish the pretense of their using them against us; to treat with them as men, and then hunt them like skunks—so long we shall have the most costly and bloody Indian wars, and the most tragical ambuscades, slaughters, and assassinations. The Indian is undoubtedly a savage, and a savage greatly spoiled by the kind of contact with civilization which he gets at the West. There is no romance, there is generally no interest whatever, in him or his fate. But there should be some interest in our own good-faith and humanity, in the lives of our soldiers and frontier settlers, and in the taxation to support our Indian policy. All this should certainly be enough to arouse a public demand for a thorough consideration of the subject, and the adoption of a system which should neither be puerile nor disgraceful, and which would tend to spare us the constant repetition of such sorrowful events as the slaughter of Custer and his brave men.

Source: Harper's Weekly, August 5, 1876.

ROMANCE AND REALITY

I.

NEVER was month like the month of June,
Her wreath of roses and lovers' moon.
Think ye "the world is out of joint?"
Then watch ye the shadows of old West Point.
See how they fall on the grassy sward;
Watch them lie on the glittering sword

Of the eager youth who longs for strife
And the stern delights of a soldier's life.
Yonder the building, old and gray,
Where he learned the warrior's art to slay.
Behind are the hours of labor done;
To-day the sweetness of triumph won;
But sweetest of all, the tender smile
That beams on a fairer face the while,
As the tale is told that, ever the same,
Fresh beauty wins from a dream of fame.
A nameless boy is her lover now,
With a beardless cheek and a childish brow.
Wait till the fearful war-drum rolls:
In the bitter hour that tries men's souls
He will win the honors that she shall wear,
Till her woman's heart grows proud to bear
A name that a nation loves to boast,
And writes with those that she honors most.
There's a rapture thrills through the lips that kiss
And lisp of fame in a scene like this.

II.

Far away on the wild frontier
Stands the cot of the pioneer.
Loud he calls to the soldier bands,
"Drive ye the savage from our lands!"
The word is given, the charge is led,
And the red soil groans with the martyr dead.
Hark ye! what is the sound that swells?
Crack of rifle and savage yells!
Poisoned arrow and hissing shot
Pour from the ambush thick and hot.
Red blood, flowing from manly veins,
Dyes with crimson the burning plains.
Look! how silent a brave form lies!
The sun glares down from the tearless skies.
No soft hand touches the matted hair,
No lips of woman are resting there.
Only a veteran, stern and grim,
Pauses a while with eyes grown dim.
There's a pictured face on the blood-stained grass;
O'er the smiling eyes no shadows pass.
There are other eyes that are dim with tears,
That will smile no more in the coming years,

That turn in pain from the cheerless moon
As the weeks bring round the month of June,
And lips that whisper a simple name
That has never rung on the blast of fame.

Source: Harper's Weekly, July 29, 1876.

9.5.   The Indian Side of the Battle of the Little Big Horn (1876)

---

*In the following account, the Cheyenne chief Two Moon gives
a firsthand account of the battle. According to Two Moon, the
annihilation of Custer's command "took about as long as a hungry man to eat his supper."*

That spring [1876] I was camped on Powder River with fifty lodges of
my people—Cheyennes. The place is near what is now Fort McKenney.
One morning soldiers charged my camp. They were in command of
Three Fingers [Colonel McKenzie]. We were surprised and scattered,
leaving our ponies. The soldiers ran all our horses off. That night the
soldiers slept, leaving the horses one side; so we crept up and stole them
back again, and then we went away.

We traveled far, and one day we met a big camp of Sioux at Charcoal
Butte. We camped with the Sioux, and had a good time, plenty grass,
plenty game, good water. Crazy Horse was head chief of the camp. Sitting Bull was camped a little ways below, on the Little Missouri River.

Crazy Horse said to me, "I'm glad you are come. We are going to fight
the white man again."

The camp was already full of wounded men, women, and children.

I said to Crazy Horse, "All right. I am ready to fight. I have fought
already. My people have been killed, my horses stolen; I am satisfied to
fight."

Here the old man paused a moment, and his face took on a lofty and
somber expression.

I believed at that time the Great Spirits had made Sioux, put them
there,—he drew a circle to the right—and white men and Cheyennes
here,—indicating two places to the left—expecting them to fight. The
Great Spirits I thought liked to see the fight; it was to them all the same
like playing. So I thought then about fighting. As he said this, he made
me feel for one moment the power of a sardonic god whose drama was
the wars of men.

About May, when the grass was tall and the horses strong, we broke

camp and started across the country to the mouth of the Tongue River.
Then Sitting Bull and Crazy Horse and all went up the Rosebud. There
we had a big fight with General Crook, and whipped him. Many soldiers
were killed—few Indians. It was a great fight, much smoke and dust.

From there we all went over the divide, and camped in the valley of
Little Horn. Everybody thought, Now we are out of the white man's
country. He can live there, we will live here. After a few days, one morning when I was in camp north of Sitting Bull, a Sioux messenger rode
up and said, "Let everybody paint up, cook, and get ready for a big
dance."

Cheyennes then went to work to cook, cut up tobacco, and get ready.
We all thought to dance all day. We were very glad to think we were
far away from the white man.

I went to water my horses at the creek, and washed them off with cool
water, then took a swim myself. I came back to the camp afoot. When I
got near my lodge, I looked up the Little Horn towards Sitting Bull's
camp. I saw a great dust rising. It looked like a whirlwind. Soon Sioux
horseman came rushing into camp shouting: "Soldiers come! Plenty
white soldiers."

I ran into my lodge, and said to my brother-in-law, "Get your horses:
the white man is coming. Everybody run for horses."

Outside, far up the valley, I heard a battle cry, Hay-ay, hay-ay! I heard
shooting, too, this way [clapping his hands very fast]. I couldn't see any
Indians. Everybody was getting horses and saddles. After I had caught
my horse, a Sioux warrior came again and said, "Many soldiers are coming."

Then he said to the women, "Get out of the way, we are going to have
hard fight."

I said, "All right, I am ready."

I got on my horse, and rode out into my camp. I called out to the
people all running about: "I am Two Moon, your chief. Don't run away.
Stay here and fight. You must stay and fight the white soldiers. I shall
stay even if I am to be killed."

I rode swiftly toward Sitting Bull's camp. There I saw the white soldiers fighting in a line [Reno's men]. Indians covered the flat. They began
to drive the soldiers all mixed up—Sioux, then soldiers, then more Sioux,
and all shooting. The air was full of smoke and dust. I saw the soldiers
fall back and drop into the river-bed like buffalo fleeing. They had no
time to look for a crossing. The Sioux chased them up the hill, where
they met more soldiers in wagons, and then messengers came saying
more soldiers were going to kill the women, and the Sioux turned back.
Chief Gall was there fighting, Crazy Horse also.

I then rode toward my camp, and stopped squaws from carrying off
lodges. While I was sitting on my horse I saw flags come up over the

hill to the east like that [he raised his finger-tips]. Then the soldiers rose all at once, all on horses, like this [he put his fingers behind each other to indicate that Custer appeared marching in columns of fours]. They formed into three bunches [squadrons] with a little ways between. Then a bugle sounded, and they all got off horses, and some soldiers led the horses back over the hill.

Then the Sioux rode up the ridge on all sides, riding very fast. The Cheyennes went up the left way. Then the shooting was quick, quick. Pop—pop—pop very fast. Some of the soldiers were down on their knees, some standing. Officers all in front. The smoke was like a great cloud, and everywhere the Sioux went the dust rose like smoke. We circled all round him—swirling like water round a stone. We shoot, we ride fast, we shoot again. Soldiers drop, and horses fall on them. Soldiers in line drop, but one man rides up and down the line—all the time shouting. He rode a sorrel horse with white face and white fore-legs. I don't know who he was. He was a brave man.

Indians keep swirling round and round, and the soldiers killed only a few. Many soldiers fell. At last all horses killed but five. Once in a while some man would break out and run toward the river, but he would fall. At last about a hundred men and five horsemen stood on the hill all bunched together. All along the bugler kept blowing his commands. He was very brave too. Then a chief was killed. I hear it was Long Hair [Custer], I don't know; and then the five horsemen and the bunch of men, may be so forty, started toward the river. The man on the sorrel horse led them, shouting all the time. He wore a buckskin shirt, and had long black hair and mustache. He fought hard with a big knife. His men were all covered with white dust. I couldn't tell whether they were officers or not. One man all alone ran far down toward the river, then round up over the hill. I thought he was going to escape, but a Sioux fired and hit him in the head. He was the last man. He wore braid on his arms [sergeant].

Source: Hamlin Garland, "General Custer's Last Fight As Seen by Two Moon," *McClure's Magazine*, September 1898, pp. 444–448.

9.6.   "The Nobility of the Redskin Is Extinguished" (1883, 1891)

In the first excerpt, outgoing General of the Army William Tecumseh Sherman (1820–1891) reports that the Indian wars have ended and that the Indian question has finally been settled. Best known for his march through Georgia during the Civil War, Sherman had been an implacable foe of the Plains Indians and a supporter of reservation policy. The second passage is from an editorial printed in the Aberdeen, South Dakota, Pioneer less than two weeks before the Wounded Knee Massacre of 1890. It is written by L. Frank Baum, the future author of The Wonderful Wizard of Oz (1900), who suggests that it is time to exterminate the remaining Indian peoples.

I now regard the Indians as substantially eliminated from the problem of the Army. There may be spasmodic and temporary alarms, but such Indian wars as have hitherto disturbed the public peace and tranquillity are not probable. The Army has been a large factor in producing this result, but it is not the only one. Immigration and the occupation by industrious farmers and miners of land vacated by the aborigines have been largely instrumental to that end, but the *railroad* which used to follow in the rear now goes forward with the picket-line in the great battle of civilization with barbarism, and has become the *greater* cause. I have in former reports, for the past fifteen years, treated of this matter, and now, on the eve of withdrawing from active participation in public affairs, I beg to emphasize much which I have spoken and written heretofore. The recent completion of the last of the four great transcontinental lines of railway has settled forever the Indian question, the Army question, and many others which have hitherto troubled the country.

Source: House Executive Document No. 1, 48th Congress, 1st session, serial 2182, 1883, pp. 45–46, reprinted in Francis Paul Prucha, ed., *Documents of United States Indian Policy* (Lincoln: University of Nebraska Press, 1993), p. 159.

The nobility of the Redskin is extinguished, and what few are left are a pack of whining curs who lick the hand that smites them. The Whites, by law of conquest, by justice of civilization, are masters of the American continent, and the best safety of the frontier settlements will be secured by the total annihilation of the few remaining Indians. Why not annihilation? Their glory has fled, their spirit broken, their manhood effaced; better that they should die than live the miserable wretches that they are.

Source: Aberdeen Saturday Pioneer (Aberdeen, South Dakota), December 20, 1891, quoted in Elliott J. Gorn, Randy Roberts, and Terry D. Bilhartz, *Constructing the American Past: A Source Book of a People's History* (New York: HarperCollins, 1991), p. 99.

9.7.   Sitting Bull's Report on the Condition of the Sioux (1883)

Just six years after the Battle of the Little Big Horn, a U.S. Senate committee visited Montana and Dakota to investigate the prog-

*ress and condition of Sioux Indians. The committee was im-
mediately bombarded with complaints, but showed little
interest. On the second day, Sitting Bull (c. 1831–1890) addressed the select committee. Among the most famous Indians
in American history, he was a leader in the warrior society, a
chief, and a holy man, known for his uncompromising stand
against the whites. While he did not actually take part in the
fighting at the Little Big Horn due to his ascendance to the chief-
taincy, he led his followers to Canada after the battle and did
not return to the States until 1881.*

If a man loses anything, and goes back and looks carefully for it he will
find it, and that is what the Indians are doing now when they ask you
to give them the things they were promised them in the past. And I do
not consider that they should be treated like beasts, and that is the reason
I have grown up with the feelings I have.

Whatever you wanted of me I have obeyed, and I have come when
you called me. The Great Father sent me word that what ever he had
against me in the past had been forgiven and thrown aside, and he
would have nothing against me in the future, and I accepted his promises and came in. And he told me not to step aside from the white man's
path, and I told him I would not, and I am doing my best to travel in
that path.

I feel that my country has gotten a bad name, and I want it to have a
good name. It used to have a good name, and I sit sometimes and wonder who it is that has given it a bad name. You are the only people now
who can give it a good name, and I want you to take care of my country
and respect it.

When we sold the Black Hills we got a very small price for it, and not
what we ought to have received. I used to think that the size of the
payments would remain the same all the time, but they are growing
smaller all the time.

I want you to tell the Great Father everything I have said, and that
we want some benefits from the promises he has made to us. And I
don't think I should be tormented with anything about giving up any
part of my land until those promises are fulfilled. I would rather wait
until that time, when I will be ready to transact any business he may
desire.

I consider that my country takes in the Black Hills, and runs from the
Powder River to the Missouri, and that all of this land belongs to me.
Our reservation is not as large as we want it to be, and I suppose the
Great Father owes us money now for land he has taken from us in the
past.

You white men advise us to follow your ways, and therefore I talk as
I do. When you have a piece of land, and anything trespasses on it, you

catch it and keep it until you get damages, and I am doing the same thing now. And I want you to tell this to the Great Father for me. I am looking into the future for the benefit of my children, and that is what I mean, when I say I want my country taken care of for me.

My children will grow up here, and I am looking ahead for their benefit and for the benefit of my children's children, too; and even beyond that again. I sit here and look around me now, and I see my people starving, and I want the Great Father to make an increase in the amount of food that is allowed us now, so that they may be able to live. We want cattle to butcher—I want you to kill 300 head of cattle at a time. That is the way you live and we want to live the same way. This is what I want you to tell the Great Father when you go back home.

If we get the things we want, our children will be raised like the white children. When the Great Father told me to live like his people I told him to send me six teams of mules, because that is the way white people make a living, and I wanted my children to have these things to help them to make a living. I also told him to send me two spans of horses with wagons, and everything else my children would need. I also asked for a horse and buggy for my children. I was advised to follow the ways of the white man, and that is why I asked for those things.

I never ask for anything that is not needed. I also asked for a cow and a bull for each family, so that they can raise cattle of their own. I asked for four yokes of oxen and wagons with them. Also a yoke of oxen and a wagon for each of my children to haul wood with.

It is your own doing that I am here. You sent me here, and advised me to live as you do, and it is not right for me to live in poverty. I asked the Great Father for hogs, male and female and for male and female sheep for my children to raise from. I did not leave out anything in the way of animals that the white men have; I asked for every one of them. I want you to tell the Great Father to send me some agricultural implements, so that I will not be obliged to work bare-handed.

Whatever he sends to this agency our agent will take care of for us, and we will be satisfied because we know he will keep everything right. Whatever is sent here for us he will be pleased to take care of for us. I want to tell you that our rations have been reduced to almost nothing, and many of the people have starved to death.

Now I beg of you to have the amount of rations increased so that our children will not starve, but will live better than they do now. I want clothing, too, and I will ask for that, too. We want all kinds of clothing for our people. Look at the men around here and see how poorly dressed they are. We want some clothing this month, and when it gets cold we want more to protect us from the weather.

That is all I have to say.

Source: 48th Congress, 1st session, 1883, Senate Report No. 283, Serial 2164, 80–81.

ANNOTATED SELECTED BIBLIOGRAPHY

Connell, Evan S. *Son of the Morning Star*. New York: Promontory Press, 1984. Part history of the Plains wars and part Custer biography. Connell's book is an extraordinary achievement, dwelling on the rare human details that historians often ignore.

Hedren, Paul L., ed. *The Great Sioux War, 1876–77*. Helena: Montana Historical Society Press, 1991. A collection of fifteen classic articles on the Sioux Wars.

Michno, Gregory F. *Lakota Noon: The Indian Narrative of Custer's Defeat*. Missoula: Mountain Press, 1997. Native American participants tell their side of the Battle of the Little Big Horn.

Sklenar, Larry. *To Hell with Honor: Custer and the Little Big Horn*. Norman: University of Oklahoma Press, 2000. Sklenar offers a fresh perspective on the last great Indian victory.

Utley, Robert M. *The Indian Frontier of the American West, 1846–1890*. Albuquerque: University of New Mexico Press, 1984. The author interprets the Indian wars from a dual perspective and with an even-handed approach.

————. *The Lance and the Shield: The Life and Times of Sitting Bull*. New York: Henry Holt, 1993. A definitive account of the life and times of the Sioux leader.

10

The Creation of Yellowstone National Park: Preserving the Natural West

Since the time of Thomas Jefferson, the American West has exerted a powerful grip on the American psyche. The natural wonders, the endless horizons, free-ranging Native American inhabitants, and the buffalo herds continue to excite the imagination of anyone once the words "West" and "frontier" are mentioned. With the opening of the railroad west to wealthy tourists in the 1870s, you did not have to be a courageous mountain man or soldier to see the U.S. version of national pride—America's answers to Old World antiquities and ancient castles.

Before the westward expansion of the 1850s, America's claims of scenic superiority rested chiefly on Niagara Falls on the New York–Canadian border. But as early as the 1830s, European visitors such as Alexis de Tocqueville noted the rampant commercialism that was already tarnishing the nation's most famous natural wonder. With the acquisition of the Far West following the U.S.-Mexican War, the nation now lay claim to the spectacular natural wonders that included the Rocky Mountains and the Pacific coast. Here now was a chance to redeem what was lost with the despoliation of Niagara Falls. Distance and the romantic imagery of artists and photographers would only add to the lure of the still "wild West."

According to a leading historian of the natural parks, "although the grandeur of the Far West inspired the national park idea, eastern men invented and shaped it."[1] In order to convince Congress to establish the national park, advocates had to persuade opponents that the region was worthless from an agricultural or ranching perspective. There was little truth in the "worthless lands" argument, but as a tactical ploy, it helped convince the public and government officials that the region would be more valuable as a tourist attraction by removing it from settlement.

The establishment of the first national park in 1872 is truly extraordinary when placed in its historical perspective. When one considers that the region is not far from the Little Big Horn, which would be the scene of Custer's demise four years in the future; that the transcontinental railroad had been completed just three years earlier; that the U.S.-Mexican War was only twenty-four years in the past; and that the Nez Perce War was some five years distant in the future—the protection of Yellowstone in 1872 seems remarkable. Taking into account that the 1870s was an era of "robber barons," conspicuous wealth and consumption, and national scandal, who could believe under such conditions that a large slice of the nation's most beautiful scenery would be preserved "for the benefit and enjoyment of the people"?

The public park concept had existed for years prior to the creation of Yellowstone National Park in 1872. Although Yellowstone was the first national park in the history of the world, plans had actually been in the works for California's Yosemite Valley to precede Yellowstone to first status in 1864. Yosemite was attracting travelers and tourists by the 1850s, and in June 1864 Congress granted this region to the state of California as a public park to protect it from private exploitation. But rather than take steps to preserve the entire valley as a park, the emphasis was placed on celebrating the giant sequoias and the precipitous cliffs, what some environmental scholars have called the park's "monumentalism."

Why Yellowstone? Why 1872? Some historians suggest that because the Upper Yellowstone region was not fully explored at an earlier date, the region was spared the fate of other natural areas. The war along the Bozeman Trail and the massacre of Fetterman's command, and the subsequent Fort Laramie Treaty in 1868, which promised the Sioux possession of the Black Hills region in perpetuity, perhaps served as a barrier to settlement. With little commercial activity and no Anglo communities in the region, it was also protected from squatters who could have preempted land before the government cast its eyes on the future national park. Fortunately, the park was created before settlers could gain a permanent foothold. The 3,300 square miles that comprise the wilderness park dwarfed Yosemite, in part because of concerns that there might be undiscovered natural wonders in the unmapped vastness of the region. So rather than attempting specifically to preserve an ecosystem, something unheard of in the nineteenth century, the goal was to protect natural curiosities that were America's "cultural heritage."

The mountain man John Colter, erstwhile member of the Lewis and Clark expedition, has been generally considered the first white man to report the spectacular grandeur of Yellowstone, in 1807. Others followed his footsteps into the wilderness and returned to "civilization" with reports of spurting geysers, hot springs that could scald a man to death, and the giant grizzly bear. Enough reports filtered back east that skepticism eventually turned to acceptance, and soon scientists, artists, and tourists alike came to see nature's majesty with their own eyes.

As early as 1833, noted western artist George Catlin (1796–1872) recognized the need for national parks, fearing that without them, much of the American wilderness would disappear. Catlin returned to the East with portraits of Indians and western landscapes and proposed setting aside the western high plains from Mexico to Lake Winnipeg as a huge reserve. Here for future generations would be "preserved in their pristine beauty and wildness, in a magnificent park" the buffalo and the Indian.[2] Although this proposition was highly unrealistic, it captured the imagination of transcendentalist writers such as Henry David Thoreau and Ralph Waldo Emerson.

Other landscape artists, including Albert Bierstadt (1830–1902) and Thomas Moran (1837–1926), followed Catlin, often exaggerating the western landscapes. Moran sometimes accompanied the pioneer landscape photographer William H. Jackson (1843–1942) on his western jaunts. Moran's emotionally charged landscapes and Jackson's photographs "became a potent new force in directing American attention to wilderness as a source of nationalism."[3]

In the years following the completion of the transcontinental railroad (1869), the public demand for more detailed information on the trans-Mississippi West led the federal government to sponsor a number of scientific surveys. While most of the expeditions were undertaken with scholarly intentions, they also showcased the natural wonders of the West thanks to the artists and photographers who accompanied the various surveys.

In the late 1860s and early 1870s, Civil War veteran and former science teacher John Wesley Powell (1834–1902) explored the Colorado River and the Grand Canyon. The self-taught geologist and ethnologist made the transition to conservationist and public lands reformer. He took to the lecture circuit to gain public support for federally sponsored scientific expeditions. Powell crusaded for a change in federal land policy, as he often found himself locked in conflict with opponents of western conservation. Although Powell was not a leader in the wilderness preservation movement, he was in the vanguard of conservationists who championed the rational use of scarce natural resources in the arid West. His three expeditions into the canyonlands of the Colorado River in the 1870s garnered tremendous interest among the public and scientists alike. While prior explorers of the region had used architectural analogies to describe the scenery, Powell admitted that the vistas were just "too vast, too complex, too grand for verbal description."[4]

When Powell first crossed the Great Plains in 1867, he found them almost devoid of white settlement. On each successive trip across the Plains he witnessed a metamorphosis, as waves of farmers dug up the land, setting the stage for the transformation of the Plains ecosystem. As more and more settlers moved out west in the nineteenth century, a number of conservationists began to feel that some regions were so spectacular that they should be set aside and left undeveloped so that future generations could enjoy their pristine beauty. In 1872 Yellowstone National Park became the first region to receive such status.

While the national park movement was widely supported outside of the West, many residents of the West feared that park legislation would close the region to settlement. According to Helena, Montana's *Rocky Mountain Gazette*, the creation of Yellowstone National Park could "keep the country a wilderness, and shut out, for many years, the travel that would seek that curious region if good roads were opened through it and hotels built therein."[5]

When Yellowstone became America's first national park in 1872, it also inaugurated the participation of the federal government in the business of managing wild lands for recreational use. The initial purchase of Yellowstone was focused more on protecting the wilderness hot springs, waterfalls, and geysers from private acquisition and exploitation. There was little consensus as to what the next step should be after the park was set aside from development. According to environmental historian Roderick Nash, the "wilderness was preserved unintentionally."[6] It would take time for park advocates to comprehend that the actual preservation of wilderness lands was the most significant result of their efforts.

Initially, proponents of the national park idea urged their creation because of the "monumental" scenery of the region. According to historian Richard White, "The United States was a young nation lacking both an ancient history and a cultural tradition rich in art, architecture, or literature."[7] Catering to the nationalism of a young country, here was an opportunity to extol the natural treasures of the Far West, which transcended the grandeur of anything the Old World had to offer.

During the first half of the nineteenth century few whites had visited the Yellowstone region, but descriptions of the wonders of the park reached the East after visits by individual fur traders and mountain men. The area was home to numerous Indian tribes, but early expeditions to explore the region and establish contact with the natives were few. During a 1870 expedition, members of one party were so impressed by the natural wonders that they intended to file land claims as soon as they could and planned to charge tourists to visit. One member, Nathaniel Pitt Langford, was reportedly appalled by the scheme and favored setting aside the lands as a "national park." But first he would have to convince Congress.

Returning to the East, Langford went on the lecture circuit, although his stories of geysers and hot springs strained credulity. Among his audience one night was Ferdinand V. Hayden (1829–1887), who was preparing to lead a scientific expedition into the West. After listening to the talk, he incorporated Yellowstone into his itinerary for the 1871 expedition. Hayden's was the first entirely civilian expedition, funded by the Department of the Interior. There was tremendous interest in the expedition in the East. The financiers of the Northern Pacific Railroad through Montana even approached Hayden to lead a crusade to make the region "a public park forever." Having the only railroad line into the region, Jay Cooke and Company saw a western version of New York's Niagara Falls and looked forward to shuttling tourists to within stagecoach distance of the future vacation hotspot.

In their efforts to publicize the wonders of the West, Hayden and Nathaniel Langford launched the campaign for Yellowstone in December 1871. Park supporters assured the opposition that the region was inhospitable to farming, and thus would by no means "harm the material interests of the people." By the 1880s the wilderness attributes of Yellowstone National Park had gained currency among government officials. But opponents still looked forward to the day when the lands could be surveyed and parceled out to speculators.

Considered a master at public relations, Hayden sought to create a visual chronicle of the expedition by persuading the artist Thomas Moran and photographer William Henry Jackson to join his retinue. Jackson's photographs would make him famous and convince Congress to approve the establishment of the world's first national park. In the month before Congress endorsed the bill, Jackson's photographs from the Hayden expedition were placed in front of almost every member of Congress. After viewing these wondrous images few were left unconvinced, and on March 1, 1872, President Ulysses S. Grant signed the bill, which described Yellowstone as a "public park or pleasuring ground." The provision that its resources be kept in their natural condition furthered the notion of wilderness preservation.

Soon after the creation of the park in 1872, officials went about removing the Lakota, Shoshone, Crow, Blackfeet, and other Indian peoples that called Yellowstone home. The Indians offered little resistance, and most were relocated to reservations. Several skirmishes with the Nez Perce and the Bannock in the late 1870s led to the removal of all Indians from Yellowstone. Government officials disseminated the widespread misconception that Indians feared national parks, particularly Yellowstone's geysers. However, this ignores the tangible reality of ancient campsites and artifacts that testify to the longtime occupation of the region by native cultures.

Although Congress had created the world's first national park, there were no provisions to prevent poaching. In fact, the park did not receive any appropriations from Congress for more than six years. Through the mid-1880s thousands of elk, deer, moose, antelope, and bighorn sheep were killed not only by hunters but also by park employees. In order to stop the rapid depletion of native animals in the Yellowstone habitat, the U.S. Army was called in beginning in 1886, and is generally credited with saving the wildlife and stamping out poaching. Many credit the creation of Yellowstone Park with allowing the region's wildlife to escape the reckless slaughter of western wildlife in the 1870s and 1880s. In 1894 Congress passed the Lacey Act, providing strict anti-poaching laws.

At the end of the twentieth century the National Park System was comprised of 369 units. Why was Yellowstone chosen as the site for the first national park? Only a decade after the passage of the Homestead Act, some argued that its physical isolation should be cause enough to remove it from the public domain, while others argued that its unique physical features, its "monumentalism," should be reserved as a tourist attraction. What started out as a campaign to save the natural wonders of the West from profiteers and business entrepreneurs led to the creation of the world's first national park. As America's environmental values evolved over the next century, so too did the goals of the park system. Formerly the purview of ecologists and scientists, wilderness preservation and wildlife protection came under the oversight of the National Park Service.

The settlement or "conquering" of the West threatened America's natural landscape at virtually every juncture. But a sea change occurred sometime toward the end of the nineteenth century, a transformation in which some Americans began to value the land as a beautiful natural tapestry rather than as a purely commercial commodity. When Langford found himself at a loss for words while attempting to describe the wonders of Yellowstone, he responded that "the scene surpasses description. It must be seen to be felt."[8]

NOTES

1. Alfred Runte, *National Parks: The American Experience* (Lincoln: University of Nebraska Press, 1979), p. 9.

2. George Catlin, *Letters and Notes on the Manners, Customs, and Conditions of the North American Indians*, vol. 1 (New York, 1842), p. 262.

3. Roderick Nash, *Wilderness and the American Mind* (New Haven: Yale University Press, 1973), p. 83.

4. John Wesley Powell, *Cañons of the Colorado* (reprint, New York, 1961), p. 329.

5. Quoted in Aubrey L. Haines, *Yellowstone National Park: Its Exploration and Establishment* (Washington, DC: National Park Service, 1974), p. 127.

6. Ibid., p. 108.

7. Richard White, *"It's Your Misfortune and None of My Own": A New History of the American West* (Norman: University of Oklahoma Press, 1991), p. 410.

8. Quoted in Anne Farrar Hyde, *An American Vision: Far Western Landscape and National Culture, 1820–1920* (New York: New York University Press, 1990), p. 193.

DOCUMENTS

10.1.   Artist George Catlin's Views on Western Preservation

More than thirty years ahead of his time, the artist-writer George Catlin proposed creating a natural park on the Great Plains as early as the 1830s. His notion of containing the buffalo and the free-ranging Plains Indians on a nature preserve for posterity was ill-conceived, but his heart was in the right place. He dedicated much of his career to preserving these images on canvas to show Americans what they had lost. He died the same year that Yellowstone became the first national park.

This strip of country, which extends from the province of Mexico to lake Winnepeg on the North, is almost one entire plain of grass, which is, and ever must be, useless to cultivating man. It is here, and here chiefly, that the buffaloes dwell; and with, and hovering about them, live and flourish the tribes of Indians, whom God made for the enjoyment of that fair land and its luxuries.

It is a melancholy contemplation for one who has travelled as I have, through these realms, and seen this noble animal in all its pride and glory, to contemplate it so rapidly wasting from the world, drawing the irresistible conclusion too, which one must do, that its species is soon to be extinguished, and with it the peace and happiness (if not the actual existence) of the tribes of Indians who are joint tenants with them, in the occupancy of these vast and idle plains.

And what a splendid contemplation too, when one (who has travelled these realms, and can duly appreciate them) imagines them as they *might* in future be seen, (by some great protecting policy of government) preserved in their pristine beauty and wildness, in a *magnificent park*, where the world could see for ages to come, the native Indian in his classic attire, galloping his wild horse, with sinewy bow, and shield and lance, amid the fleeting herds of elks and buffaloes. What a beautiful and thrilling specimen for America to preserve and hold up to the view of her refined citizens and the world, in future ages! A *nation's Park*, containing man and beast, in all the wild and freshness of their nature's beauty!

I would ask no other monument to my memory, nor any other enrolment of my name amongst the famous dead, than the reputation of having been the founder of such an institution.

Such scenes might easily have been preserved, and still could be cherished on the great plains of the West, without detriment to the country or its borders; for the tracts of country on which the buffaloes have assembled, are uniformly sterile, and of no available use to cultivating man.

It is on these plains, which are stocked with buffaloes, that the finest specimens of the Indian race are to be seen. It is here, that the savage is decorated in the richest costume. It is here, and here only, that his wants are all satisfied, and even the *luxuries* of life are afforded him in abundance. And here also is he the proud and honourable man (before he has had teachers or laws), above the imported wants, which beget meanness and vice; stimulated by ideas of honour and virtue, in which the God of Nature has certainly not curtailed him.

Source: George Catlin, *Letters and Notes on the Manners, Customs, and Conditions of the North American Indians*, Vol. 1 (New York, 1841), pp. 261–262.

10.2.   Debate over Creating Yellowstone National Park (1872)

Several months before President Ulysses S. Grant signed the bill creating Yellowstone National Park, a debate took place in the Senate over the provisions of the bill to create the park. Much of the debate revolved around the traditional American sports of hunting and fishing. The argument that the land to be preserved was worthless for agricultural use was used to demonstrate that the region could not be settled anyway.

Mr. POMEROY. The Committee on Public Lands, to whom was referred the bill (S. No. 392) to set apart a tract of land lying near the headwaters of the Yellowstone as a public park, have directed me to report it back without amendment, to recommend its passage, and to ask that it have the present consideration of the Senate.

The VICE PRESIDENT. The Senator from Kansas asks unanimous consent of the Senate for the present consideration of the bill reported by him. It will be reported in full, subject to objection.

The Chief Clerk read the bill.

The Committee on Public Lands reported the bill with an amendment in line nineteen to strike out the words "after the passage of this act," and in line twenty, after the word "upon", to insert the words "or occupying a part of:" so as to make the clause read, "and all persons who shall locate or settle upon or occupy any part of the same, or any part thereof, except as hereinafter provided, shall be considered as trespassers and removed therefrom."

The VICE PRESIDENT. Is there objection to the present consideration of this bill?

Mr. CAMERON. I should like to know from somebody having charge of the bill, in the first place, how many miles square are to be set apart, or how many acres, for this purpose, and what is the necessity for the park belonging to the United States.

Mr. POMEROY. This bill originated as the result of the exploration, made by Professor Hayden, under an appropriation of Congress last year. With a party he explored the headwaters of the Yellowstone and found it to be a great natural curiosity, great geysers, as they are termed, water-spouts, and hot springs, and having platted the ground himself, and having given me the dimensions of it, the bill was drawn up, as it was thought best to consecrate and set apart this great place of national resort, as it may be in the future, for the purposes of public enjoyment.

Mr. MORTON. How many square miles are there in it?

Mr. POMEROY. It is substantially forty miles square. It is north and south forty-four miles, and east and west forty miles. He was careful to make a survey so as to include all the basin where the Yellowstone has its source.

Mr. CAMERON. That is several times larger than the District of Columbia.

Mr. POMEROY. Yes, Sir. There are no arable lands: no agricultural lands there. It is the highest elevation from which our springs descend, and as it cannot interfere with any settlement for legitimate agricultural purposes, it was thought that it ought to be set apart early for this purpose. We found when we set apart the Yosemite valley that there were one or two persons who had made claims there, and there has been a contest, and it has finally gone to the Supreme Court to decide whether persons who settle on unsurveyed lands before the Government takes possession of them by any special act of Congress have rights as against the Government. The court has held that settlers on unsurveyed lands have no rights as against the Government. The Government can make an appropriation of any unsurveyed lands, notwithstanding settlers may be upon them. As this region would be attractive only on account of preempting a hot spring or some valuable mineral, it was thought such claims had better be excluded from the bill.

There are several Senators whose attention has been called to this matter, and there are photographs of the valley and the curiosities, which Senators can see. The only object of the bill is to take early possession of it by the United States and set it apart, so that it cannot be included in any claim or occupied by any settlers.

Mr. TRUMBULL. Mr. President—

The VICE PRESIDENT. The Chair must state that the Senate have not yet given their consent to the present consideration of the bill. The Senator from Pennsylvania desired some explanation in regard to it. Does he reserve the right to object?

Mr. CAMERON. I make no objection.

Mr. THURMAN. I object.

Mr. SHERMAN. I will not object if it is not going to lead to debate.

Mr. TRUMBULL. It can be disposed of in a minute.

Mr. THURMAN. I object to the consideration of this bill in the morning hour. I am willing to take it up when we can attend to it, but not now.

· · ·

The VICE PRESIDENT. The bill (S. No. 392) to set apart a certain tract of land lying near the headwaters of the Yellowstone river as a public park, taken up on the motion of the Senator from Kansas, which was reported by the Committee on Public Lands, is now before the Senate as in Committee of the Whole.

The bill was read—[followed by a restatement of the amendments previously reported by the Committee on Public Lands].

The VICE PRESIDENT. These amendments will be regarded as agreed to unless objected to. They are agreed to.

Mr. ANTHONY. I observe that the destruction of game and fish for gain or profit is forbidden. I move to strike out the words "for gain or profit," so that there shall be no destruction of game there for any purpose. We do not want sportsmen going over there with their guns.

Mr. POMEROY. The only object was to prevent the wanton destruction of the fish and game; but we thought parties who encamped there and caught fish for their own use ought not to be restrained from doing so. The bill will allow parties there to shoot game or catch fish for their own subsistence. The provision of the bill is designed to stop the wanton destruction of game or fish for merchandise.

Mr. ANTHONY. I do not know but that that covers it. What I mean is that this park should not be used for sporting. If people are encamped there, and desire to catch fish and kill game for their own sustenance while they remain there, there can be no objection to that; but I do not think it ought to be used as a preserve for sporting.

Mr. POMEROY. I agree with the Senator, but I think the bill as drawn protects the game and fish as well as can be done.

Mr. ANTHONY. Very well; I am satisfied.

The VICE PRESIDENT. The Senator does not insist on his amendment?

Mr. ANTHONY. No, sir.

Mr. TIPTON. I think if this is to become a public park, a place of great national resort, and we allow the shooting of game or the taking of fish without any restriction at all, the game will soon be utterly destroyed. I think, therefore, there should be a prohibition against their destruction for any purpose, for if the door is once opened I fear there will ultimately be an entire destruction of all the game in that park.

Mr. POMEROY. It will be entirely under the control of the Secretary of the Interior. He is to make the rules that shall govern the destruction and capture of game. I think in that respect the Secretary of the Interior whoever he may be, will be as vigilant as we would be.

The VICE PRESIDENT. Perhaps the Secretary had better report the sentence referred to by Senators as bearing on this question, and then any Senator who desires to amend can move to do so.

The Chief Clerk read as follows:

"He shall provide against the wanton destruction of the fish and game found within said park, and against their capture or destruction for the purposes of merchandise or profit."

Mr. EDMUNDS. I hope this bill will pass. I have taken some pains to make myself acquainted with the history of this most interesting region. It is so far elevated above the sea that it cannot be used for private occupation at all, but it is probably one of the most wonderful regions in that space of territory which the globe exhibits anywhere, and therefore we are doing no harm to the material interests of the people in endeavoring to preserve it. I hope the bill will pass unanimously.

Mr. COLE. I have grave doubts about the propriety of passing this bill. The natural curiosities there cannot be interfered with by anything that man can do. The geysers will remain, no matter where the owner-ship of the land may be, and I do not know why settlers should be excluded from a tract of land forty miles square, as I understand this to be, in the Rocky mountains or any other place. I cannot see how the natural curiosities can be interfered with if settlers are allowed to ap-proach them. I suppose there is very little timber on this tract of land, certainly no more than is necessary for the use and convenience of per-sons going upon it. I do not see the reason or propriety of setting apart a large tract of land of that kind in the Territories of the United States for a public park. There is abundance of public park ground in the Rocky mountains that will never be occupied. It is all one great park, and never can be anything else; large portions of it at all events. There are some places, perhaps this is one, where persons can and would go and settle and improve and cultivate the grounds, if there be ground fit for culti-vation.

Mr. EDMUNDS. Has my friend forgotten that this ground is north of latitude forty, and is over seven thousand feet above the level of the sea? You cannot cultivate that kind of ground.

Mr. COLE. The Senator is probably mistaken in that. Ground of a greater height than that has been cultivated and occupied.

Mr. EDMUNDS. In that latitude?

Mr. COLE: Yes, sir. But if it cannot be occupied and cultivated, why should we make a public park of it? If it cannot be occupied by man, why protect it from occupation? I see no reason in that. If nature has excluded men from its occupation, why set it apart and exclude persons from it? If there is any sound reason for the passage of the bill, of course I would not oppose it; but really I do not see any myself.

Mr. TRUMBULL. I think our experience with the wonderful natural curiosity, if I may so call it, in the Senator's own State, should admonish us of the propriety of passing such a bill as this. There is the wonderful Yosemite valley, which one or two persons are now claiming by virtue of preemption. Here is a region of country away up in the Rocky mountains, where there are the most wonderful geysers on the face of the earth; a country that is not likely ever to be inhabited for the purposes of agriculture; but it is possible that some person may go there and plant himself right across the only path that leads to these wonders, and charge every man that passes along between the gorges of these mountains a fee of a dollar or five dollars. He may place an obstruction there, and toll may be gathered from every person who goes to see these wonders of creation.

Now this tract of land is uninhabited; nobody lives there; it was never trod by civilized man until within a short period. Perhaps a year or two ago was the first time that this country was ever explored by anybody. It is now proposed, while it is in this condition, to reserve it from sale and occupation in this way. I think it is a very proper bill to pass, and now is the time to enact it. We did set apart the region of country on which the mammoth trees grow in California, and the Yosemite valley also we have undertaken to reserve, but there is a dispute about it. Now, before there is any dispute as to this wonderful country, I hope we shall except it from the general disposition of the public lands, and reserve it to the Government. At some future time, if we desire to do so, we can repeal this law if it is in anybody's way: but now I think it a very appropriate bill to pass.

The bill was reported to the Senate as amended: and the amendments were concurred in. The bill was ordered to be engrossed for a third reading, read a third time, and passed.

Source: The Congressional Globe, 42nd Cong., 2nd Sess., January 22–23, 1872, p. 697, reprinted in Aubrey L. Haines, *Yellowstone National Park: Its Exploration and Establishment* (Washington, DC: U.S. Department of the Interior, National Park Service, 1974), pp. 116–119.

10.3.   Legislation Establishing Yellowstone National Park (1872)

On March 1, 1872, Congress established Yellowstone National Park, the nation's first national park. Created out of more than 2 million acres of the public domain, it is still the largest park in the United States. The following Act of Dedication states specifically that the land was being set aside "as a public park" for "the benefit and enjoyment of the people," setting a precedent for future natural parks.

AN ACT to set apart a certain tract of land lying near the headwaters of the Yellowstone River as a public park.

Be it enacted by the Senate and House of Representatives of the United States of America in Congress assembled, That the tract of land in the Territories of Montana and Wyoming lying near the headwaters of the Yellowstone River, and described as follows, to wit: commencing at the junction of Gardiner's River with the Yellowstone River and running east of the meridian, passing ten miles to the eastward of the most eastern point of Yellowstone Lake; thence south along the said meridian to the parallel of latitude, passing ten miles south of the most southern point of Yellowstone Lake; thence west along said parallel to the meridian, passing fifteen miles west of the most western point of Madison Lake; thence north along said meridian to the latitude of the junction of the Yellowstone and Gardiner's Rivers; thence east to the place of beginning, is hereby reserved and withdrawn from settlement, occupancy, or sale under the laws of the United States, and dedicated and set apart as a public park or pleasuring ground for the benefit and enjoyment of the people; and all persons who shall locate, or settle upon, or occupy the same or any part thereof, except as hereinafter provided, shall be considered trespassers and removed therefrom.

SEC. 2. That said public park shall be under the exclusive control of the Secretary of the Interior, whose duty it shall be as soon as practicable, to make and publish such rules and regulations as he may deem necessary or proper for the care and management of the same. Such regulations shall provide for the preservation from injury or spoliation of all timber, mineral deposits, natural curiosities, or wonders within said park, and their retention in their natural condition.

The Secretary may, in his discretion, grant leases for building purposes, for terms not exceeding ten years, of small parcels of ground, at such places in said park as shall require the erection of buildings for the accommodation of visitors; all of the proceeds of said leases, and other revenues that may be derived from any source connected with said park, to be expended under his direction in the management of the same and the construction of roads and bridle-paths therein. He shall provide against the wanton destruction of the fish and game found within said park and against their capture or destruction for the purposes of merchandise or profit. He shall also cause all persons trespassing upon the same after the passage of this act to be removed therefrom, and generally shall be authorized to take all such measures as shall be necessary or proper to fully carry out the objects and purposes of this act.

Approved March 1, 1872.

Signed by:

JAMES G. BLAINE, *Speaker of the House*

SCHUYLER COLFAX, *Vice-President of the United States and President of the Senate*

ULYSSES S. GRANT, *President of the United States*

Source: "The Act of Dedication," *U.S. Statutes at Large* 17 (1872): 350.

10.4.   John Wesley Powell Describes the Grand Canyon (1875)

Explorers and scientists such as John Wesley Powell created interest in the natural West after several heroic voyages down the Colorado River through the uncharted Grand Canyon. Having lost an arm during the Civil War, Powell became a folk hero while championing conservation policy in the West. As an advocate of land reform, he was often pitted against the opponents of the national parks, which included mining, cattle, and timber corporate interests. In the following passages from his classic book Exploration of the Colorado River, *he seems at a loss for words to describe the wonders of the Grand Canyon.*

The longest cañon through which the Colorado runs is that between the mouth of the Colorado Chiquito and the Grand Wash, a distance of two hundred and seventeen and a half miles. But this is separated from another above, sixty-five and a half miles in length, only by the narrow cañon-valley of the Colorado Chiquito.

All the scenic features of this cañon land are on a giant scale, strange and weird. The streams run at depths almost inaccessible; lashing the rocks which beset their channels; rolling in rapids, and plunging in falls, and making a wild music which but adds to the gloom of the solitude.

· · ·

Through these tables the Colorado runs, in an easterly and westerly direction, in a deep gorge, known as the Grand Cañon.

The varying depths of this cañon, due to the varying altitudes of the plateaus through which it runs, can only be seen from above. As we wind about in the gloomy depths below, the difference between 4,000 and 6,000 feet is not discerned, but the characteristics of the cañon—the scenic features—change abruptly with the change in the altitude of the walls, as the faults are passed. In running the channel, which divides the twin plateaus, we pass around the first great southern bend. In the very depths of the cañon we have black granite, with a narrow cleft, through which a great river plunges. This granite portion of the walls is carved with deep gulches and embossed with pinnacles and towers. Above are broken, ragged, nonconformable rocks, in many places sloping back at a low angle. Clambering over these, we reach rocks lying in horizontal beds. Some are soft; many very hard; the softer strata are washed out; the harder remain as shelves. Everywhere there are side gulches and cañons, so that these gulches are set about ten thousand dark, gloomy alcoves. One might imagine that this was intended for the library of the gods: and it was. The shelves are not for books, but form the stony leaves of one great book. He who would read the language of the universe may dig out letters here and there, and with them spell the words, and read, in a slow and imperfect way, but still so as to understand a little, the story of creation.

Source: John Wesley Powell, *Exploration of the Colorado River of the West and Its Tributaries* . . . (Washington, DC: Government Printing Office, 1875), pp. 5, 193–194.

10.5.   Indian Removal from Yellowstone National Park (1879)

The Indians of Yellowstone offered little resistance to removal from the national park. Initially, Shoshone Indians either left on their own or were relocated to the Wind River and Fort Hall reservations. After a conflict with the Nez Perce in 1877, the superintendent of Yellowstone National Park ordered all Indians to leave the park. In order to support Indian removal, Superintendent Philetus Norris resorted to widespread misconceptions that "Yellowstone is not Indian country" and that Indians stayed away from the park because of primal fear of geysers. Both claims were preposterous. The following passage is from Hiram M. Chittenden's (1858–1917) book The Yellowstone National Park. *Trained as a civil engineer, Chittenden also proved to be*

*an able historian after he left the U.S. Army Corps of Engineers.
In this excerpt, Chittenden recounts the series of treaties and
land claims that expelled Native Americans from America's first
national park.*

In 1880, Col. P. W. Norris, Second Superintendent of the Park, had a
long interview on the shore of the Yellowstone Lake with We-Saw, "an
old but remarkably intelligent Indian" of the Shoshone tribe, who was
then acting as guide to an exploring party under Governor Hoyt, of
Wyoming, and who had previously passed through the Park with the
expedition of 1873 under Captain W. A. Jones, U. S. A. He had also been
in the Park region on former occasions. Colonel Norris records the following facts from this Indian's conversation.

"We-Saw states that he had neither knowledge nor tradition of any
permanent occupants of the Park save the timid Sheepeaters. . . . He said
that his people (Shoshones) the Bannocks and the Crows, occasionally
visited the Yellowstone Lake and River portions of the Park, but very
seldom the geyser regions, which he declared were *'heap, heap, bad,'* and
never wintered there, as white men sometimes did with horses."

It seems that even the resident Sheepeaters knew little of the geyser
basins. General Sheridan, who entered the Park from the south in 1882,
makes this record in his report of the expedition:

"We had with us five Sheep Eating Indians as guides, and, strange to
say, although these Indians had lived for years and years about Mounts
Sheridan and Hancock, and the high mountains south-east of the Yellowstone Lake, they knew nothing about the Firehole Geyser Basin, and
they exhibited more astonishment and wonder than any of us."

Evidence like the foregoing clearly indicates that this country was *terra
incognita* to the vast body of Indians who dwelt around it, and again this
singular fact presents itself for explanation. Was it, as is generally supposed, a "superstitious fear" that kept them away? The incidents just
related give some color to such a theory; but if it were really true we
should expect to find well authenticated Indian traditions of so marvel-
ous a country. Unfortunately history records none. It is not meant by
this to imply that reputed traditions concerning the Yellowstone are unknown. For instance, it is related that the Crows always refused to tell
the whites of the geysers because they believed that whoever visited
them became endowed with supernatural powers, and they wished to
retain a monopoly of this knowledge. But traditions of this sort, like most
Indian curiosities now offered for sale, are evidently of spurious origin.
Only in the names "Yellowstone" and "Burning Mountains" do we find
any original evidence that this land of wonders appealed in the least
degree to the native imagination.

The real explanation of this remarkable ignorance appears to us to rest on grounds essentially practical. There was nothing to induce the Indians to visit the Park country. For three-fourths of the year that country is inaccessible on account of snow. It is covered with dense forests, which in most places are so filled with fallen timber and tangled underbrush as to be practically impassable. As a game country in those early days it could not compare with the lower surrounding valleys. As a highway of communication between the valleys of the Missouri, Snake, Yellowstone, and Bighorn Rivers, it was no thoroughfare. The great routes, except the Bannock trail already described, lay on the outside. All the conditions, therefore, which might attract the Indians to this region were wanting. Even those sentimental influences, such as a love of sublime scenery and a curiosity to see the strange freaks of nature, evidently had less weight with them than with their pale-face brethren.

Summarizing the results of such knowledge, confessedly meager, as exists upon this subject, it appears:

(1.) That the country now embraced in the Yellowstone National Park was occupied, at the time of its discovery, by small bands of Sheepeater Indians, probably not exceeding in number one hundred and fifty souls. They dwelt in the neighborhood of the Washburn and Absaroka Ranges, and among the mountains around the sources of the Snake. They were not familiar with the geyser regions.

(2.) Wandering bands from other tribes occasionally visited this country, but generally along the line of the Yellowstone River or the Great Bannock Trail. Their knowledge of the geyser regions was extremely limited, and very few had ever seen or heard of them. It is probable that the Indians visited this country more frequently in earlier times than since the advent of the white man.

(3.) The Indians avoided the region of the Upper Yellowstone from practical, rather than from sentimental, considerations.

The legal processes by which the vast territory of these various tribes passed to the United States, are full of incongruities resulting from a general ignorance of the country in question. By the Treaty of Fort Laramie, dated September 17, 1851, between the United States on the one hand, and the Crows, Blackfeet and other northern tribes on the other, the Crows were given, as part of their territory, all that portion of the Park country which lies east of the Yellowstone River; and the Blackfeet, all that portion lying between the Yellowstone River and the Continental Divide. This was before any thing whatever was known of the country so given away. None of the Shoshone tribes were party to the treaty, and the rights of the Sheepeaters were utterly ignored. That neither the Blackfeet nor the Crows had any real claim to these extravagant grants is evidenced by their prompt relinquishment of them in the first subsequent treaties. Thus, by treaty of October 17, 1855, the Blackfeet agreed that all of their portion of the Park country, with much other territory, should be and remain a common hunting ground for certain designated tribes; and by treaty of May 17, 1868, the Crows relinquished all of their territory south of the Montana boundary line.

That portion of the Park country drained by the Snake River was always considered Shoshone territory, although apparently never formally recognized in any public treaty. By an unratified treaty, dated September 24, 1868, the provisions of which seem to have been the basis of subsequent arrangements with the Shoshonean tribes, all this territory and much besides was ceded to the United States, and the tribes were located upon small reservations.

It thus appears that at the time the Park was created, March 1, 1872, all the territory included in its limits had been ceded to the United States except the hunting ground above referred to, and the narrow strip of Crow territory east of the Yellowstone where the north boundary of the Park lies two or three miles north of the Montana line. The "hunting ground" arrangement was abrogated by statute of April 15, 1874, and the strip of Crow territory was purchased under an agreement with the Crows, dated June 12, 1880, and ratified by Congress, April 11, 1882, thus extinguishing the last remaining Indian title to any portion of the Yellowstone Park.

Source: Hiram Martin Chittenden, *The Yellowstone National Park: Historical and Descriptive* (Cincinnati: Robert Clarke Company, 1895), pp. 14–19.

10.6.   Tourists in Yellowstone (1923)

By the 1920s, thanks to advances in transportation, shorter work days, and a growing middle class, Americans had more time to visit national parks and to vacation. In the following passage the now-familiar and ubiquitous tourists are described at Yellowstone, hectically rushing through the requisite tour of physical wonders. The writer compares the park to when he first visited it years earlier.

Probably more than ninety-five per cent of the tourists visiting the Yellowstone are fluttered folk and wild being rushed through on a four-day schedule. This imposes a terribly hectic program, which, however, is not the fault of the transportation or hotel people, (who offer all facilities and inducements for a calmer survey), but of the tourist himself, who seems imbued with the idea that the more he sees in the day the more he is getting for his money. The American tourist, doubtless a quite mild-

demeanoured and amenable person on his native heath, when observed
flagrante delicto touring is by long odds the worst-mannered of all of
God's creatures. Collectively, that is; individually many of him and her
turn out far from offensive. Strangely—perhaps because, for the moment,
they are all more or less infected with the same form of hysteria—they
never seem to get much on each other's nerves. To a wanderer, however,
habituated to the kindness, consideration, dignity and respect for age
commonly displayed by such peoples as the Red Indian, the South Sea
Islander and the Borneo Dyak, the tourist at close range is rather trying.
I proceeded with the regular convoy to Old Faithful, then took a car to
the crest of the Continental Divide, and proceeded from there down the
Yellowstone on foot in comparative peace and contentment.

With the large and rapidly increasing number of railway tourists coming to the Park every year, each intent upon making the round and
getting away in the minimum of time, there is probably no better plan
devisable than the present one of shooting them in and out, and from
camp to camp, in large busses. The most annoying and unsatisfactory
feature of this system is the great amount of time which the tourist must
stand by waiting for his bus-seat and room to be allotted. This, however,
can hardly be helped with daily shipments numbering several hundred
being made from and received at each camp and hotel. Under the circumstances the most satisfactory way of touring the Park is in one's own
car, stopping at either hotel or camp, according to one's taste and pock-
etbook. Delightful as the auto camping grounds are, tenting is hardly to
be recommended on account of the mosquitoes.

Allowing for the difference in season, there was little change observ-
able in the natural features of the Park since my former visit. Things
looked different, of course, but that was only because there was less
snow and more dust. The only appreciable natural changes were in the
hot spring and geyser areas, where here or there a formation had aug-
mented or crumbled to dust according to whether or not its supply of
mineral-charged water had been maintained or not. The cliffs and
mountains, waterfalls, and gorges could have suffered no more than the
two decades, infinitesimal geologic modifications—mostly erosive. Even
in the geyser basins the changes of a decade are such as few save a
scientific observer would note. The first authentic written description of
the Fire Hole geysers basins was penned nearly eighty years ago by
Warren Angus Ferris, a clerk of the American Fur Company. It describes
that region of the present as accurately as would the account of a last
summer's tourist.

Source: Lewis R. Freeman, *Down the Yellowstone* (London: William Heinemann,
1923), pp. 101–104.

ANNOTATED SELECTED BIBLIOGRAPHY

Bartlett, Richard A. *Nature's Yellowstone: The Story of an American Wilderness that Became Yellowstone National Park in 1872.* Albuquerque: University of New Mexico Press, 1974. Narrative history of Yellowstone Park by a well-known authority.

———. *Yellowstone: A Wilderness Besieged.* Tucson: University of Arizona Press, 1985. Bartlett looks at politics, personalities, and public attitudes that have shaped Yellowstone.

Chase, Alston. *Playing God in Yellowstone: The Destruction of America's First National Park.* New York: Harcourt Brace Jovanovich, 1987. Examines park policy at Yellowstone in the aftermath of devastating forest fires that were allowed to burn out of control.

Keller, Robert H., and Michael F. Turek. *American Indians and National Parks.* Tucson: University of Arizona Press, 1998. The previously untold story of the impact of national parks on native peoples.

Meyer, Judith L. *The Spirit of Yellowstone: The Cultural Evolution of a National Park.* Lanham, MD: Rowman and Littlefield, 1996. Meyer examines 125 years of attitudes toward nature.

Runte, Alfred. *National Parks: The American Experience.* Lincoln: University of Nebraska Press, 1979. One of the best overviews of the history of the national parks, beginning with Congress's unwritten rule of preserving only "worthless land."

Schullery, Paul. *Searching for Yellowstone: Ecology and Wonder in the Last Wilderness.* Boston: Houghton Mifflin, 1997. Schullery looks at a century of debate over what the real purposes of national parks should be and our changing relationship with nature.

11

Chinese Exclusion: Race Relations in California

Chinese immigrants began landing on American shores soon after the discovery of gold in California. At first they stayed close to San Francisco and the mines in the Sierra Nevadas. The initial immigration of the Chinese to the United States coincided with the national controversy over the emancipation of the slaves and agitation over Spanish Americans. However, as free workers of color, willing to work for low wages, the Chinese earned the enmity of white workers.

Between 1848 and 1882, more than 300,000 Chinese immigrants entered the United States. Most of them were Cantonese-speaking people from southwestern China who arrived in San Francisco and then scattered throughout California, Oregon, and Washington. They tended to be "birds of passage," immigrant men who traveled to the New World without their families and intended to stay only temporarily, long enough to accumulate capital to be used back in China for the benefit of their families. The Chinese were Asians in a white society, and many were Buddhists in a Christian society, and whites tended to resent them. Working-class whites especially feared the repressive effect an over supply of Chinese labor would have on wages. In 1882 Congress responded to their demands by passing the first immigration restriction law in the United States.

By the time free Chinese immigration to the United States was terminated in 1882, almost 100,000 Chinese men and 5,000 Chinese women resided in the West, the majority of them in California. Unfortunately, the Chinese men found that U.S. immigration laws made it difficult for their families, particularly females, to join them in their new land. For many years a predominantly male Chinese population would characterize Chinese communities in the West.

During the 1850s and 1860s, the western mining frontier expanded into the Rocky Mountains. Together with transcontinental railroad construction, new opportunities were opened for Chinese immigrants, and soon Chinese communities could be found across the West. Chinese immigration continued to grow into the second half of the nineteenth century. Most intended to return to China with enough savings to live with their families in unaccustomed luxury. Unlike Hispanics, African Americans, and other non-Anglo westerners in the Far West, the Chinese retained a separateness from the dominant white society that often led to suspicion, prejudice, and sometimes violence. Combined with their intentions to make their fortunes and leave the continent, the Chinese seemed the inalterable alien to many white Americans. It would not be until after the Chinese directed their goals toward remaining in America that they would slowly be accepted by Americans in the West.

Anti-Chinese violence began almost as soon as they came to America during the early stages of the Gold Rush. Efforts to remove the Chinese from California began as early as the 1850s. After the state of California ruled in 1854 that the Chinese could not testify against whites in courts, they were regularly preyed on by whites who knew they would not be held legally accountable for their actions. Some of the most serious violence took place in the 1870s and 1880s as the "Chinese Question" entered national politics. Demagogues used slogans such as "The Chinese Must Go" to turn isolated acts of disorganized violence into full-scale riots.

The farther the Chinese relocated from California's urban centers the less protected they were. However, cities would only provide an illusion of security, with many of the worst riots taking place in Los Angeles (1871) and San Francisco (1877). None surpassed the ferocity of the 1885 murder of twenty-eight Chinese coal miners by a mob of 150 whites in Rock Springs, Wyoming. The remainder of the Chinese population was forced out of town. The riot was precipitated by the Chinese refusal to join white coal miners in a strike against the Pacific Coal Department. In 1887 the U.S. government reimbursed the Chinese government for the outrage, paying indemnities of almost $150,000.

The Chinese were a target for discrimination and abuse throughout the nineteenth-century West. Although they were welcomed in the heady days of the California Gold Rush as manual labor, when the mines played out and Chinese continued to immigrate to California, they often became the target of white frustration and despair over their own declining economic prospects. A pattern emerged in which the Chinese were not excluded from certain occupations until there was a downturn in the economy and competition for jobs grew acute. Into the 1870s Anglo Californians saw the Chinese as hopelessly different and unassimilative. Sensational reports of Chinese prostitution and opium use fed the anti-Chinese sentiments of the era.

For their part, wherever there was a large enough community in the West, the Chinese created a Chinatown. A Chinatown offered the Chinese immigrants an illusion of home where they could find solace in the company of their countrymen, Chinese foods, and familiar customs and languages, though distorted by the absence of women. Over time Chinatowns became home to tongs (Chinese benevolent societies established in 1850s San Francisco) and other power brokers who provided exploited Chinese workers some relief from the monotony of their working lives.

The immigration of many Chinese was facilitated by the architects of the transcontinental railroad, who viewed them as docile and dependable laborers. In 1868 the United States negotiated the Burlingame Treaty with China, which made immigration easier by recognizing the reciprocal right of Chinese and American citizens to immigrate to either country without limitations. The main attraction that Chinese labor had for America's railroad tycoons and other business leaders was that they would work for much lower wages than whites. In the years following the Civil War, the price of white labor increased, as did new opportunities for homesteading and mining personal claims, allowing for a growing force of self-employed independent workers. But when the more productive mining claims and homesteads were taken up and after the federal government awarded huge land grants to the railroads, more and more formerly independent citizens were forced onto the labor market. Soon white workers were vying with Chinese workers for unskilled jobs.

By the 1870s Chinese workers were underbidding Anglo workers for jobs. Exploited in California and elsewhere, Chinese laborers could be found in agriculture, service trades, and manufacturing. According to one estimate, in 1872 Chinese workers made up half of the factory work force of San Francisco. But with no voting rights and few political supporters in the West, Chinese immigrants were targeted for restrictions by western congressmen, who needed to protect their constituents. Nevertheless, the Chinese were not without their supporters, few though they were. In the congressional debate that followed, the only political allies the Chinese could muster were idealists in the East, such as Congressman Martin I. Townsend of New York, who in 1879 compared the treatment of Chinese workers to that of earlier immigrants: "I remember the day when the cry was against the Catholic Irish, against the condemned Germans, because they were coming here to take away the labor of the American citizen."[1]

The "problem of Chinese immigration" was mainly played out in California, the most populous western state in the nineteenth century. During the late 1860s anti-Chinese clubs were formed throughout California. Ranging from the Workingmen's Alliance and the Supreme Order of the Caucasians to the Anti-Chinese Association and the People's Protective Alliance, their main goal was to intimidate officials into discriminating against the Chinese. When legal pressure lagged behind, workers could resort to violent measures such as in October 1871, when Los Angelenos murdered at least twenty Chinese during a race riot.

Economic recession is often coupled with the search for a scapegoat, and with the lean economic times of the late 1870s anti-Chinese agitation became more violent around San Francisco. By 1877 at least 16,000 white workingmen were unemployed. When not castigating their former employers, they looked elsewhere for an explanation for their hard times. Once they noticed Chinese workers filling their jobs for lower wages on farms and in factories, the next step was to target the Chinese.

While vigilantes and unemployed workers found an outlet for their tensions in racist violence, others turned to political action. In 1877 Denis Kearney (1847–1907), a business entrepreneur and Irish immigrant, organized and became president of the Workingman's Party of California as organized labor made exclusion a crusade. Running on a populist platform that featured such radical issues as the direct election of U.S. senators, an eight-hour work day, and state regulation of banks and railroads, the party also exhibited an undercurrent of xenophobia. During the state constitutional convention of the late 1870s the Workingmen's Party capitulated on a number of these planks in order to obtain several anti-Chinese clauses. After the Workingmen's Party fell apart after 1879, the only plank from the party's initiatives to survive was the anti-Chinese provision, which prohibited corporations and public works projects from hiring Chinese workers. By the 1880s the only defenders of the Chinese in California were business entrepreneurs who needed cheap labor and missionaries who needed "heathen" souls to save.

Beginning in the late 1870s anti-Chinese agitation on the federal level heated up. In October 1879 Congress passed a bill limiting the number of Chinese who could arrive on one vessel to fifteen, but the president vetoed it. Two years later the 1868 Burlingame Treaty was renegotiated, with China acceding to American requests to "regulate, limit, or suspend" the immigration of Chinese laborers. However, nonlaborers such as merchants, teachers, and students were allowed to immigrate of their own accord. The Chinese Exclusion Act, which was passed the following year, suspended the immigration of Chinese laborers for ten years but continued to allow other categories of persons as specified by the treaty.

In the often rancorous debate over Chinese immigration in the late 1870s and early 1880s, a number of interesting claims were put forth by proponents of both sides that perhaps make the debate more understandable in contemporary perspective. There were real fears by American leaders that the Chinese could take over the Pacific Coast, which was still rather thinly populated. Senator James G. Blaine, confronting a Chinese supporter in the Senate, claimed that "the incalculable hordes in China are much nearer to the Pacific Coast of the United States, in point of expense of reaching it, than the people of Kansas," and that "either the Anglo-Saxon race will possess the Pacific slope or the Mongolians will possess it."[2] Although there was little argument that China was farther away than Kansas, in the 1870s it was still cheaper to sail from China to California than to cross overland from Kansas.

Most Anglo Americans were racially prejudiced in the nineteenth century, believing that they were superior to nonwhites. Why did the Chinese engender so much racial hatred in the nineteenth-century West? The California Gold Rush drew gold seekers from many cultures, races, and ethnicities, including Chileans, African Americans, Mexicans, Native Americans, Irish, and a panoply of others, yet in the years after the gold strikes the Chinese continued to arouse deep animosity in the Anglo West. There are several possible explanations for this phenomenon. In the past, marginalized minorities would accept assimilation or subordination; others might just pack up and leave for more hospitable climes. But in California the Chinese, who saw themselves as culturally superior and distinct from other Asian peoples, accepted neither assimilation nor subordination while continuing to arrive in ever increasing numbers between the 1850s and 1870s.

The nineteenth-century Chinese population in America, mostly located in California and the West, peaked in the early 1880s. Of the 105,000 Chinese in the United States in 1880, 75,132 lived in California, 9,540 in Oregon, 5,416 in Nevada, 3,379 in Idaho, 3,186 in Washington, 1,765 in Montana, 1,630 in Arizona, 914 in Wyoming, 612 in Colorado, 501 in Utah, and 57 in New Mexico. The passage of the Chinese Exclusion Act by Congress in 1882 virtually ended legal Chinese immigration. Ten years after the passage of the 1882 Exclusion Act, California passed the Geary Act, which led to ten more years of exclusion. As historian Patricia Limerick perceptively noted, "The Chinese Exclusion Act of 1882 arose out of a West Coast pattern of immigration and nativism and set a crucial precedent for the limiting of immigration on the basis of race and ethnicity."[3]

In 1943, at the height of hostilities in the Pacific theater of World War II, Congress finally repealed Chinese exclusion laws, established a quota, and permitted Chinese to become naturalized citizens. The immigration act of 1965 opened the door for Asian immigrants by abolishing "national origin" as the basis for allocating immigration quotas to various countries, effectively putting Asian countries on an equal footing with other nations. This new policy not only inaugurated a major shift in historic immigration patterns, but also substantially altered the numbers and variety of immigrants. During the 1970s and 1980s the influx of new immigrants from Asia, South America, the Middle East, and other parts of the non-Western world remade the cultural map of many parts of the West and elsewhere in the nation, and led to a resurgence in nativism in the United States.

NOTES

1. Marion Mills Miller, ed., *Great Debates in American History*, Vol. 11 (New York: Current Literature Publishing Co., 1913), pp. 224–225.

2. Ibid., p. 247.

3. Patricia N. Limerick, *Something in the Soil* (New York: W. W. Norton, 2000), p. 90.

DOCUMENTS

11.1. Early Anti-Chinese Immigration Legislation (1862)

With the nation's largest Chinese population in 1862, California was the first to introduce legislation "to protect white labor" from Chinese competition. California had already passed a law to bar entry of Chinese and "Mongolians" in 1858. During the 1850s the California legislature introduced several taxes to discourage Chinese immigration. According to the following 1862 act, the state of California imposed a "police tax" of $2.50 a month on every Chinese resident over the age of eighteen. However, the state supreme court declared the law unconstitutional soon after.

The People of the State of California, represented in Senate and Assembly, do enact as follows:

SECTION 1. There is hereby levied on each person, male and female, of the Mongolian race, of the age of eighteen years and upwards, residing in this State, except such as shall, under laws now existing, or which may hereafter be enacted, take out licenses to work in the mines, or to prosecute some kind of business, a monthly capitation tax of two dollars and fifty cents, which tax shall be known as the Chinese Police Tax; provided, That all Mongolians exclusively engaged in the production and manufacture of the following articles shall be exempt from the provisions of this Act, viz: sugar, rice, coffee, tea. . . .

SECTION 4. The Collector shall collect the Chinese police tax, provided for in this Act, from all persons liable to pay the same, and may seize the personal property of any such person refusing to pay such tax, and sell the same at public auction, by giving notice by proclamation one hour previous to such sale; and shall deliver the property, together with a bill of sale thereof, to the person agreeing to pay, and paying, the highest therefor, which delivery and bill of sale shall transfer to such person a good and sufficient title to the property. And after deducting the tax and necessary expenses incurred by reason of such refusal, seizure, and sale of property, the Collector shall return the surplus of the proceeds of the sale, if any, to the person whose property was sold; provided, That should any person, liable to pay the tax imposed in this

Act, in any county in this State, escape into any other County, with the intention to evade the payment of such tax, then, and in that event, it shall be lawful for the Collector to pursue such person, and enforce the payment of such tax in the same manner as if no such escape had been made. And the Collector, when he shall collect Chinese police taxes, as provided for in this section, shall deliver to each of the persons paying such taxes a police tax receipt, with the blanks properly filled; provided, further, That any Mongolian, or Mongolians, may pay the above named tax to the County Treasurer, who is hereby authorized to receipt for the same in the same manner as the Collector. And any Mongolian, so paying said tax to the Treasurer of the County, if paid monthly, shall be entitled to a reduction of twenty percent on said tax. And if paid in advance for the year next ensuing, such Mongolian, or Mongolians, shall be entitled to a reduction of thirty-three and one third percent on said tax. But in all cases where the County Treasurer receipts for said tax yearly in advance, he shall do it by issuing receipts for each month separately; and any Mongolian who shall exhibit a County Treasurer's receipt, as above provided, to the Collector, shall be exempted from the payment of said tax to the Collector for the month for which said receipt was given.

SECTION 5. Any person charged with the collection of Chinese police taxes, who shall give any receipt other than the one prescribed in this Act, or receive money for such taxes without giving the necessary receipt therefor, or who shall insert more than one name in any receipt, shall be guilty of a felony, and, upon conviction thereof, shall be fined in a sum not exceeding one thousand dollars, and be imprisoned in the State Prison for a period not exceeding one year.

SECTION 6. Any Tax Collector who shall sell, or cause to be sold, any police tax receipt, with the date of the sale left blank, or which shall not be dated and signed, and blanks filled with ink, by the Controller, Auditor, and Tax Collector, and any person who shall make any alteration, or cause the same to be made, in any police tax receipt, shall be deemed guilty of a felony, and, on conviction therof, shall be fined in a sum not exceeding one thousand dollars, and imprisoned in the State prison for a period not exceeding 2 years; and the police tax receipt so sold, with blank date, or which shall not be signed and dated, and blanks filled with ink, as aforesaid, or which shall have been altered, shall be received in evidence in any Court of competent jurisdiction.

SECTION 7. Any person or company who shall hire persons liable to pay the Chinese police tax shall be held responsible for the payment of the tax due from each person so hired; and no employer shall be released from this liability on the ground that the employee is indebted to him (the employer), and the Collector may proceed against any such employer in the same manner as he might against the original party owing the taxes. The Collector shall have power to require any person or company believed to be indebted to, or to have any money, gold dust, or property of any kind, belonging to any person liable for police taxes, or in which such person is interested, in his or their possession, or under his or their control, to answer, under oath, as to such indebtedness, or the possession of such money, gold dust, or other property. In case a party is indebted, or has possession or control of any moneys, gold dust, or other property, as aforesaid, of such person liable for police taxes, he may collect from such party the amount of such taxes, and may require the delivery of such money, gold dust, or other property, as aforesaid; and in all cases the receipt of the Collector to said party shall be a complete bar to any demand made against said party, or his legal representatives, for the amounts of money, gold dust, or property, embraced therein.

SECTION 8. The Collector shall receive for his service, in collecting police taxes, twenty percent of all moneys which he shall collect from persons owing such taxes. And of the residue, after deducting the percentage of the Collector, forty percent shall be paid into the County Treasury, for the use of the State, forty percent into the general County Fund, for the use of the County, and the remaining twenty percent into the School Fund, for the benefit of schools within the County; provided, That in counties where the Tax Collector receives a specific salary, he shall not be required to pay the percentage allowed for collecting the police tax into the County Treasury, but shall be allowed to retain the same for his own use and benefit; provided, That where he shall collect the police tax by Deputy, the percentage shall go to the Deputy....

SECTION 10. It is hereby made the duty of the various officers charged with the execution of the provisions of this Act, to carry out said provisions by themselves of Deputies; and for the faithful performance of their duties in the premises, they shall be liable on their official bonds, respectively. The Treasurers of the respective counties shall make their statements and settlements under this Act with the Controller of State, at the same times and in the same manner they make their settlements under the general Revenue Act.

SECTION 11. This Act shall take effect and be in force from and after the first day of May, next ensuing.

Source: "An Act to Protect Free White Labor Against Competition with Chinese Coolie Labor, and to Discourage the Immigration of the Chinese into the State of California," April 26, 1862. Reprinted in William L. Tung, The Chinese in America, 1820–1973: A Chronology and Fact Book (Dobbs Ferry, NY: Oceana Publications, 1974).

11.2.   Denis Kearney's Workingmen's Party Manifesto (1877)

During the late 1870s, Denis Kearney, the leader of the Work-ingmen's Party in California, called for the expulsion of the Chi-nese. He argued that they took jobs away from Americans because they were willing to work for lower pay. Opponents to his policy noted that Kearney himself was an immigrant from Ireland. He had moved to San Francisco in 1868 and operated a carting business. He was arrested for inciting violence on sev-eral occasions, but was repeatedly acquitted. Although he met with limited political success, by the end of the 1870s he and his party had vanished into obscurity. The following principles of the Workingmen's Party, adopted on October 5, 1877, offer a strong Populist message.

The following were the principles declared: "The object of this associa-tion is to unite all the poor and working men and their friends into one political party for the purpose of defending themselves against the dan-gerous encroachments of capital on the happiness of our people, and the liberties of our country. We propose to wrest the gov't from the hands of the rich and place it in those of the people where it properly belongs. We propose to rid the country of cheap Chinese labor as soon as possible, and by all the means in our power, because it tends still more to degrade labor and aggrandize capital. We propose to destroy land monopoly in our state by such laws as will make it impossible. We propose to destroy the great money power of the rich by a system of taxation that will make great wealth impossible in the future. We propose to provide decently for the poor and unfortunate, the weak, the helpless, and especially the young, because the country is rich enough to do so, and religion, hu-manity, and patriotism demand we should do so. We propose to elect none but competent workingmen and their friends to any office what-ever. The rich have ruled us till they have ruined us. We will now take our own affairs into our own hands. The republic must and shall be preserved, and only workingmen will do it. Our shoddy aristocrats want an emperor, and a standing army to shoot down the people. For these purposes we propose to form ourselves into the Workingmen's Party of California, and to pledge and enroll therein all who are willing to join us in accomplishing these ends. When we have 10,000 members we shall have the sympathy and support of 20,000 other workingmen. The party will then wait upon all who employ Chinese, and ask for their discharge; and it will mark as public enemies those who refuse to comply with their request. This party will exhaust all peaccable [*sic*] means of attaining its ends; but it will not be denied justice when it has the power to enforce it. It will encourage no riot or outrage, but it will not volunteer to repress or put down, or arrest, or prosecute the hungry and impatient who manifest their hatred of the Chinaman by a crusade against John or those who employ him. Let those who raise the storm by their selfishness suppress it themselves. If they dare raise the devil let them meet him face to face. We will not help them."

Source: Hubert Howe Bancroft, *The Works of Hubert Howe Bancroft*, vol. 24 (San Francisco: History Company, 1890), p. 356, n. 20.

11.3.   Congressional Debate over Chinese Immigration (1879)

According to the 1868 Burlingame Treaty, Chinese laborers had the right of unlimited immigration to the United States. But by the late 1870s a new political and economic climate led once more to the discussion of restricting Chinese immigration. In the following debate over a House bill to restrict Chinese immigration, Albert S. Willis of Kentucky defends the anti-immigration proposal. Representing the opposition to the bill is Martin I. Townsend of New York, who blames much of the anti-Chinese agitation on Denis Kearney and the Workingmen's Party.

[Albert S. Willis (Kentucky)]: The evils of Chinese immigration have been fully recognized upon the Pacific slope for many years. Welcomed at first as a unique addition to the society and a valuable ally in the development of the material resources of their new home, the Chinese, by their sordid, selfish, immoral, and non-amalgamating habits, within a very short time reversed the judgment in their favor and came to be regarded as a standing menace to the social and political institutions of the country.

The State laws which had been enacted having been declared unconstitutional by the Supreme Court, and every other means of relief proving ineffectual, it was finally determined to appeal to Congress. Accordingly, as early as the 22d of December, 1869, an effort was made, but without success, to secure restrictive legislation. In the Forty-second Congress, and also in the Forty-third Congress, numerous memorials, resolutions of public meetings, and petitions were presented to the same effect and with the same result. At the first session of the Forty-fourth Congress these renewed appeals for relief met for the first time with a favorable response. A joint resolution was introduced and passed calling upon the President of the United States to "open negotiations with the Chinese Government for the purpose of modifying the provisions of the treaty between the two countries and restricting the same to commercial purposes."

Subsequently, at the same session, another joint resolution was passed, requesting the President to present to the Chinese Government an additional article to the treaty of July 28, 1868, reserving mutually to the two governments the right to regulate, restrict, or prevent immigration to their respective countries. These authoritative requests on the part of Congress failed to secure the desired relief. In the meanwhile the question had assumed dangerous proportions. The conviction that Chinese immigration was a great evil was so deep-seated and unanimous that mob violence was openly threatened, and in many instances the arm of the law seemed powerless to protect. Recognizing the exigency, the legislature of California appointed a special committee, whose report, based upon the testimony of witnesses familiar with the subject, ably and graphically sets forth the objections to the Chinese. Subsequently to this a joint committee appointed by the Forty-fourth Congress collected voluminous testimony upon the same subject, and by a majority report urged upon the Executive Department the necessity for an immediate change of the Burlingame treaty, to the end that such immigration might be restricted or prevented. These reports, together with other official documents upon the subject, were laid before the present Congress.

Your committee consider that further delay would work great injustice to a large portion of our country, provided the evils whereof they complain are well founded.

This whole question is not one of right, but of policy. There is no principle upon which we are compelled to receive into our midst the natives of Asia, Africa, or any other part of the world. The character, source, and extent of immigration should be regulated and controlled with reference to our own wants and welfare. The difficult problems, economic and political, resulting from the presence of the red and black races would be renewed in a more aggravated and dangerous form by the yellow race. The Mongolian, unlike the Indian, is brought in daily contact with our social and political life; and, unlike the African, does not surrender any of his marked pecularities by reason of that contact. It is neither possible nor desirable for two races as distinct as the Caucasian and Mongolian to live under the same government without assimilation. The degradation or slavery of one or the other would be the inevitable result. Homogeneity of ideas and of physical and social habits is essential to national harmony and progress. Equally grave objections may be urged against the Chinese from an industrial standpoint. Our laboring people cannot and ought not to be subjected to a competition which involves the surrender of the sacred and elevating influences of home and the sacrifice of the ordinary appliances of personal civilization. The question, therefore, is not one of competition, but of a substitution of one kind of labor for another.

No self-governing country can afford to diminish or destroy the dignity, the welfare, and independence of its citizens. Justice to the people of the Pacific slope, the dictates of common humanity and benevolence, as well as the plainest suggestions of practical statesmanship, all demand that the problem of Chinese immigration shall be solved while it is yet within the legislative control.

. . .

[Martin I. Townsend (New York)]: I have nothing to charge against the dominant party in this House, although the first treaty under which these immigrations have occurred was negotiated in good old Democratic days [under Buchanan], but it was in days when the light of heaven sometimes reached the brain of the Democracy. [Laughter.] And, sir, I credit to the Democracy not only the making of the treaty but the prosperity which has accrued to the Pacific coast from the adoption of it. California owes what she is in the agricultural world, her grains, her fruits, her agricultural prosperity, to the treaty of 1858 and the one subsequently negotiated. It was before Kearney came and before Kearney was represented in the national halls.

But it is said we must take unusual ground for the benefit of the laboring classes in this country. The laboring classes in this country, the gentleman from Pennsylvania [Hendrick B. Wright] said, are starving. "Two hundred millions of them" [laughter], said the gentleman from Pennsylvania, "are starving!" Two hundred millions in this country are starving! [Great laughter.] And he said, besides, that there are in Pennsylvania five thousand in the lunatic asylum from the hardness of the times. Let me say to the gentleman from Pennsylvania that lunatics sometimes are made by hardness of the times, sometimes by unrequited love, and lunatics are sometimes made from unsatisfied ambition [laughter] and the Pennsylvania lunatics made by the latter cause do not always stay at home within the State of Pennsylvania. [Great laughter.]

I stand here not to disparage, not to underrate, the suffering of the laboring classes or other classes in this country. It has been very great; it is very great to-day; it has been always very great in the world. The struggle to keep the wolf away from the door is the hardest struggle humanity has to make, and yet it is what has made humanity what it has come to be in the better portions of Christendom. The hard soils of Pennsylvania—there are some good soils there—the hard soils of the hardest part of New York, and the hard soils of New England have made a body of men whom we may be proud of before the world and before Heaven.

But, sir, do not let us forget another thing, that in the midst of these hard times the year 1878 in the United States of America was the year of the greatest prosperity that has ever occurred to any people since the dawn of creation. There never has been a period in any land when labor could buy with its rewards so much to eat, to drink, and to wear and with which to provide for its loved ones, as the year 1878; and all this has occurred to a great degree because we have overridden the fanatics of the olden time. It is the "Heathen Chinee" to-day that we are called to suppress. I say to the gentleman from Kentucky [Mr. Willis], who has charge of this bill and who represents Louisville, Kentucky, that I remember the day when the cry was against the Catholic Irish, against the condemned Germans, and when the streets of his city flowed with blood and when the streets of St. Louis, in Missouri, flowed with blood in the riots against the Irish and the Germans because they were coming here to take away the labor of the American citizen and rob his children of their bread. Those who got up those riots were overruled. Thank God, I had a hand in it. I was in a minority. The great men of the Democratic party, many of them of the State of New York, were on the other side. Erastus Brooks, of the *Evening Express*, a trusted leader of the party to-day, was, if I remember rightly, the head of what was called the American Order, organized to protect the country against the inroads of what they deemed hordes of Irish and Germans. But, sir, we put them down by the use of hard common sense. We beat them, though we were in a minority. My State gave 200,000 majority in favor of oppression and exclusion. But, sir, our unparalleled prosperity which has crowned us in this country has been due in a great degree to the sturdy, stalwart labor of the Irish and the Germans.

Source: Marion Mills Miller, ed., *Great Debates in American History*, Vol. 11 (New York: Current Literature Publishing Co., 1913), pp. 221–225.

11.4.   The Chinese Exclusion Act (1882)

Working-class whites feared the repressive effect excess Chinese labor would have on wages. In 1882 Congress responded with the first immigration law aimed at restricting a specifically named ethnic group in the United States. The Chinese exclusion bill not only banned the immigration of Chinese laborers to the United States for a period of ten years, but also excluded all Chinese (residents included) from American citizenship. The other provisions of the act follow.

An act to execute certain treaty stipulations relating to Chinese.

WHEREAS, in the opinion of the Government of the United States the coming of Chinese laborers to this country endangers the good order of certain localities within the territory thereof: Therefore,

Be it enacted . . . That from and after the expiration of ninety days next after the passage of this act, and until the expiration of ten years next after the passage of this act, the coming of Chinese laborers to the United States be, and the same is hereby, suspended; and during such suspension it shall not be lawful for any Chinese laborer to come, or, having so come after the expiration of said ninety days, to remain within the United States.

SEC. 2. That the master of any vessel who shall knowingly bring within the United States on such vessel, and land or permit to be landed, any Chinese laborer, from any foreign port or place, shall be deemed guilty of a misdemeanor, and on conviction thereof shall be punished by a fine of not more than five hundred dollars for each and every such Chinese laborer so brought, and may be also imprisoned for a term not exceeding one year.

SEC. 3. That the two foregoing sections shall not apply to Chinese laborers who were in the United States on the seventeenth day of November, eighteen hundred and eighty, or who shall have come into the same before the expiration of ninety days next after the passage of this act, and who shall produce to such master before going on board such vessel, and shall produce to the collector of the port in the United States at which such vessel shall arrive, the evidence hereinafter in this act required of his being one of the laborers in this section mentioned; nor shall the two foregoing sections apply to the case of any master whose vessel, being bound to a port not within the United States, shall come within the jurisdiction of the United States by reason of being in distress or in stress of weather, or touching at any port of the United States on its voyage to any foreign port or place: *Provided*, That all Chinese laborers brought on such vessel shall depart with the vessel on leaving port.

SEC. 4. That for the purpose of properly identifying Chinese laborers who were in the United States on the seventeenth day of November, eighteen hundred and eighty, or who shall have come into the same before the expiration of ninety days next after the passage of this act, and in order to furnish them with the proper evidence of their right to go from and come to the United States of their free will and accord, as provided by the treaty between the United States and China dated November seventeenth, eighteen hundred and eighty, the collector of customs of the district from which any such Chinese laborer shall depart from the United States shall, in person or by deputy, go on board each vessel having on board any such Chinese laborer and cleared or about to sail from his district for a foreign port, and on such vessel make a list of all such Chinese laborers, which shall be entered in registry-books to be kept for that purpose, in which shall be stated the name, age, occupation, last place of residence, physical marks or peculiarities, and all facts necessary for the identification of each of such Chinese laborers, which books shall be safely kept in the custom-house; and every such Chinese laborer so departing from the United States shall be entitled to, and shall receive, free of any charge or cost upon application therefor, from the collector or his deputy, at the time such list is taken, a certificate, signed by the collector or his deputy and attested by his seal of office, in such form as the Secretary of the Treasury shall prescribe, which certificate shall contain a statement of the name, age, occupation, last place of residence, personal description, and facts of identification of the Chinese laborer to whom the certificate is issued, corresponding with the said list and registry in all particulars. In case any Chinese laborer after having received such certificate shall leave such vessel before her departure he shall deliver his certificate to the master of the vessel, and if such Chinese laborer shall fail to return to such vessel before her departure from port the certificate shall be delivered by the master to the collector of customs for cancellation. The certificate herein provided for shall entitle the Chinese laborer to whom the same is issued to return to and re-enter the United States upon producing and delivering the same to the collector of customs of the district at which such Chinese laborer shall seek to re-enter; and upon delivery of such certificate by such Chinese laborer to the collector of customs at the time of re-entry in the United States, said collector shall cause the same to be filed in the custom-house and duly cancelled.

SEC. 5. [Certificate to issue on departure from United States, by land, free of cost.]

SEC. 6. That in order to the faithful execution of articles one and two of the treaty in this act before mentioned, every Chinese person other than a laborer who may be entitled by said treaty and this act to come within the United States, and who shall be about to come to the United States, shall be identified as so entitled by the Chinese Government in each case, such identity to be evidenced by a certificate issued under the authority of said government, which certificate shall be in the English language or (if not in the English language) accompanied by a translation into English, stating such right to come, and which certificate shall state the name, title, or official rank, if any, the age, height, and all physical peculiarities, former and present occupation or profession, and place of residence in China of the person to whom the certificate is issued and that such person is entitled comformably to the treaty in this act mentioned to come within the United States. Such certificate shall be prima-facie evidence of the fact set forth therein, and shall be produced to the collector of customs, or his deputy, of the port in the district in the United States at which the person named therein shall arrive.

SEC. 7. [Fraudulent certificates.]

SEC. 8. That the master of any vessel arriving in the United States from any foreign port or place shall, at the same time he delivers a manifest of the cargo, and if there be no cargo, then at the time of making a report of the entry of the vessel pursuant to law, in addition to the other matter required to be reported, and before landing, or permitting to land any Chinese passengers, deliver and report to the collector of customs of the district in which such vessels shall have arrived a separate list of all Chinese passengers taken on board his vessel at any foreign port or place, and all such passengers on board the vessel at that time. Such list shall show the names of such passengers (and if accredited officers of the Chinese Government traveling on the business of that government, or their servants, with a note of such facts), and the names and other particulars, as shown by their respective certificates; and such list shall be sworn to by the master in the manner required by law in relation to the manifest of the cargo. Any willful refusal or neglect of any such master to comply with the provisions of this section shall incur the same penalties and forfeiture as are provided for a refusal or neglect to report and deliver a manifest of the cargo.

SEC. 9. That before any Chinese passengers are landed from any such vessel, the collector, or his deputy, shall proceed to examine such passengers, comparing the certificates with the list and with the passengers; and no passenger shall be allowed to land in the United States from such vessel in violation of law.

SEC. 10. [Forfeiture of vessels for violation of provisions of act.]

SEC. 11. That any person who shall knowingly bring into or cause to be brought into the United States by land, or who shall knowingly aid or abet the same, or aid or abet the landing in the United States from any vessel of any Chinese person not lawfully entitled to enter the United States, shall be deemed guilty of a misdemeanor, and shall, on conviction thereof, be fined in a sum not exceeding one thousand dollars, and imprisoned for a term not exceeding one year.

SEC. 12. That no Chinese person shall be permitted to enter the United States by land without producing to the proper officer of customs the certificate in this act required of Chinese persons seeking to land from a vessel. And any Chinese person found unlawfully within the United States shall be caused to be removed therefrom to the country from whence he came, by direction of the President of the United States, and at the cost of the United States, after being brought before some justice, judge, or commissioner of a court of the United States and found to be one not lawfully entitled to be or remain in the United States.

SEC. 13. That this act shall not apply to diplomatic and other officers of the Chinese Government traveling upon the business of that government, whose credentials shall be taken as equivalent to the certificate in this act mentioned, and shall exempt them and their body and household servants from the provisions of this act as to other Chinese persons.

Sec. 14. That hereafter no State court or court of the United States shall admit Chinese to citizenship; and all laws in conflict with this act are hereby repealed.

Sec. 15. That the words, "Chinese laborers," wherever used in this act, shall be construed to mean both skilled and unskilled laborers and Chinese employed in mining.

Approved, May 6, 1882.

Source: William MacDonald, ed., *Select Statutes and Other Documents Illustrative of the History of the United States* (New York: Macmillan, 1922), pp. 323–328.

11.5.   In Support of Chinese Immigration

In the first passage travel-writer John Codman (1814–1900) speaks out on behalf of Chinese immigration. The second excerpt is by a former missionary to China, Mrs. S. L. Baldwin. Her widely read pamphlet argued for the repeal of anti-Chinese legislation.

The great social question agitating San Francisco, and to a certain extent the State of California, is, "Shall the Chinese go?" Their presence is objected to because they teach immorality and because they "take the bread out of the mouths" of white laborers.

Now the danger of immoral teaching from a class who keep their immorality, which is exaggerated to the last degree, chiefly pent up in their own quarter of the city, is very slight in the way of contagion, and the pretence of their "taking bread from other people's mouths" is very feeble, so long as white hotel-waiters can obtain thirty dollars per month, and chambermaids twenty five dollars per month, including the bread for their mouths and all the dainties offered to the guests.

There is no part of the United States where labor of all kinds commands higher wages than in California, and none where living is less expensive. Food is cheap, and rents not exhorbitant, while people, if they choose, may live out of doors, with advantage to health, the greater part of the year. The Chinese confer a positive benefit upon the State in keeping labor within reasonable bounds, and thus enabling it to raise and export immense crops of grain. It would be well if they should occupy all the servile positions in the cities and drive aristocratic white servants and troublesome "hoodlums" into the country, where they can always find employment.

The worst that can be said of the Mongol is, that he is a labor-saving machine, which is very much needed while labor rules at its present high price. He may be classed with sewing machines, reapers and headers. These are composed of needles, springs and iron teeth, whereas he is a thing of bone and muscle. They are the offspring of art; he is the off-spring of nature. *Voilà tout.* The advantages of employing either kind of machinery are equal, and the objections against the one are as forcible as they are against the other.

Our sympathies were certainly with the Chinese when we were told at a large wheat ranche, in reply to the question why none of them were employed: "We dare not do it. If we did, our crops and buildings would be burned, as for the same cause they were burned at Chico."

Last summer I met a sociably disposed gentleman on the boat running from Vallejo to San Francisco. We drifted on to the Chinese question, upon which he appeared to be thoroughly informed. He was decidedly in favor of importing more Chinese, instead of limiting the immigration. He said that as house servants they were invaluable. He was confident that without their competition the Irish waiters and chambermaids would demand such wages that families in moderate circumstances would be compelled to do all their own work. He thought that instead of interfering with American mechanics they were a positive advantage to the home industry of California.

He gave a forcible illustration of this. A large boot and shoe factory in Sacramento was competing favorably with the eastern market and lessening the demand from that quarter. One hundred and fifty white men and fifty Chinamen were employed in the establishment. About that time Kearney came to Sacramento and said that "those Chinese must go." They went accordingly, and the result was that white men not being able to do the work for which they were appointed, the whole concern was run at a loss and finally broken up, so that the hundred and fifty white men were thrown out of employment by their own act. This was only one of many cases in point.

If I had not been convinced already that the Chinese are profitable to California as railroad builders and fruit-growers this intelligent reasoner would have satisfied me.

On parting at the wharf we exchanged cards, and I found that he was the editor of the—well, I will not "go back" on the profession—but he was the editor of a newspaper having as wide a circulation as any other in the State. "May I use your name in my correspondence?" I asked.

"Good heavens, no!" he exclaimed, "this is only private talk; I don't utter such sentiments in my newspaper!" I found that he did not, for in all California there was not a more violent anti-Chinese newspaper than the ———!

The senseless nature of the excitement against the Chinese should be at once apparent when we reflect that their number is absolutely decreasing in a considerable ratio, while that of the white population is increasing so fast that the next census is relied upon to give California 900,000 inhabitants.

At the close of 1876 there were in the United States altogether 104,963 Chinese. They have since decreased 7,900, leaving 97,063, of whom there are computed to be in California and Oregon 62,500, and in San Francisco and its neighborhood 25,450. What a fearful "invasion of pauper labor" is this!

. . .

There are twenty-five thousand four hundred and fifty Chinese, most of whom it is admitted are mere sojourners without families, who are expected to capture a city of three hundred thousand people, to reduce its laborers to starvation and to demoralize them utterly! . . .

We have no statistics of the employment of the other 37,050 Chinese who are about to subjugate a million people in California and Oregon, or of the remaining 34,563 who are scattered like incendiary fire-brands among the 45,000,000 people of the United States. But it is fair to take the same divisions that exist in San Francisco.

Source: John Codman, *The Round Trip by Way of Panama Through California, Oregon, Nevada, Utah, Idaho, and Colorado* (New York: G. P. Putnam's Sons, 1882), pp. 126–130.

"Now then, let us study a moment the excuses given for this agitation. . . . We are being overwhelmed by a great multitude of Chinese laborers, in opposition to and defiance of the restriction law. But the census statistics do not bear out this statement. *There are only thirty-three more Chinamen to-day*, when our population is one hundred and thirty thousand, than there were five years ago, when we had only seventy thousand people. If *twenty-five* white people were able to get along peaceably and prosperously in competition with *one* Chinaman five years ago, there is no reason to believe *forty-five* white citizens are in danger of being overwhelmed by the same Celestial at the present time. . . . The one great bar to the general advancement and prosperity of the Pacific-coast section is that labor is so high that it practically prohibits home manufacture. The butter on our table was made in an Iowa creamery. The lard used to shorten our pie-crust was canned in Chicago. The cheese we eat was pressed in New York. Our shoes, made from hides which originally grew on Puget Sound cattle, have twice crossed the continent before they are ready for our use. The wool sheared from our sheep this season will be shipped back next year in ready-made clothing, with two freight rates added. And other things innumerable might be mentioned. The greatest need we have is the importation of cheap labor, backed by capital to sustain manufactories. . . . The Chinaman has one peculiarity; *he lives according to his income.* If he makes but fifty cents a day, he lives on vegetable-soup and boiled rice, and keeps out of debt, and steers clear of the gout. If he gets a dollar a day, he has beef, pork, potatoes, fish, and wheat-bread. And if you raise his wages to a dollar and a half or two dollars, he will eat more chickens, turkeys, geese, and fruit, out of his wages, than any other class of foreigners the writer has yet seen in America."

My own personal experience since I returned to this land has not been of the most enjoyable, up-lifting kind. The "spirit moves me" to give it to my readers. I have nothing to be thankful for in this experience, save that it is not worse, as it surely would have been had I lived on the Pacific Coast. For many years we lived in China. At last failing health brought me and mine back to this favored Christian land, the traditional home of the "free and brave." We brought with us a Chinese servant. He was a Christian, gentle, kind, and most courteous to all. On our way home we travelled through many lands, heathen, papal, and Christian. This Chinese servant received not an unkind word or insult in any of those lands. We at last arrived in the United States. We settled for the winter in the parsonage of a church in a city proud of its churches and Christian institutions. Three days after, I sent my Chinaman out with my little boy in his carriage. In an hour they returned with such an unsightly, dirty, hooting rabble after them, that I was shocked, and hastened to bring baby and nurse in. I then kindly told them that I did not want them to follow my baby and his nurse in that style, and requested them to leave.

In return I received only insult and the grossest impertinence. I then told them if it occurred again I would certainly call the police. That ended their coming to our door, for they evidently understood that I would do as I said; but during our stay of some months in that city, I had no comfort in taking my nurse or baby down town for any purpose, and rarely did I do it save from necessity. On one such occasion I stood in the main street waiting for a car. We were directly opposite an elegant church, with steeple pointing heavenward. The pastor, no doubt, gave his audience sound doctrine as to the brotherhood of man, Christ's love and sacrifice for all, and the duty to love our neighbor as ourselves. Our Chinaman stood admiring the church, now and then making a remark to me. Just then a man passed us. He was dirty and ragged, and puffing a filthy pipe. He evidently had been drinking too much of his native lager or something stronger. As he passed he gave a look of hatred at the quiet, clean, gentlemanly Chinaman standing there holding my baby.

The man passed on, crossed the street, then stopped, reconsidered, turned round, and came back to where we stood, and deliberately circled us round and round, with eyes bent full of hate upon the Chinaman, who seemed utterly unconscious of the evil spirit he excited.

Source: S. L. Baldwin, *Must the Chinese Go? Examination of the Chinese Question* (New York: H. B. Elkins, 1890), p. 62–63.

11.6.   The Chinese Question (1888)

The "Chinese question" became a national political issue in the 1870s. However, from the very beginning of Chinese immigration to the West, the Chinese were persecuted due to stereotypes and misconceptions about their culture. Best known for his book on Jesse James in 1882, published just weeks after the outlaw's murder, Frank Triplett explores the differences between Chinese and European cultures in the following passage. Triplett deflects the various prejudices against the Chinese by putting them in a more rational context.

His worst enemies allow to him sobriety, patience and frugality. They admit that he neither meddles with the social, moral, or political affairs of his neighbors. They say that he is adaptable and if he cannot find employment at his regular trade, whatever that may be, he turns his hand to something else—in fact, that he is the American of Asia.

They say that, while inferior in physique to the white man, he is superior in diligence and patient energy. They say that he doesn't get drunk, attends no club, has no elections and parades, belongs to no societies, organizes no strikes, and raises no riots. How they could make out a better character for this much abused heathen we can hardly see.

They speak of his filthy habits, and yet cleanliness is a part of his religion and rigidly practiced. They say that he sleeps in crowded quarters and poisons himself with the foul exhalations from dozens of his fellows, and yet his death rate is lower than any of our other immigrants. They speak of his cheap labor, and yet his washing and his cooking are better paid than those of any other of our domestics.

It is true that his patience and industry enable him to work out fortunes from the "tailings," from which the American has already taken their richest deposits of the precious metals, and in household work the Chinese easily displace our Bridgets and our Lenas, from the fact that they are not inquisitive, demand no "Sundays and afternoons out," attend to their own business, do not pry into that of their employers, and ask but a single question, when seeking employment—"is the pay certain!"

To think of asking the number of children in a family, as if the production of offspring were the unpardonable sin; to dictate as to the management of the household, or any part of it, are things which never enter their minds, and they were welcomed in California (when the servant girl had become the domestic autocrat), as a God-send.

.   .   .

In amusements, the Chinese keep rigidly their New Year, their festival lasting with them a week. This celebration does not occur on a certain, fixed date, as our first of January, but is governed by the moon, as is our Easter and falls somewhere between the 21st of January and the 20th of February. They are regular patrons to their theatres, where interminable plays hold the stage for weeks; their dramas being on the plan of our continued stories. Their plays are all tragedies; of comedy they have no idea. Gambling is followed by all classes, it not being accounted by them wrong to spend their own money in any way they choose.

Their peculiarities are many; they smoke cigars and pipes, but never chew tobacco. They never drink cold water. They never walk abreast, but one after the other. They use no animals in their labors. Their carriages are sedan chairs. They have no politics. Widows must wait three years after the death of their husbands before re-marriage, and even then the man who marries a widow is held in contempt. No display is allowed to the widow-bride. White is their badge of mourning. They do no courting, their marriages being arranged by old women, who follow matchmaking as a profession. In the street the wife must walk at a suitable distance behind her "lord and master," as her husband truly is. In China polygamy is somewhat practiced, and the killing of female children is common, though generally denounced.

The idle stories of their "rice-and-rat eating" propensities are easily disproved by any candid inquirer, who will take the trouble to consult the butcher, patronized by these queer people. Pork and chickens are their favorite meats; peas and potatoes their preference in vegetables, and they are partial to all kinds of sweetmeats. They use a great deal of fruit, but little bread. Tea is their universal table beverage and this they drink scalding hot and without sugar or milk.

How long these strange beings have maintained their exclusive civilization, within the walls of their unchanging empire, we will never know, but it is certain that thousands of years ago, when the ancestors of the Saxon and the Celt, the Anglo-Norman and the Teutonic races were rude barbarians, clad only in the skins of wild beasts and living by the chase, the progenitor of the California Chinaman of to-day enjoyed his printing press and his tillage, and clad in silken fabrics, was familiar with gun-powder and mechanic arts, some of which are new to us even at the present time. All the mutations of time have failed to change him in character, physiognomy or habits, and while the rest of the world has been revolutionized by the onward rush of the hours and the steady march of progress, this gigantic empire alone has known no change.

. . .

Years of continued residence in San Francisco have failed to confirm the alleged danger of his spreading amongst the whites the dread disease of leprosy. It is, in fact, probable, that under his better sanitary conditions and with the more generous food he is able to obtain in this country, this disease will disappear entirely from his race.

As to the female prostitution, so prevalent amongst Chinawomen in California, that is due to the fact that none, save prostitutes, are brought to this country. That courtesans exist in China was certainly to be expected, as the "strange woman" has at all times and ages and in all countries, been regarded as one of the necessary evils of society.

Source: Frank Triplett, *Conquering the Wilderness* (New York: N. D. Thompson Publishing Co., 1888), pp. 594–598.

ANNOTATED SELECTED BIBLIOGRAPHY

Chan, Sucheng. *Asian Americans: An Interpretive History*. Boston: Twayne, 1991. Chan offers a rich blend of statistics and informative history as she discusses the Chinese transition from immigrant to Asian American.

————. *The Bittersweet Soil: The Chinese in California Agriculture, 1860–1910*. Berkeley: University of California Press, 1986. Unlike most books on the Chinese in nineteenth-century America, which dwell on the urban experience, Chan examines the agricultural saga.

Kingston, Maxine Hong. *China Men*. New York: Alfred A. Knopf, 1980. The author chronicles the lives of three generations of Chinese men in America, woven from memory, myth, and fact.

Saxton, Alexander. *The Indispensable Enemy: Labor and the Anti-Chinese Movement in California*. Berkeley: University of California Press, 1971. Saxton explores the development of the anti-Chinese labor movement during the late nineteenth century.

Takaki, Ronald. *Iron Cages: Race and Culture in Nineteenth Century America*. New York: Oxford University Press, 1990. An exhaustively researched history of immigration and racial attitudes in America during the 1800s.

Yung, Judy. *Unbound Voices: A Documentary History of Chinese Women in San Francisco*. Berkeley: University of California Press, 1999. This volume brings together the voices of Chinese American women in a collection of documents, telling the story of their experiences in San Francisco from the Gold Rush years to World War II.

Zhu, Liping. *A Chinaman's Chance: The Chinese on the Rocky Mountain Mining Frontier.* Niwot: University Press of Colorado, 1997. Zhu challenges the stereotypical image of the Chinese pioneers.

12

Wounded Knee, 1890

The last bloody encounter of any consequence between whites and Indians occurred at Wounded Knee Creek, Dakota Territory, in the waning days of 1890. The Lakota Sioux had been embroiled in hostilities with American forces since Sitting Bull refused to recognize the 1868 Fort Laramie Treaty, which recognized fixed boundaries to prevent future conflict between the Sioux and white intruders. Unwilling to accept the confines of the Great Sioux Reserve on an expanse of land reaching from the Missouri River to the Dakota Territory, Sitting Bull opted for autonomy. With the discovery of gold in the Black Hills of the Dakotas, the fragile peace was shattered and the Great Sioux War of 1876–1877 broke out. Its most famous battle took place at the Little Big Horn in the summer of 1876, culminating in the destruction of George Armstrong Custer's command (see Chapter 9). In reality, the battle was a Pyrrhic victory for the combined Lakota-Cheyenne forces. A massive effort by the U.S. Army soon sealed the fate of the Sioux, forcing them onto the rapidly diminishing lands of the Great Sioux Reserve. Together with the buffalo herds, the Lakota way of life was on the brink of annihilation. Hope soon appeared in the guise of a new religious movement.

The Ghost Dance was an Indian messianic movement that emerged in the West in 1870. Initially, it was active in California, Oregon, and parts of Nevada. Intrinsic to its doctrine was the notion that all white people would be swallowed up by the earth and that dead Indians would return to life on earth, hence the Ghost Dance imagery. The first wave of the messianic movement abated after a few years when the prophecies of the Ghost Dance prophet failed to materialize. The movement was resurrected more successfully in the 1880s by the Paiute messiah Wovoka (c. 1856–1932), also known by his English name, Jack Wilson. Influenced by the earlier prophets, in 1889 Wovoka experienced a vision in which a Supreme Being instructed him to inform his people that if they lived in harmony with one another and with the whites, worked hard, and took part in ceremonial dances, they could be reunited with the dead and the whites would disappear forever.

The resurrection of the Ghost Dance in the 1880s had little appeal for the California Indians who had seen the movement come and go, or for Southwest Indian tribes, who were traditionally unreceptive to doctrines involving ghosts. However, by 1890 the Ghost Dance found allure among the Rocky Mountain tribes and then the peoples of the Great Plains. The Sioux added another ingredient to the basic dance and chanting ceremonies, adopting "ghost shirts" that were thought to be impervious to bullets and would protect the wearer from harm.

The adoption of the white muslin ghost shirts, garnished with celestial images by the Plains Indian tribes, was not coincidental, but was a response to their rapidly changing environment. The world of the Plains Indians was undergoing a rapid transformation. Defeated on the battlefields, besieged by contagious diseases, and with the once numerous buffalo depleted, the demoralized Sioux were faced with confinement on reservations and the disintegration of their culture. Without the great herds of buffalo providing their basics of food and shelter, the end of their nomadic way of life was on the horizon.

The Ghost Dance reached the Sioux Indians of the Great Plains in 1890. Prophesying the return of the dead and the immense bison herds, the messianic movement instantly found adherents among a people who deeply resented the destruction of their culture at the hands of a government with a track record of breaking treaties and other promises. Ultimately, the spread of the religion would lead to a series of tragedies that resulted first in the killing of Sitting Bull and then the carnage at Wounded Knee. What is rather ironic about the tragedy following the introduction of the Ghost Dance was the lack of hostility directed toward whites. Although it included predictions of the demise of the white man, this messianic movement remained pacifist in nature.

In 1890 a new treaty cut the Sioux reservation almost by half, and economizing by Congress insured that Indians on the reservation would be poorly fed. Wovoka's promises of a revitalization of the Sioux way of life led to frenzied activity among the Sioux. Military authorities misconstrued the intent of the Ghost Dance "craze" and overreacted. At the Standing Rock Reservation, the ever skeptical Sitting Bull, one of the last chiefs to surrender, distanced himself from the Ghost Dance, but refused to intervene on behalf of the authorities. Best known for his conflict with

Sitting Bull, the Indian agent James McLaughlin (1842–1923) contended without substantiation that the great Indian leader had triggered the religious frenzy. As a result, orders were sent to the Sioux Indian police to arrest Sitting Bull. In the fracas that followed, Sitting Bull, considered by many to be the architect of Custer's defeat, and six followers, along with six Indian policemen, were killed. Tensions were exacerbated by the death of the Sioux leader. Many of the chief's followers decamped to join Big Foot, another Sioux chief who was preparing his own followers to surrender at the Pine Ridge Reservation, several hundred miles to the south.

Meanwhile, members of the Seventh Cavalry, the very same unit that had been vanquished fourteen years earlier, pursued Big Foot's band, finally catching up with them on December 28, 1890. Some of the officers with the regiment had fought with Major Marcus Reno at the Little Big Horn in 1876. The soldiers escorted the Indians toward the Pine Ridge Agency, roughly twenty miles away. Night was approaching, and Big Foot's band was instructed to camp temporarily at Wounded Knee Creek. Since night was falling, the soldiers decided that the Indians, two-thirds of whom were women and children, could be disarmed the following morning. But to be safe and to make sure the prisoners did not attempt to escape, two cavalry troops were assigned to guard the perimeter of the camp. In addition, two Hotchkiss guns were strategically placed overlooking the Sioux camp. This weapon of destruction, if needed, could discharge fifty explosive charges per minute more than two miles away. But for the time being the guns were aimed so that they would take out the nearby Indian lodges in the event of hostilities.

As the night wore on, members of the Seventh Cavalry reportedly enjoyed rounds of whiskey and began to talk of revenging Custer's ignominious defeat. Later in the evening more troops arrived, and Colonel James W. Forsyth, in command of Custer's former regiment, took charge of the operation and informed the other officers that Big Foot's band would be taken to the Union Pacific Railroad and transported to the military prison in Omaha. Two more Hotchkiss guns were placed alongside the others, and Forsyth joined his men in their celebration around the keg of whiskey. At that very moment, Big Foot, perilously ill from pneumonia, was enjoying his last night of rest. Before bedding down for the night, he set up a white flag in the middle of the encampment.

On the morning of December 29, the soldiers made the rounds of the Sioux camp to collect any weapons. Although most of the men owned weapons, few volunteered to give them up. In response the soldiers became agitated and began wreaking havoc in the camp, tearing up belongings and abusing the women and children. Some accounts suggest the gunfire began after the zealous medicine man Yellow Bird encouraged the young men to resist. Yellow Bird exhorted the warriors, reminding them that the ghost shirts would protect them. He then threw a handful of dirt in the air, a traditional call to battle.

Other reports indicate that as the soldiers conducted a meticulous search one became involved in an animated discussion with a deaf warrior named Black Coyote over his weapon. Black Coyote resisted attempts to take his rifle, and in the ensuing struggle it accidentally fired. The already nervous soldiers, most of whom had never been involved in actual battle, responded to the gun's report by opening fire on the Indian encampment. The first volley killed or wounded at least two-thirds of the Indians.

The Wounded Knee episode remains controversial to this day. There is no consensus as to who actually fired the first shot, although many authorities believe it was an accidental shot. But what followed was brutal close-quarters combat between the perimeter guard and the Indians. After breaking through the troops the Indians were mowed down by the Hotchkiss guns, and after a short series of skirmishes in the village and in the peripheral ravines the bloodshed ended. Estimates of Indian dead ranged from 146 to 300, while the army suffered 25 deaths. The indelible photographs of Big Foot and other contorted Indian bodies frozen to the ground, half covered by snow, led to an outpouring of sympathy for the Plains Indians. These photographs were taken three days after the battle when troops were sent out to gather up and bury the dead after the blizzard following the carnage. To the horror of the soldiers, a number of women and children were found still alive, but most died before being brought back to camp. The dead warriors from Big Foot's camp along with the women and children were finally unceremoniously buried by civilians at two dollars per corpse in a mass grave on the same hill from which the Hotchkiss guns unleashed their withering fire (the burial of the dead at Wounded Knee was recorded by photographer George Trager).

Events at Wounded Knee were reported by a contingent of war correspondents. Some interviewed survivors before telegraphing dispatches to various newspapers. There having been little in the way of war news to report before this incident, the public hungered for information from the Dakotas. Newspapers demonstrated little moderation in their coverage. There was no consensus on whether the events of December 29, 1890, constituted a battle or a massacre. Some newspapers saw Wounded Knee as an opportunity for bloodthirsty members of the Seventh Cavalry to even the score from 1876. The deaths of helpless women and children gave credence to this interpretation. Other papers saw the conduct of the soldiers as meritorious as they endeavored to prevent a recurrence of the Custer debacle. Although a number of cavalrymen were awarded the Congressional Medal of Honor for their supposed heroism at Wounded Knee, their merit is dubious, since thirteen of the twenty-five soldiers who died in the confrontation were killed by friendly fire.

Perhaps there is some truth to both interpretations. This was an event that neither group expected. Witnesses testified that when soldiers attempted to disarm the warriors, one fanatical medicine man incited the more militant young men to open fire on the soldiers. The soldiers returned fire, and although there is no proof that soldiers targeted women and children, there was nowhere for them to escape the deadly fusillade. Additional stimuli for this clash emanated from other factors as well— Seventh Cavalry members bent on revenge, fear of recurring Indian hostilities, inept Indian policy, and the rebirth of the Indian religious movement known as the Ghost Dance. As 1890 ended the Ghost Dance lost its luster for the dejected Sioux, and the Plains Wars had ended after a half-century of confrontations.

More bloodshed was narrowly averted. After hearing of the massacre just twenty miles away, the 4,000 Indians from the Pine Ridge Reservation gathered north of the agency. For a short time they were able to trap the Seventh Cavalry, which was on a reconnaissance mission. But before hostilities erupted 3,5000 troops led by General Nelson Miles appeared to defuse the potentially explosive situation on January 15, 1891.

The sensational reports of Wounded Knee led Indian reform groups and humanitarians to put so much pressure on President Benjamin Harrison that he had no choice but to open an inquiry into the killing. On January 4, 1891, General Miles relieved Colonel Forsyth of command of the Seventh Cavalry and convened a full-scale court of inquiry. The vast majority of witnesses who testified supported Forsyth's actions. According to historian Robert Utley, an objective reading of the court transcripts suggests that the soldiers tried to avoid killing women and children, but because the Indian combatants were mixed in with the noncombatants this was almost impossible. On January 18, the court concluded that Forsyth had indeed demonstrated "incompetence" and had disobeyed orders. Despite the ruling, Forsyth's career continued to flourish, and in 1897 he rose from brigadier general to major general.

The massacre at Wounded Knee corresponded with a new era in U.S. Indian policy. The well-meaning but poorly conceived attempts to assimilate Indians into the American mainstream had begun with the passage of the Dawes Act of 1887. By this act reform-minded Indian rights organizations, as well as land speculators, hoped to undermine traditional tribal authority, eradicate tribal culture, and destroy the reservation system by breaking up Indian tribal lands and redistributing the land in small allotments to individual Indian families. This would diminish the power of tribal governments. In return, Native Americans were offered individual land ownership, legal rights and protections, and the responsibilities of full citizenship. The news of the tragedy at Wounded Knee further convinced reformers that the Dawes Act was the right solution for assimilating and preserving the remaining Native Americans. As a result of the Dawes Act, Indian lands dwindled to less than half of their 1887 level. The failure of this policy led to its termination in 1934.

Although there is a tendency to view the carnage of Wounded Knee as the last incident of the Indian wars, its context is more complicated than that. Symbolically, it has also become linked with the closing of the American West. In 1893 the young historian Frederick Jackson Turner delivered his seminal paper, "The Significance of the Frontier in American History," to the American Historical Association in Chicago. Turner noted that the 1890 census showed that there was no more frontier line. Although he never formally made the connection between the census and Wounded Knee, both signified the end of a chapter in the history of the American West. According to the 1890 census, there was no longer a frontier of free land, and after Wounded Knee there were no more free-ranging Indian bands. The last major campaign against the American Indians has since come to symbolize the deficiencies of federal Indian policy and the disintegration of the traditional Indian way of life.

Since 1890, Wounded Knee has become a lightning rod for Indian activism, most notably during the 1973 siege by members of the American Indian Movement (AIM). The armed standoff between activists and federal agents brought international attention to the symbolic site. The confrontation lasted for more than seventy days, fueled by a media blitz that did much to dramatize the plight of the American Indian. This time, though, the Indians achieved a substantial propaganda victory, as AIM leaders negotiated a peaceful withdrawal.

In December 1990, on the centennial of the massacre, 300 Sioux Indians set out on a journey to commemorate the last journey of Chief Big Foot and his followers. During their five-day expedition, they endured freezing temperatures and arctic winds, but they persisted in their goal of reaching Wounded Knee, South Dakota, exactly one hundred years after the massacre. When they reached their destination, they found that the historical marker, which had previously read "Battle of Wounded Knee, 1890," had been replaced to reflect the new era with a sign that read "Massacre of Wounded Knee, 1890." The Sioux who made this ride, who referred to themselves collectively as Sitanka Wokiksuye (Chief Big Foot Memorial Ride) saw their gesture as more than a memorial. As historian James Wilson so poignantly explained, "By ending a hundred years of mourning, they would simultaneously free both the massacre victims and their descendants,"[1] allowing the process of national renewal to move forward as Indians trapped on reservations coped with new concerns such as drugs, alcohol, threats to the environment, and domestic violence.

NOTE

1. Jack Wilson, *The Earth Shall Weep: A History of Native America* (New York: Grove Press, 1998), p. xix.

DOCUMENTS

12.1.   The Indian Story of Wounded Knee

The following testimony of Turning Hawk, Spotted Horse, and American Horse, all survivors of Wounded Knee, was given to the commissioner of Indian affairs on February 11, 1891. These reports were included in the published investigation into the slaughter.

TURNING HAWK. When we heard that these people were coming toward our agency we also heard this. These people were coming toward Pine Ridge agency, and when they were almost on the agency they were met by the soldiers and surrounded and finally taken to the Wounded Knee creek, and there at a given time their guns were demanded. When they had delivered them up, the men were separated from their families, from their tipis, and taken to a certain spot. When the guns were thus taken and the men thus separated, there was a crazy man, a young man of very bad influence and in fact a nobody, among that bunch of Indians fired his gun, and of course the firing of a gun must have been the breaking of a military rule of some sort, because immediately the soldiers returned fire and indiscriminate killing followed.

SPOTTED HORSE. This man shot an officer in the army; the first shot killed this officer. I was a voluntary scout at that encounter and I saw exactly what was done, and that was what I noticed; that the first shot killed an officer. As soon as this shot was fired the Indians immediately began drawing their knives, and they were exhorted from all sides to desist, but this was not obeyed. Consequently the firing began immediately on the part of the soldiers.

TURNING HAWK. All the men who were in a bunch were killed right there, and those who escaped that first fire got into the ravine, and as they went along up the ravine for a long distance they were pursued on both sides by the soldiers and shot down, as the dead bodies showed afterwards. The women were standing off at a different place from where the men were stationed, and when the firing began, those of the men who escaped the first onslaught went in one direction up the ravine, and then the women, who were bunched together at another place, went entirely in a different direction through an open field, and the women fared the same fate as the men who went up the deep ravine.

AMERICAN HORSE. The men were separated, as has already been said, from the women, and they were surrounded by the soldiers. Then came next the village of the Indians and that was entirely surrounded by the soldiers also. When the firing began, of course the people who were standing immediately around the young man who fired the first shot were killed right together, and then they turned their guns, Hotchkiss guns, etc., upon the women who were in the lodges standing there under a flag of truce, and of course as soon as they were fired upon they fled, the men fleeing in one direction and the women running in two different directions. So that there were three general directions in which they took flight.

There was a woman with an infant in her arms, who was killed as she almost touched the flag of truce, and the women and children of course were strewn all along the circular village until they were dispatched. Right near the flag of truce a mother was shot down with her infant; the child not knowing that its mother was dead was still nursing, and that especially was a very sad sight. The women as they were fleeing with their babes were killed together, shot right through, and the women who were very heavy with child were also killed. All the Indians fled in these three directions, and after most all of them had been killed a cry was made that all those who were not killed or wounded should come forth and they would be safe. Little boys who were not wounded came out of their places of refuge, and as soon as they came in sight a number of soldiers surrounded them and butchered them there.

Of course we all feel very sad about this affair. I stood very loyal to the government all through those troublesome days, and believing so much in the government and being so loyal to it, my disappointment was very strong, and I have come to Washington with a very great blame on my heart. Of course it would have been all right if only the men were killed; we would feel almost grateful for it. But the fact of the killing of the women, and more especially the killing of the young boys and girls who are to go to make up the future strength of the Indian people, is the saddest part of the whole affair and we feel it very sorely.

I was not there at the time before the burial of the bodies, but I did go there with some of the police and the Indian doctor and a great many of the people, men from the agency, and we went through the battlefield and saw where the bodies were from the track of the blood.

Source: J. W. Powell ed., Fourteenth Annual Report of the Bureau of Ethnology, Part 2 (Washington, DC: U.S. Government Printing Office, 1896), pp. 885–886.

12.2.   The Aftermath

Dr. Charles Eastman, a full-blooded Sioux from Boston, visited Wounded Knee after the fight and recorded his impressions of the carnage. The field was still littered with the dead and wounded several days after the hostilities. Eastman was admittedly not an eyewitness but received his information by interviewing several Indian prisoners.

A ghastly account of the battle-ground has been given by Dr. Charles A. Eastman, of Boston, a full blooded Sioux, who visited it after the conflict. He wrote on January 3:

"On Thursday morning I visited the field of battle, where all those Indians were killed, on the Wounded Knee, last Monday. I went there to get the wounded, some who were left out. The soldiers brought with them about twenty-five, and I found eleven who were still living. Among them were two babies, about three months old, and an old woman who is totally blind, who was left for dead. Four of them were found out in a field in the storm, which was very severe. They were half buried in the snow. It was a terrible and horrible sight to see women and children lying in groups, dead. I suppose they were of one family. Some of the young girls wrapped their heads with shawls and buried their faces in their hands. I suppose they did that so that they would not see the soldiers come up to shoot them. At one place there were two little children, one about one year old, the other about three, lying on their faces, dead, and about 30 yards from them a woman lay on her face, dead. These were away from the camp about an eighth of a mile.

"In front of the tents, which were in a semi-circle, lay dead most of the men. This was right by one of the soldiers' tents. Those who were still living told me that that was where the Indians were ordered to hold a council with the soldiers. The accounts of the battle by the Indians were simple, and confirmed one another, that the soldiers ordered them to go into camp, for they were moving them, and told them that they would give them provisions. Having done this they (the Indians) were asked to give up their arms, which was complied with by most of them, in fact all the old men, but many of the younger men did not comply, because they either had no arms or concealed them in their blankets. Then a order was given to search their persons and their tents as well, and when a search was made of a wretch of an Indian, who was known as Good-for-Nothing, he fired the first shot, and killed one of the soldiers. They fired upon the Indians instantaneously. Shells were thrown among the women and children, so that they mutilated them most horribly. I tried to go to the field the next day, with some Indians, but I was not allowed to. I think it was a wise thing not to go so early. Even Thursday I thought I would be shot. Some of the Indians (friendly) found their relations lying dead. They waited and began to put out their guns. My friend, Louis De Coteau, was with me, but left me when they acted in this manner. Before he left me the hostiles appeared. We did not take in all the wounded. Those we could not carry away we left in a log house and gave them food."

A little Indian baby girl about three months old, one of the survivors of the battle of Wounded Knee, who lay for three days beside the dead body of its mother, was adopted by Mrs. Allison Nailor, a wealthy lady of Washington. Major John Burke, manager of Buffalo Bill's Wild West Combination, stood as god-father to the child, and had it christened Maggie C. Nailor, the first name and initial being those of the child's new found benefactress.

Miss Elaine Goodale, the poet, who had devoted some years to educational work among the Indians, made this report to the Commissioner of Indian affairs, concerning the battle at Wounded Knee:

"I was not an eye-witness of the fight and my information has been obtained chiefly from Indian prisoners who engaged in it and half-breeds who were present, and from parties who visited the battlefield several days after the encounter.

"The testimony of the survivors of Big Foot's band is unanimous on one important point, namely, that the Indians did not deliberately plan a resistance. The party was not a war party, according to their statements (which I believe to be true), but a party intending to visit the agency at the invitation of Red Cloud.

"The Indians say that many of the men were unarmed. When they met the troops they anticipated no trouble. There was constant friendly intercourse between the soldiers and the Indians, even women shaking hands with the officers and men. The demand for their arms was a surprise to the Indians, but the great majority of them chose to submit quietly. The tepees had already been searched and a large number of guns, knives and hatchets confiscated when the searching of the persons of the men was begun. The women say that they too were searched and their knives (which they always carry for domestic purposes) taken from them. A number of the men had surrendered their rifles and cartridge belts when one young man (who is described by the Indians as a good-for-nothing young fellow) fired a single shot. This called forth a volley from the troops and the firing and confusion became general."

I do not credit the statement which has been made by some that the women carried arms and participated actively in the fight. The weight of testimony is overwhelmingly against this supposition. There may have been one or two isolated cases of this kind, but there is no doubt that the great majority of the women and children, as well as many unarmed men and youths, had no thought of anything but flight. They were pursued up the ravines, and shot down indiscriminately by the soldiers.

It is reported that one of the officers called out, "Don't shoot the squaws," but the men were doubtless too much excited to obey. The killing of the women and children was in part unavoidable, owing to the confusion, but I think there is no doubt that it was in many cases deliberate and intentional. The 7th Cavalry, Custer's old command, had an old grudge to repay.

The party of scouts who buried the dead, report sixty-four bodies of men and boys, forty-four of women and eighteen of young children. Some were carried off by the hostiles. A number of prisoners, chiefly women, have since died of their wounds, and more will soon follow. The party who visited the battlefield on January 1st, to rescue any wounded who might have been abandoned, and brought in seven, report that nearly all the bodies of the men were lying close about Big Foot's Sibley tent while the women and children were scattered along a distance of two miles from the scene of the encounter.

Source: W. Fletcher Johnson, *Life of Sitting Bull and History of the Indian War of 1890–91* (Edgewood Publishing Co., 1891), pp. 453–457.

12.3.   A Ghost Dance Ballad

Private W. H. Prather's participation in the Ghost Dance troubles and the subsequent Wounded Knee Massacre inspired him to write the following ballad. Prather was a member of the African American troop of the Ninth Cavalry. This ballad became a popular song among frontiersmen and soldiers on the Great Plains in the late nineteenth century.

The Indian, Ghost Dance and War

The Red Skins left their Agency, the Soldiers left their Post,
All on the strength of an Indian tale about Messiah's ghost
Got up by savage chieftains to lead their tribes astray;
But Uncle Sam wouldn't have it so, for he ain't built that way.
They swore that this Messiah came to them in visions sleep,
And promised to restore their game and Buffalos a heap,
So they must start a big ghost dance, then all would join their
    band,
And may be so we lead the way into the great Bad Land.

Chorus:

    They claimed the shirt Messiah gave, no bullet could go through,
    But when the Soldiers fired at them they saw this was not true.
    The Medicine man supplied them with their great Messiah's
        grace,
    And he, too, pulled his freight and swore the 7th hard to face.

    About their tents the Soldiers stood, awaiting one and all,
    That they might hear the trumpet clear when sounding General
        call
    Or Boots and Saddles in a rush, that each and every man
    Might mount in haste, ride soon and fast to stop this devilish
        band
    But Generals great like Miles and Brooke don't do things up that
        way,
    For they know an Indian like a book, and let him have his sway
    Until they think him far enough and then to John they'll say,
    "You had better stop your fooling or we'll bring our guns to
        play."

Chorus.—They claimed the shirt, etc.

    The 9th marched out with splendid cheer the Bad Lands to ex-
        plo'e—
    With Col. Henry at their head they never fear the foe;
    So on they rode from Xmas eve 'till dawn of Xmas day;
    The Red Skins heard the 9th was near and fled in great dismay;
    The 7th is of courage bold both officers and men,
    But bad luck seems to follow them and twice has took them in;
    They came in contact with Big Foot's warriors in their fierce
        might
    This chief made sure he had a chance of vantage in the fight.

Chorus.—They claimed the shirt, etc.

    A fight took place, 'twas hand to hand, unwarned by trumpet
        call,
    While the Sioux were dropping man by man—the 7th killed them
        all,
    And to that regiment be said "Ye noble braves, well done,
    Although you lost some gallant men a glorious fight you've
        won."
    The 8th was there, the sixth rode miles to swell that great com-
        mand
    And waited orders night and day to round up Short Bull's band.
    The Infantry marched up in mass the Cavalry's support,

And while the latter rounded up, the former held the fort.
Chorus.—They claimed the shirt, etc.

E battery of the 1st stood by and did their duty well,
For every time the Hotchkiss barked they say a hostile fell.
Some Indian soldiers chipped in too and helped to quell the fray,
And now the campaign's ended and the soldiers marched away.
So all have done their share, you see, whether it was thick or
   thin,
And all helped break the ghost dance up and drive the hostiles
   in.
The settlers in that region now can breathe with better grace;
They only ask and pray to God to make John hold his base.
Chorus.—They claimed the shirt, etc.

Source: J. W. Powell, ed., *Fourteenth Annual Report of the Bureau of Ethnology*, Part
2 (Washington, DC: U.S. Government Printing Office, 1896), p. 883.

12.4.   M. L. Johnson at Wounded Knee

---

*The following is an account of the Wounded Knee Massacre by
a participant from Texas, M. L. Johnson, who privately printed
his autobiography in 1923. Johnson captures the confusion, excitement, and carnage of the thirty-minute massacre.*

In the decline of all nations of people a "Saviour" has arisen from among
the people with prophesies false or true, they sought to better the conditions of their race.

Thus it was that a Messiah came among the Brule Sioux from Idaho
with the wondrous tale that the plains of Nebraska and Dakota were
now to be given back to their primeval condition of the buffalo and
Indian—that these scenes were to be actually viewed by going into a
dance or something like a hypnotic state produced by physical exhaustion; so when these tales of a reproduction of their barbaric splendor
were told them at this time of distress, they believed it to be a divine
revelation and so accepted it. The Messiah painted hieroglyphics on cotton shirts and assured his followers that they would turn the bullets of
the white man. They now had nothing to fear, and so nearly 6,000 of
them went on the war-path. Chief Two Strikes was at the head of them.
Their first hostile act was the killing of the government cattle herder.
Then they took a Northwesterly course toward the Bad Lands, leaving

destruction in their wake. The Indian agent at Pine Ridge, fearing for his life, deserted his post. United States troops were telegraphed for and soon 3,000 soldiers were in the field under General Miles. On the North of Pine Ridge Agency 6,000 Indians were depredating—one mile South there was encamped a band of Indians under Chief American Horse— settlers were deserting their homes—Rushville was filled with fright and fugitives.

The state troops were ordered out and consisted of 2,000 men. They were commanded by Brig. General L. W. Colby. On the 28th day of December, 1890, Col. Forsythe of the U. S. A. was ordered out to round up Big Foot's band then depredating in the hills. We came on to them on the evening of December 28th, and marched them some eight miles to Wounded Knee Creek. 93 soldiers stood guard all night with the intention of disarming the Indians at day break—the weather was intensely cold.

I sat in a tent eating some hard tack and coffee when a volley of 100 rifles was heard to come from down the creek where the Indians were being guarded. In an instant the heavier boom of musketry followed the deafening sound of the Hotchkiss gun—the long expected battle was on!

Does memory in any one ever serve to describe a battle accurately? I think not—the strain on the nervous system is so great that memory refuses to retain all the eye sees.

I saw a cloud of smoke, puffs of blue smoke, as the deadly triangle of soldiers poured bullets into the struggling mass of Indinans [sic] about the tepees. Wavering ranks of the blue as the withering fire was returned—frantic horses dashing riderless over the plain—forms in red blankets running hither and thither. Swift retreat of small parties followed by swifter pursuit of horsemen.

There were hand-to-hand conflicts here and there—the men in blue extemporizing boxes and sacks of grain for breastworks.

I heard the bugle notes sounding "Charge;" again their mellow cadence said "Fire at Will." Above the sound of the rifle shots and cannonade came the weird shrill "Hi, Yi, Hip, Zi," and anon, after an effective volley, rose the sullen roar of voices whose cry was, "Remember Custer."

Indians were pinned to earth with bayonets; squaws dashed here and there with long knives attempting to stab the soldiers—they too, were shot. Thirty minutes of the hottest fight and the Indians were fleeing to the hills—they gained the gullies and shot the soldiers in pursuit.

The trench at the Wounded Knee fight was dug 60 feet long, 9 feet wide and 6 feet deep, and 251 bodies were piled "pell mell" into it.

The field of carnage is the most dreadful thing the human eye can dwell on, and I wish it were effaced from my memory for in after years

I have heard in fitful slumber those dying yells and piteous cries of agony.

I know of but one survivor, a sucking Indian baby girl, found strapped on the back of her stiff, frozen, dead mother, four days after the battle. How that infant could stand, and live, in that condition no one could even guess, but such is the fact and she was taken from her dead mother by Gen. L. W. Colby, of Beatrice, Nebraska, and taken to his home and adopted. I have her picture when she was about 12 years old, and the last time I heard from her, she was still living.

Now if this account does not appeal to the reader as being the plain truth, and nothing but the truth I ask the reader to send to the Indian agent at Washington, D. C., and I am positive he will verify every word of it, the most exciting, horrible account of an Indian fight that a human eye has ever witnessed, and I shall offer proof positive that every word of it is the truth and nothing but the truth.

Source: M. L. Johnson, *True History of the Struggles with Hostile Indians* (Dallas: Privately printed, 1923), pp. 12–15.

12.5.   The Ghost Dance

The following passage is from a lecture the newspaper reporter George H. Harries of the Washington Star *gave on his experiences in the Dakotas during the Ghost Dance troubles. He paints a sympathetic portrait of the dispossessed Sioux.*

The ghost dance, Mr. Harries said, "was undoubtedly religious, the ghost song a prayer. In all of that song there was not an improper expression. The singers, clad in ghost shirts and leggings, circled around the medicine man, each one chanting the rude melody to which hunger had set words that appealed to every feeling heart. "Give us to eat," was their cry. "Let us have health," they sang. "Allow not our wives and children to starve, but, O Great Spirit, fill the land with the buffalo and the bear and the fleet-footed deer," they prayed in unison." And why should they not pray? Has it come to pass in these United States that the right of any man to petition the Almighty in a harmless manner is to be abridged by force of arms? Must the Indian talk with his Creator only through the medium of a ready-made prayer book and bow before the throne of grace after a fashion that accords with the requirements of fine spun civilization? When the red man's soul writhes and chafes in the fetters a beneficent government has provided, must the Indian agent alone be the receptacle into which the story of grief can legally be poured? Could these questions be cried aloud so that the whole world might hear, millions on millions of voices would answer, No! And yet our government answered in the affirmative because an Indian agent, inexperienced and terrorized by fears that his feeble nature could not subdue, insisted that the presence of troops at Pine Ridge was absolutely necessary. The Indian police could have attended to the whole matter and the soldiers need never have been called from their posts. The power of the Indian police was never tested; troops were injudiciously summoned and open rebellion followed.

The Sioux is very tenacious of his rights—long and painful experience has taught him that laxity in dealing with the white race results disastrously for himself—so he felt as though his reservation had been invaded when the soldiers came and camped thereon. And yet he did not go on the warpath. He insisted that the great father was without jurisdiction as to the ghost dance and had sent soldiers on the reservation without cause. He protested, vainly and then, with great unanimity, left Pine Ridge for the comparative seclusion of the Bad Lands. That was rank rebellion. The Sioux simply said: "If you want my reservation you can have it," and retired leaving the troops and the agency employees in possession. Diplomacy, threats and the prospect of a hard winter brought the rebels back to Pine Ridge. Then Big Foot's band of Minnecongues from Cheyenne river made its appearance on the Porcupine and their arrival complicated the situation somewhat, for they were known to be vile characters. The seventh cavalry immediately moved out to intercept this aggregation of imported deviltry and when the troops and the Indians collided the battle of Wounded Knee was the result.

In less than two hours from the time of that fight the Ogallalas and Brules at Pine Ridge knew what had happened. Tepees were hurriedly struck, ponies caught and either saddled or hitched to wagons, guns were taken out of their hiding places, stores of ammunition opened up. There was the rattle of wheels, the dust-provoking but almost noiseless movement of unshod hoofs, the disappearance of the women and children, the appearance of mounted warriors on the hills just north of the agency, the yells of enraged men, the whistling of many bullets and the Sioux were at last on the warpath!

The ills of thirteen years—some imaginary, many very real—had borne fruit and for a while it seemed as though the deeds which crimsoned the frontier thirty or forty years ago were about to be more than duplicated. Wise counsel from friendly Indians proved, however, to be more powerful than the thirst for blood, and by nightfall the five or six thousand Ishmaelites were well on their way to the Bad Lands for the second time in a month. Only for a brief time was the Indian on the warpath. Theoretically he was a hostile until he made an alleged surrender of himself to Gen. Miles on January 15, but as a matter of fact he was not on the warpath but for a few hours on December 29. So far as the troops were concerned the Sioux would have fought at any moment, that was apparent at all times, but had he gone on the warpath his animosity would have been directed at every white settler within reach. Hundreds of the frontiersmen would have gone down in the strife, and a thousand blazing cabins and a score of desolated settlements would have marked the hostile course in South Dakota and Nebraska. Three thousand five hundred soldiers of the regular army and a thousand Nebraska militiamen must necessarily have failed to surround even an equal number of Indians had those Indians been intent on a general war. There was no general war. Not a single settler was killed, not a white man's home disturbed during the whole of the trouble. A few people lost cattle and horses—picked up by small bands of wandering Brules—and that was the greatest damage done the frontiersman by the Sioux in the winter of 1890–'91.

Why, even now the greater proportion of the soldiers who served in this last campaign sympathize heartily with the Indian. An officer of exalted rank, who commanded one of the bravest regiments on the reservation, said to me; "This whole proceeding is an outrage. The Government so treats these Indians that they can do nothing else than fight, and then it orders us out here to kill the victims of its duplicity. I have," said he, "been fighting Indians for many years, and personally have nothing on which to base anything like affection for them, yet there are times when I feel like throwing aside the uniform that honors me with its covering and donning in its place the blanket of the savage. Then I could fight and be sure that my cause had a just foundation."

Source: T. A. Bland, ed., *A Brief History of the Late Military Invasion of the Home of the Sioux* (Washington, DC: National Indian Defence Association, 1891), pp. 23–24.

12.6.   The Death of Sitting Bull and Wounded Knee

> *This early account from the popular press, in this case* Scribner's Magazine, *makes the connection between Sitting Bull's killing, Wounded Knee, and the deficiencies of government Indian policy. It is surprisingly even-handed for its time.*

There are two prominent events subsequent to the arrival of troops at Pine Ridge which have especially excited inquiry in the public mind and to which I will refer. The first is the arrest and death of Sitting Bull; the second is the affair of Wounded Knee. The limits of this article will only permit an outline of these incidents.

The arrest of Sitting Bull was, no doubt, a measure necessary to prevent further spreading of a revolt which largely emanated from him. Concerning his own dangerous intentions there can be no doubt. The evidence on this point is abundant and specific. The arrest was attempted under telegraphic instructions from General Ruger, at St. Paul, to Colonel Drum, commanding Fort Yates, the military post adjoining the Standing Rock Agency, under date of December 12th. It was the expressed wish of General Ruger that the military and the civil agent should co-operate in effecting the arrest. Fortunately entire harmony existed between Colonel Drum and Major McLaughlin. The agent wished to effect the arrest by means of the Indian police, so as to avoid unnecessary irritation to the followers of Sitting Bull, and at a time when the majority of these Indians would be absent from their camp drawing rations at the agency. This wise intention was frustrated by the unexpected attempt of Sitting Bull to leave the reservation. Therefore the arrest, instead of being attempted December 20th, was precipitated December 14th. Sitting Bull evidently intended to submit to his captors peaceably, but, while dressing, in his tent for the journey, he was incited to resistance by the outcries of his son, who berated the Indian policemen and exhorted his father not to allow himself to be taken. Upon coming out of his tent, under charge of the police, Sitting Bull yielded to his son's advice and called on his people to rescue him. In an instant a savage crowd of one hundred and fifty Indians attacked and fired upon the police. Almost immediately six of the police were killed or mortally wounded, and Sitting Bull was himself killed by one of the wounded police. The fight lasted about half an hour. The police soon drove the Indians, who far outnumbered them, from around the adjoining buildings and into the surrounding woods. During the fight women attacked the police with knives and clubs, but in every instance the latter simply disarmed and placed them under guard until the troops arrived, after which they were given their liberty. The highest praise for courage and ability was accorded the police for their part in this affair by the military officer commanding the troops who supported them.

Can American patriotism see nothing in the devotion of these men to duty, their loyalty to the flag, their constancy even unto death, which is worthy an enduring monument? Can American art find no inspiration, no elements of true dramatic emotion, in this pre-eminently American tragedy?

It were well if the same chisel which recorded in "eternal bronze" the sad and patient nobility of Lincoln might also fashion some memorial to the humble heroes of Standing Rock! The genius of Thorwaldsen and the fidelity of the Swiss Guard breathe forever in the dying Lion of Lucerne. May not the genius of some American sculptor and the fidelity of the Indian police find similar expression?

What is to be said of Wounded Knee, with its two hundred dead, its slaughtered women and children? Evidence from various reliable sources shows very clearly that Colonel Forsythe, the veteran officer in charge, did all that could be done by care, consideration, and firmness to prevent a conflict. He had provided a tent warmed with a Sibley stove for Big Foot, who was ill with pneumonia. He assured the Indians of kind treatment, but told them also that they must surrender their arms. He tried to avoid a search for weapons, but to this they forced him to resort. The explosion came during the process of search, and when a medicine-man incited them to resist and appealed to their fanaticism by assuring them that their sacred shirts were bullet-proof. Then one shot was fired by the Indians, and another and another. The Indians were wholly responsible in bringing on the fight. Whether in the desperate struggle which ensued there was or was not an unnecessary sacrifice of the lives of women and children is another question. From the fact that so many women and children were killed, and that their bodies were found far from the scene of action, and as though they were shot down while fleeing, it would look as though blind rage had been at work, in striking contrast to the moderation of the Indian police at the Sitting Bull fight when they were assailed by women.

But responsibility for the massacre of Wounded Knee, as for many another sad and similar event, rests more upon the shoulders of the citizens of the United States who permit the condition of savage ignorance, incompetent control, or Congressional indifference and inaction, than upon those of maddened soldiers, who having seen their comrades shot at their side are tempted to kill and destroy all belonging to the enemy within their reach. That the uprising ended with so little bloodshed the country may thank the patience and ability of General Miles. Perhaps had he taken the field earlier there might have been still less to mourn.

What is the remedy? What must be done to prevent such occurrences in future? The remedy is not far to seek nor does it require many words to state its essentials.

First, the people as a body must desire and demand of the President and of Congress better things. There must be a substantial unity of opinion among various bodies of citizens as to the main points of a remedy, and unity of action in securing it; a willingness to abandon minor points in order to secure the greater ones. The necessity for abandoning partisanship in considering this great national question should be frankly recognized. The words Democrat and Republican should be forgotten in dealing with Indian affairs. Even now there are sincere friends of the

Indians who are very sensitive to any criticism, no matter how just it may be, which reflects on their own party. This is a fatal block to progress. The great religious bodies, the Roman communion on the one side, and the Protestant communions on the other, should try to recognize the value of each other's work, at least as an instrument of civilization. There should be greater co-operation between the civil and military branches of the Government, less drawing into hostile camps with the idea that there is a military severity and inhumanity on the one side, and unmitigated rascality on the other. There are military officers who would make capital Indian agents, and civil agents could be found, if the right way were taken to seek them, who can manage Indians without the intrusion of troops.

If, then, a public sentiment can be aroused on this question at once powerful, intelligent, united, and persistent, these are the simple principles and the flexible system which it should demand:

1. A single, intelligent, experienced, responsible head to control the Indian service under the President—a man who shall be permitted to form his plans and to carry them to fruition along the lines of well-defined and sound principles, and free from partisan interference.

2. An Indian service conducted in absolute harmony with the principles of Civil Service Reform—the principle of merit, not of spoils. Only thoroughly qualified men, should be appointed to serve as Indian agents.

3. The prompt appropriation of funds by Congress to permit the education of all Indian youth, and the effective management of the service. No more Indian boys and girls should be permitted to grow up in ignorance and savagery; also the prompt passage of laws recommended by the Indian Department and requisite to protect the interests of the Indians.

But to do these things, as Bishop Hare has well said, and to solve "the problem that remains, the spoils system, will require 'the uprising of a great people.'"

Source: Herbert Welsh, "The Meaning of the Dakota Outbreak," *Scribner's Magazine*, April 1891, pp. 451–452.

12.7.   The Aftermath of Wounded Knee

Following the battle Indian casualties were unceremoniously dumped into a mass grave, much like the treatment of Nazi concentration camp victims during World War II. According to this account, the soldiers perform their duties, but not without a degree of compassion.

A long trench was dug and into it were thrown all the bodies, piled one upon another like so much cordwood, until the pit was full, when the earth was heaped over them and the funeral was complete. Many of the bodies were stripped by the whites, who went out in order to get the "ghost shirts," and the frozen bodies were thrown into the trench stiff and naked. They were only dead Indians. As one of the burial party said, "It was a thing to melt the heart of a man, if it was of stone, to see those little children, with their bodies shot to pieces, thrown naked into the pit." The dead soldiers had already been brought in and buried decently at the agency. When the writer visited the spot the following winter, the Indians had put up a wire fence around the trench and smeared the posts with sacred red medicine paint.

A baby girl of only three or four months was found under the snow, carefully wrapped up in a shawl, beside her dead mother, whose body was pierced by two bullets. On her head was a little cap of buckskin, upon which the American flag was embroidered in bright beadwork. She had lived through all the exposure, being only slightly frozen, and soon recovered after being brought in to the agency. Her mother being killed, and, in all probability, her father also, she was adopted by General Colby, commanding the Nebraska state troops. The Indian women in camp gave her the poetic name of Zitkala-noni, "Lost Bird," and by the family of her adoption she was baptized under the name of Marguerite. She is now (1896) living in the general's family at Washington, a chubby little girl 6 years of age, as happy with her dolls and playthings as a little girl of that age ought to be.

Another little girl about 5 years of age was picked up on the battlefield and brought in by the Indian police on the afternoon of the fight. She was adopted by George Sword, captain of the Indian police, and is now living with him under the name of Jennie Sword, a remarkably pretty little girl, gentle and engaging in her manners.

A little boy of four years, the son of Yellow Bird, the medicine man, was playing on his pony in front of a tipi when the firing began. As he described it some time ago in lisping English: "My father ran and fell down and the blood came out of his mouth [he was shot through the head], and then a soldier put his gun up to my white pony's nose and shot him, and then I ran and a policeman got me." As his father was thus killed and his mother was already dead, he was adopted by Mrs Lucy Arnold, who had been a teacher among the Sioux and knew his family before the trouble began. She had already given him his name, Herbert Zitkalazi, the last word being the Sioux form of his father's name, "Yellow Bird." She brought him back with her to Washington, where he soon learned English and became a general favorite of all who knew him for his affectionate disposition and unusual intelligence, with genuine boyish enthusiasm in all he undertook. . . . His adopted mother having resumed her school work among his tribe, he is now back with her, attending school under her supervision at Standing Rock, where, as in Washington, he seems to be a natural leader among those of his own age. When we think of these children and consider that only by the merest accident they escaped the death that overtook a hundred other children at Wounded Knee, who may all have had in themselves the same possibilities of affection, education, and happy usefulness, we can understand the sickening meaning of such affairs as the Chivington massacre in Colorado and the Custer fight on the Washita, where the newspaper reports merely that "the enemy was surprised and the Indian camp destroyed."

Source: J. W. Powell, ed., *Fourteenth Annual Report of the Bureau of Ethnology*, Part 2 (Washington, DC: U.S. Government Printing Office, 1896), pp. 878–881.

ANNOTATED SELECTED BIBLIOGRAPHY

Brown, Dee. *Bury My Heart at Wounded Knee: An Indian History of the American West*. New York: Holt, Rinehart and Winston, 1970. Brown struck a chord with the 1960s generation with this best-selling history of the West from the Indian perspective.

Mooney, James. *The Ghost Dance and the Sioux Outbreak of 1890*. 1896. Reprint. North Dighton, MA: JG Press, 1996. First published in 1896, this is James Mooney's firsthand account of the background, development, and practice of the Ghost Dance as he spent two years working for the U.S. Bureau of Ethnology.

Neihardt, John G. *Black Elk Speaks*. New York: Morrow, 1932. Reprint. Lincoln: University of Nebraska Press, 1961. The legendary "book of visions" by the Sioux warrior and medicine man, who witnessed the life and death of the Plains Indian in the late nineteenth century.

Smith, Paul Chaat, and Robert Allen Warrior. *Like a Hurricane: The Indian Movement from Alcatraz to Wounded Knee*. New York: New Press, 1996. Gripping account of Indian activism in the late 1960s.

Utley, Robert. *The Last Days of the Sioux Nation*. New Haven: Yale University Press, 1963. Excellent treatment of the complex and controversial relationship between the Sioux and the white invaders.

Wilson, Jack, *The Earth Shall Weep: A History of Native America*. New York: Grove Press, 1998. A critically acclaimed history of the Native Americans' struggle for survival against the tide of invading peoples and cultures.

13 _____

The Dust Bowl: Transition on the Farming Frontier

The Dust Bowl of the 1930s was an environmental, economic, and social disaster all wrapped up in one. It focused attention on American farm policy and on the scarce resources farmers could expect as they moved beyond the 100th meridian. But, most of all, it put an end to an American tradition and dream—a farming frontier where individuals and families could fashion a better life using traditional farming skills that had succeeded in the well-watered East. Perhaps presidential candidate Franklin D. Roosevelt summed it up best while on the campaign trail in 1932, when he noted, "Our last frontier has long since been reached and there is practically no more free land."[1]

Roosevelt's bleak declaration was only partly true. The frontier era may have indeed ended, but there were still millions of uninhabited acres in the West. Conditioned to a land of inexhaustible resources, farmers compensated for falling prices in the 1930s by breaking more sod for wheat, giving little thought to soil conservation practices. They paid a price for that neglect.

The Dust Bowl would prove to be the era's greatest conservationist challenge. After nine years of drought, exacerbated by decades of overplowing and overgrazing, the federal government was forced to come to the aid of Plains farmers. Although new soil conservation strategies were introduced by government agronomists, the main aid came in the form of public assistance. According to historian Walter P. Webb, the public domain was the "original relief fund for farmers," but by the 1930s Plains farmers had been transformed into a new dependent class.[2]

The Plains region east of the Rocky Mountains, which explorers had dismissed as the Great American Desert, unsuited to agriculture, proved a formidable barrier to settlement prior to the Civil War. Following the war, cattlemen dominated the Great Plains until the late 1880s. Agricultural development came in fits and starts before new technology, irrigation and dry farming, and other innovations made agriculture possible and even profitable on the Plains by the end of the century.

Farmers were at first put off by the harsh climate and tough prairie sod, but these hardships would not squelch the land fever engendered by prospects of free or cheap land under the Homestead Act. The act worked relatively well in the East, where rainfall was plentiful and dependable. But past the 100th meridian water was a scarce commodity. Despite the early spring rains on the Plains, months could pass before the next deluge.

Periodically between 1870 and the 1930s the rains stopped. Cycles of drought have taken their toll on Great Plains farmers since the 1870s, when unscrupulous land promoters lured thousands of homesteaders to the region. Between 1870 and 1900, major agricultural attention focused on the formerly reviled Great American Desert, which included the semiarid grasslands that stretched between the 98th meridian and the Rocky Mountains, and from Canada to the Rio Grande. This region of low rainfall and generally diverse climate was unlike any prospective farming frontier. Still, the intrepid farmer came. Between 1870 and 1900 "more farm land was brought under cultivation . . . than in the entire previous history of the nation,"[3] with most of the increase taking place on the central Plains.

In the 1870s Plains farmers made the transition from subsistence to commercial agriculture, leading to intensive exploitation of the environment. The land was denuded of the natural grasses that had covered the rich soils for centuries and irreparably damaged by the new farming technologies that cut the root system in order to turn over the sod. Once the soil was exposed to the elements, millions of acres faced erosion. Wind and drought were the great scourge of Plains farming. Hot winds scorched the crops and then lifted dry topsoil, creating immense swirls of dust that sometimes landed hundreds of miles away.

In eastern Colorado a searing drought in 1889 and 1890 wiped out crops, leaving hundreds of farmers impoverished. During the late 1880s a widespread and damaging drought halted the land and agricultural boom on the central Great Plains of Nebraska, Kansas, and Colorado. In 1890 an even worse drought stretched from the Texas Panhandle to the Canadian border, leading many farmers to abandon the land. While rainfall came the following year, within three years drought and crop failure would return once more.

Many farmers moved onto the Plains during the great wheat bonanza of World War I, when good crop prices and a string of wet years resulted in thousands of acres of grasslands being plowed up. Farmers were encouraged by federal subsidies to increase production to keep up with the war effort. As a consequence, more lands were opened for wheat and cotton growing. Following the war, high American tariffs, together with the resumption of European food production, drastically reduced American exports of grain and fibers, creating an agricultural depression in the West. In order to make more money, farmers had to plow up more land, and in the process further reduced the native grasses.

Natural disaster only added to the economic hardships. The introduction of new farm machinery during the war years (1917–1918) reduced the amount of human labor needed to produce crops. The topography of the Great Plains was perfectly suited to mechanized agriculture, and by the 1930s what took fifty-eight hours to plant and harvest one hundred years earlier could be accomplished in just three hours. As a result, farmers could till more land in less time, leading to the creation of larger farms and increased production.

When drought hit, the exposed topsoil was lifted into dark clouds that filled the horizon. By the time the weather cycle of the 1930s hit, the stage already had been set for the Dust Bowl disaster. The storms began in 1931. Topsoil on the northern Great Plains just blew away. For the next ten years the dust storms hit other sections of the Plains as well—the southern Plains worst of all. By late morning it was pitch dark, like nightfall. Everything was covered with dirt and dust. No matter how one covered a window or a door, the dust came in. The storms continued through 1935. According to the Soil Conservation Service, by the time the dust storms ended perhaps 300 million tons of topsoil had been swept off the Great Plains.

In April 1935, an Associated Press reporter coined the term "dust bowl," after a turbulent dust storm blew across the southern Great Plains region stretching through Kansas, Colorado, Oklahoma, Texas, and New Mexico. The Dust Bowl of the 1930s is generally considered one of the worst environmental disasters in the nation's history. However, there is some argument as to the exact cause of the calamity. Some scholars suggest that it was caused by the agricultural practices of the day, noting that in less than fifty years rapacious, unsophisticated farmers, through overgrazing and careless plowing, turned 97 million acres of the richest soil in America into a great dust bowl that darkened the skies and swept soil hundreds of miles away. During the proceedings of one drought committee convened to study the problem, an official seemed to have hit the nail right on the head, stating, "The basic cause of the present Great Plains situation is our attempt to impose upon the region a system of agriculture to which the Plains are not adapted or to bring into a semi-arid region methods which are suitable . . . only for a humid region."[4]

Others saw it differently, viewing the farmers as "innocent victims" of severe drought. Beginning in 1928, the Plains faced a seven-year drought,

perhaps the most prolonged in American history. What was most per-
plexing to the failed farmers of the Great Plains, as they watched the
rich topsoil blow away, was how earlier generations had gotten away
with turning the high Plains "grass side down,"[5] and escaped punishment. Most of the farmers who moved onto the Plains in the 1920s were
indeed skilled professionals who had moved to the wrong place at the
wrong time. Lured by the artificially high prices of the war years and
scheming land promoters, many felt, when the dust years hit, that the
government had a hand in their dilemma and should share the blame
for encouraging the settlement of the arid grasslands.

Continuing a tradition that has existed in the West since the first settlers asked the federal government to build roads and protect them from
Indians, during the 1920s and 1930s western farmers lent their voices to
the chorus requesting federal relief. President Roosevelt did adopt several agricultural relief measures as part of his New Deal program, but
Roosevelt was pragmatic when dealing with land policy. He understood
that agricultural overproduction stimulated in part by World War I had
encouraged the farming of millions of acres of land unsuited for agriculture. By the 1930s New Dealers were calling for a reduction of crop
production. In order to do this, the federal government would have to
curtail expectations of success among prospective farmers. The drought
of the 1930s was unparalleled in recent history. In one program the federal government purchased livestock and either shipped them to better
watered regions or slaughtered them. Otherwise the cattle would slowly
die where they were. According to one historian, most of the income
received by Plains farmers in 1934 came from government programs that
purchased their cattle or paid them to restrict crop production. Federal
aid saved the farmer and the cattleman. By doing so, westerners paid a
price—more federal control of public lands. Soon cattle grazing on the
public domain came under federal supervision. The next step was re-
ducing the amount of land being farmed in an attempt to bring back the
native grasses and reduce erosion. However, when the rains returned,
farmers reverted to their old destructive ways. As one environmental
historian stated, "The government's programs had become a means of
relief in bad times and something to be ignored in good times."[6]

When Dust Bowl victims were not blaming the government or the
weather, they were pointing their fingers at nefarious land promoters
who promised something that nature could not bring—dependable farming conditions. For many Plains settlers and a legion of future homesteaders, the Dust Bowl put an end, at least temporarily, to the frontier
optimism that had so dominated the American consciousness for generations. For potential westerners, the onset of the Dust Bowl years
meant that "the dreaming is finished."[7]

The Dust Bowl was not just an environmental disaster but a human

one as well, causing thousands of farmers to leave their homesteads. Soon after the first hint of drought, "Okies" from Oklahoma and "Arkies" from Arkansas joined the procession of farmers, businessmen, oil workers, and other Depression casualties hitting the road for California. As many as 300,000 residents of Missouri, Oklahoma, Texas, and Arkansas headed for California, in one of the largest migrations west since the California Gold Rush.

Despite the stereotypical portrait of the Joad family in John Steinbeck's novel *The Grapes of Wrath* (1939), the majority of those moving to California were not farmers but were more urban types who opted for urban areas. During lean economic times California was not a favorable destination for Asian and Hispanic laborers seeking opportunity, and it proved no more inviting to the rural migrants in the Depression years than it had in the 1880s, when Chinese workers were barred from immigrating.

In years past, when the California gold fields played out or Indians forced farmers from their lands, fortune seekers returned to the East. But the exodus of the 1930s was different, with destinations now in the West, ranging from the Rocky Mountains to the Pacific Coast. A tremendous demographic shift occurred during this period, with many people giving up farming altogether and moving to more urban areas. Once part of an optimistic homesteading population, many moved on with broken dreams. Photographers such as Margaret Bourke-White captured their plight in shantytowns strewn across the West. The reputation of the American West suffered in the 1930s. All of the scientific and technical explanations in the world could not salvage the luster that had been lost to the Dust Bowl years. Several lines in poet Archibald MacLeish's ode to the "vanishing" West, *Land of the Free*, refer to a legendary West that "is behind us now." This theme would resonate in the years following the New Deal, until a "New West" emerged as the Sun Belt in the post–World War II era. But that West no longer included the Plains in its promise.

Did western farmers suffer more than farmers in other regions of the country? All farmers experienced a decline in agricultural prices, high interest rates and surpluses, and indebtedness. But with western farming taking place under marginal environmental conditions, together with a decade of drought, the 1930s were a disaster on the Plains.

While agricultural conservation proved a failure on the Great Plains during the New Deal years, farmers slowly made the transition to new farming techniques as ecological principles of land use became more acceptable. In the 1970s deep well irrigation was seen as the new panacea for aridity. While irrigation had been introduced to the Great Plains in the 1870s, the rivers it depended on proved an unreliable source of water. One hundred years later farmers were able to tap reservoirs deep un-

derground (up to 600 feet or more). Irrigated farming has proved rewarding for farmers in the Dust Bowl region. According to one source, one former Dust Bowl county in Kansas during the 1970s "was consistently ranked as one of the wealthiest in per capita income in the United States."[8] By the 1980s, though, farmers were again leaving the Plains, driven down by high credit costs and driven away by low agricultural prices. According to the 2000 census, the Plains states suffered the largest percentage of population loss in the previous decade.

Drought and dust were nothing new to the arid West. Nor were cycles of boom and bust. Once-booming mining towns from Tombstone to Nevada City offer mute testimony to the illusory riches that led thousands to follow the gold and silver rushes of the nineteenth century. So, too, do the silent grasses now flourishing on the Great Plains offer homage to the once-booming towns that grew up in the shadow of land speculators, who counted on their guile and inexpensive farm equipment to "buck the odds against the Great American Desert."[9] What farmers did not count on were the rains that never came. Ignoring the warnings of Pike, Long, Powell, and others who knew better, intrepid farmers cast their lot with the miners, cattlemen, and timber men who had come to the Plains before them. One can only wonder how Zebulon Pike or Stephen Long would have replied to one American in the 1930s who commented, "Isn't it astonishing that in America it should take one generation to reduce its prolific nature to a condition like the Gobi Desert, which was a million years in the making."[10]

NOTES

1. Quoted in Robert V. Hine and John Mack Faragher, *The American West: A New Interpretative History* (New Haven: Yale University Press, 2000), p. 461.

2. Robert G. Athearn, Quoted in *The Mythic West in Twentieth-Century America* (Lawrence: University Press of Kansas, 1986), p. 83.

3. John F. Stover, *American Railroads* (Chicago: University of Chicago Press, 1961), p. 98.

4. Quoted in Richard Lowitt, *The New Deal and the West* (Bloomington: Indiana University Press, 1984), p. 42.

5. Quoted in Athearn, *Mythic West*, p. 85.

6. Richard White, *"It's Your Misfortune and None of My Own": A New History of the American West* (Norman: University of Oklahoma Press, 1991), p. 481.

7. Athearn, *Mythic West*, pp. 78–104.

8. Donald Worster, *Dust Bowl: The Southern Plains in the 1930s* (New York: Oxford University Press, 1979), p. 235.

9. Athearn, *Mythic West*, p. 80.

10. Quoted in Lowitt, *New Deal and the West*, pp. 34–35.

DOCUMENTS

13.1.   A Remedy for Agricultural Overproduction (1933)

---

*In 1933 President Franklin Roosevelt and more than thirty ad-
visors grappled with producing a farm bill that combined crop
controls designed to cut production and increase prices. It was
hoped that at the same time the bill would introduce new conservation practices to restore the soil. The result was the Agricultural Adjustment Act of 1938. It would be declared
unconstitutional by the Supreme Court in 1936. However, two
years later the act of 1938 proved acceptable and constitutional
and would provide the foundation for farm policy for several
decades. This act was enacted as an alternative and replacement
for the farm subsidy policies found unworkable in the 1933
AAA. The following passage from the 1933 act declares a state
of emergency and describes the new federal agricultural policy.*

DECLARATION OF EMERGENCY

That the present acute economic emergency being in part the consequence of a severe and increasing disparity between the prices of agricultural and other commodities, which disparity has largely destroyed
the purchasing power of farmers for industrial products, has broken
down the orderly exchange of commodities, and has seriously impaired
the agricultural assets supporting the national credit structure, it is
hereby declared that these conditions in the basic industry of agriculture
have affected transactions in agricultural commodities with a national
public interest, have burdened and obstructed the normal currents of
commerce in such commodities, and render imperative the immediate
enactment of title I of this Act.

DECLARATION OF POLICY

Sec. 2. It is hereby declared to be the policy of Congress—
(1) To establish and maintain such balance between the production
and consumption of agricultural commodities, and such marketing conditions therefor, as will reestablish prices to farmers at a level that will
give agricultural commodities a purchasing power with respect to articles that farmers buy, equivalent to the purchasing power of agricultural
commodities in the base period. The base period in the case of all agricultural commodities except tobacco shall be the prewar period, August

1909–July 1914. In the case of tobacco, the base period shall be the post-war period, August 1919–July 1929.

(2) To approach such equality of purchasing power by gradual correction of the present inequalities therein at as rapid a rate as is deemed feasible in view of the current consumptive demand in domestic and foreign markets.

(3) To protect the consumers' interest by readjusting farm production at such level as will not increase the percentage of the consumers' retail expenditures for agricultural commodities, or products derived therefrom, which is returned to the farmer, above the percentage which was returned to the farmer in the prewar period, August 1909–July 1914.

Source: U.S. Statutes at Large 48 (1933):31–38.

13.2.   Letters from a Dust Bowl Farmer (1933–1936)

The following passages are excerpted from letters submitted by Caroline A. Henderson (1877–1966) to the Atlantic Monthly *during the 1930s. Some of the published letters were part of an ongoing correspondence with a friend in Maryland named Evelyn Harris. They offer a poignant chronicle of one of the darkest eras in Great Plains agriculture. What differentiates Henderson from the typical farmer's wife was that she was a graduate of Mt. Holyoke College (1901), a prestigious college in Massachusetts, in an era when most women did not go to college. Brought up on a farm in Iowa, Henderson taught school after college before a serious illness forced her to give up her teaching career. In 1906 she returned to her roots, taking up a homestead in Oklahoma. She soon married a farmer, and both worked the ranch until the 1950s. They died in 1966 and their ashes were laid to rest in the center of the land that they had sweated over most of their adult lives.*

The September 17, 1932 letter from Caroline to Evelyn describes her plight in the context of widespread Depression conditions. In the 1935 and 1936 letters Henderson describes Dust Bowl conditions and then comments on the realities of pioneering on the twentieth-century Great Plains.

EVA, OKLAHOMA
September 17, 1932

MY DEAR EVELYN,

Lest you think that we are the sole darlings of misfortune, I might mention the neighboring farmer who sold his crop from 75 acres at 30

cents and had $12 left above combining expenses to pay for his seed, for the use of his land, for the labor of preparing the ground, drilling the wheat, marketing the crop, and for board for the combine hands; or another neighbor who sold $49 worth of wheat from 250 acres and owed one fourth of it for rent. Sadder still, I might tell of the man who kept on persistently trying to raise wheat before anyone else here thought it practicable. He did at last succeed in showing that over a series of years wheat is probably our most dependable crop. But troubles in his family, some years of short crops, and the low prices of the past three seasons have broken him. He has lost his 960 acres of land and most of his stock. He is now trying desperately, and I think without much chance of success, to get a government loan to buy back a few of his cattle and start all over again—old, half-blind, almost barehanded—in a Texas valley, where, as he told us, he hopes to avoid the mistakes he has made here.

The rain for which we were hoping so eagerly when I wrote last has never come. Indeed, we have had no effective moisture since early in June. One good rain during the summer would have given us at least roughage for our stock. As it is, the sowed cane and Sudan grass died down when it was six inches high, and our crops of maize and Kafir corn are little better—hardly a start on what we shall require for winter feed. I really do not know what we shall do. Our choice seems to lie between sacrificing the cattle at the ruinous prices now prevailing—we recently sold five well-grown young steers for $122.50—or trying in some as yet unthought-of way to get roughage for them through the winter.

The situation throughout the country is much more serious, I believe, than many people suppose. Think of the loss of homes, the decrease in land values, the idle shops and idle men, the closed banks, delinquent taxes, rents hopelessly overdue, children deprived of school privileges, thousands of young men and women roaming over the country freed from the normal restraints of orderly social conditions. A neighbor recently told us that he had counted eighty-five such wanderers on one freight train in northern Texas. Just a few days ago I talked with a merchant who was elated because, as he said, even the most destitute folk in St. Louis are making no complaints about their condition. He regarded this as a hopeful sign, but it seems to me a sign of lethargy unworthy of a people with the history and traditions of America behind them.

. . .

EVA, OKLAHOMA
June 30, 1935

MY DEAR EVELYN:—

. . . Wearing our shade hats, with handkerchiefs tied over our faces and vaseline in our nostrils, we have been trying to rescue our home from the accumulations of wind-blown dust which penetrates wherever air can go. It is an almost hopeless task, for there is rarely a day when at some time the dust clouds do not roll over. "Visibility" approaches zero and everything is covered again with a silt-like deposit which may vary in depth from a film to actual ripples on the kitchen floor. I keep oiled cloths on the window sills and between the upper and lower sashes. They help just a little to retard or collect the dust. Some seal the windows with the gummed-paper strips used in wrapping parcels, but no method is fully effective. We buy what appears to be red cedar saw-dust with oil added to use in sweeping our floors, and do our best to avoid inhaling the irritating dust.

In telling you of these conditions I realize that I expose myself to charges of disloyalty to this western region. A good Kansas friend suggests that we should imitate the Californian attitude toward earthquakes and keep to ourselves what we know about dust storms. Since the very limited rains of May in this section gave some slight ground for renewed hope, optimism has been the approved policy. Printed articles or statements by journalists, railroad officials, and secretaries of small-town Chambers of Commerce have heralded too enthusiastically the return of prosperity to the drouth region. And in our part of the country that is the one durable basis for any prosperity whatever. There is nothing else to build upon. But you wished to know the truth, so I am telling you the actual situation, though I freely admit that the facts are themselves often contradictory and confusing.

Early in May, with no more grass or even weeds on our 640 acres than on your kitchen floor, and even the scanty remnants of dried grasses from last year cut off and blown away, we decided, like most of our neighbors, to ship our cattle to grass in the central part of the state.

· · ·

January 28, 1936

Dear Evelyn:—

· · ·

On the whole it is not surprising that here and there some bitterness should have been felt and expressed, perhaps immoderately, over the recent AAA [Agricultural Adjustment Act] decision in the Supreme Court. People here, business men as well as the farmers themselves, realize that the benefit payments under the AAA and the wage payments from Federal work projects are all that have saved a large territory here from abandonment. A December statement by the Soil Conservation service reports an area in five states, including part or all of sixty-eight counties and 87,900 square miles of territory, as in need of active measures for protection and control of the dust-storm menace. Mr. Bennett, director of the service, regards this as the greatest "physical problem facing the country to-day." I was astonished to find by a little primary arithmetic that the area involved is equal to that of all the New England States, with New Jersey and Maryland and about half of Delaware added for good measure.

The desolation of the countryside would admittedly have meant the ruin of the small towns, entirely dependent as they are upon country patronage. It will also mean—if it must ever be abandoned through utter exhaustion of resources and sheer inability to hang on any longer—a creeping eastward into more settled and productive territory of the danger and losses originating in the arid wastelands. It is a problem now that no merely individual action can handle successfully.

But to return briefly to the Supreme Court decision. It has naturally been the cause of much regrettable confusion. It would probably have caused even more disturbance had there not been a background of hope that something may yet be done to compensate for the disappointments necessarily involved.

Farmers are not asking for special favors. They ask only an even chance as compared with other workers. But people don't understand.

Perhaps the many books on pioneer life with the usual successful and happy outcome have helped to give a wrong impression and perpetuate the idea that country people live on wild game and fish and fruits and in general on the free bounty of heaven. Many people have no idea of the cash expense of operating a farm to-day, or the work and planning required to keep the wheels going round, to say nothing of a decent living or suitable education for the children. This year we are keeping a separate account of expenses for car, truck, and tractor, all of which are old and frequently in need of repair. I fear we shall be horrified and discouraged by the close of the year. Not that I should willingly return to the long, slow trips of fifteen miles to town in a jolting wagon. Not that I want to take it out of the flesh and blood of horses in the hot heavy work of seed time and harvest—if they come again. But we can't combine the modern methods of work with the income of our early pioneering, when $200 used to cover all of a year's expense.

Sources: Caroline Henderson to Evelyn Harris, "Letters of Two Women Farmers," *Atlantic Monthly*, Vol. 152, August 1933, p. 355; Caroline Henderson, "Letters from the Dust Bowl," *Atlantic Monthly*, Vol. 157, May 1936, pp. 540–541, 545–547.

13.3.   A Farmer Criticizes New Deal Agricultural Policy (1935)

Not everything Caroline Henderson wrote was accepted for publication. The following passage, edited by Virginia C. Purdy, is from an essay by Henderson that was rejected by the Atlantic

Monthly in 1935. Henderson demonstrates a keen understand-
ing of New Deal agricultural policies, recognizing their strengths
and weaknesses.

I did not vote for the New Deal and certainly not for the old one. I can
therefore claim no credit for its accomplishments or responsibility for its
mistakes. I am not appointed to defend it. But I do like fair play. There
are certain accusations made against the present attempts at social reconstruction that are wickedly unjust so far as we can determine from
local conditions.

One of these criticisms relates to the alleged wastefulness of relief administration and the useless or damaging work projects attempted. In
our county with a population of 14,000, between November 15, 1933,
and December 27, 1934, the public work pay rolls under CWA [Civil
Works Administration] and FERA [Federal Emergency Relief Adminis-
tration] are reported as totaling $331,760.69. The sum expended seems
to us truly enormous, and the extent of aid required is most unusual in
a section where pioneer traditions of self-help and neighborly assistance
are still strong. Yet certain facts should be considered. In the late summer
of 1934 the county relief administration reported that they had been operating on about a 3% margin. In one week when the total expense
amounted to $7222, of this sum $214 had been expended on office force,
supervision, all administrative expenses! This, too, in a county of "magnificent distances" requiring much driving over an area 34 miles wide
and 60 long, almost twice as large as the state of Rhode Island and nearly
as large as Delaware. Even if this 3% overhead expense were doubled
or quadrupled, it would still be far below the cost alleged by some severe
critics.

Of highways ruined, of projects resulting in actual damage to their
communities, we have seen nothing. On the contrary, our roads have
been immensely improved, steep hills cut down, valleys filled and reservoirs constructed; the crooked has been made straight "and the rough
places plain." If mere dollars were to be considered, the actually destitute
in our section could undoubtedly have been fed and clothed more
cheaply than the work projects have been carried out. But in our national
economy manhood must be considered as well as money. People employed to do some useful work may retain their self-respect to a degree
impossible under cash relief. My own personal resentment has been
roused, not so much by the fact of this type of work as by our national
inability so to regulate our affairs that we can make full use of the machines devised to relieve men of their most crude and exhausting labors.
The sight of a large group of men building up a graded road by pick
and shovel is indeed a reproach to all of us. I feel ashamed to drive by
and see our own neighbors so employed. The correction of such obvious

mismanagement may require us to accept a fundamentally different theory of the meaning and the rewards of labor, a new system of more fairly distributed opportunities for wholesome and creative leisure for all.

There is possibly an anomaly about the construction of wide and expensive roads in an area not at present entirely self-supporting. Yet they remain as a permanent and forward-looking type of improvement which helps us still to cling to our dreams for the future. We hope that as the years go by they may not be used exclusively by the jackrabbits. And such work has made state and national governments and the possibility of cooperation for human need a vivid reality in the homes of our people as no policy of direct relief could possibly have done—this too, without humiliation or the fostering of habits of dependence.

A second anxiety, whether real or assumed, relates to the fear of widespread and serious degradation of moral character, resulting from the various relief projects. In my own judgment such anxiety is quite unwarranted; though I can speak only of the conditions with which we are familiar. We have not personally asked for any of the relief work—yet. But we know that people are eager for it. When a man will drive several miles to some FERA project, work with his horses for the required time under any weather conditions, spend most of his earnings for high-priced stock feed so as to conserve the means of his family's livelihood and be ready for farming again whenever rain may come, the danger of his becoming a habitual pauper through government aid seems to me quite negligible. If we must worry so much over the ruinous effects of "made work" on people of this type, why haven't we been worrying for generations over the character of the idlers to whom some accident of birth or inheritance has given wealth unmeasured, unearned and unappreciated? If we must continue to protest against the AAA efforts to effect some fair balance between prices of farm and industrial products because of increased cost to the consumer, why haven't we for a century been crying out against the similar effect of protective tariffs, imposed with the conscious purpose of maintaining prices sufficient to build up and increase enormous fortunes for a comparatively few?

A third criticism is based on the overworked idea of "regimentation," concerning which certain syndicate writers and politicians have wasted too much ink and breath. It would be interesting to trace the recent history of this formidable word and determine if possible the true cause of all the professional shuddering over this alleged menace to American liberties. It might be enlightening to one of these prophets of gloom if he could drop into some little country schoolhouse crowded with farmers assembled to consider some of the control programs for agriculture. I have attended nearly all of the wheat meetings in our own district and the most distinct impression received was the entire absence of anything like standardization or compulsion. To be sure, most of the men wore blue denim overalls and blue or gray shirts. But there uniformity ended. Each man's problems were considered individually and no two were exactly alike. All sorts of human relationships were involved, obligations to tenants, landlords, or relatives. Everyone's interest was thoroughly considered. There was nothing approaching violent partisanship or over-urgency in presenting the plans. We were among our neighbors and friends, trying to do what was best for all. One who could attend such a meeting and then go out and lament over the "regimentation" of agriculture would have to be either dull or insincere. If our experience is exceptional, then it is at least worth recording as a hint of what might be accomplished by more general cooperation. Signers of the acreage control contracts are asked to report on their production at the close of the year as a basis for further planning. If this business-like procedure is "regimentation," anyone who feels inclined remains of course quite free to become excited about it. Many of these self-appointed defenders of freedom seem to know nothing of the loss of liberty attendant upon seriously adverse economic conditions. No regimentation is more cruel than that of extreme poverty. The cramped and barren lives of millions of share-croppers in the southern states, the deplorable conditions in some of the coal-mining areas, the slum districts in almost any large city, are a pitiful contradiction to our boasted "inalienable right to life, liberty, and the pursuit of happiness."

Source: Virginia C. Purdy, ed., " 'Dust to Eat': A Document from the Dust Bowl," *Chronicles of Oklahoma*, Vol. 58 No. 4 (Winter 1980–1981), pp. 448–451.

13.4.   Margaret Bourke-White Reports the Dust Bowl (1935)

Some of the most memorable images of the Dust Bowl years came from the camera and pen of noted photojournalist Margaret Bourke-White. In a report for The Nation *magazine, Bourke-White describes the impact of the mid-1930s drought on a 300,000 square mile area as she offers a memorable report from both airplane and ground transport.*

Vitamin K they call it—the dust which sifts under the door sills, and stings in the eyes, and seasons every spoonful of food. The dust storms have distinct personalities, rising in formation like rolling clouds, creeping up silently like formless fog, approaching violently like a tornado. Where has it come from? It provides topics of endless speculation. Red, it is the topsoil from Oklahoma; brown, it is the fertile earth of western Kansas; the good grazing land of Texas and New Mexico sweeps by as a murky yellow haze. Or, tracing it locally, "My uncle will be along pretty soon," they say; "I just saw his farm go by."

The town dwellers stack their linen in trunks, stuff wet cloths along the window sills, estimate the tons of sand in the darkened air above them, paste cloth masks on their faces with adhesive tape, and try to joke about Vitamin K. But on the farms and ranches there is an attitude of despair.

By coincidence I was in the same parts of the country where last year I photographed the drought. As short a time as eight months ago there was an attitude of false optimism. "Things will get better," the farmers would say. "We're not as hard hit as other states. The government will help out. This can't go on." But this year there is an atmosphere of utter hopelessness. Nothing to do. No use digging out your chicken coops and pigpens after the last "duster" because the next one will be coming along soon. No use trying to keep the house clean. No use fighting off that foreclosure any longer. No use even hoping to give your cattle anything to chew on when their food crops have literally blown out of the ground.

It was my job to avoid dust storms, since I was commissioned by an airplane company to take photographs of its course from the air, but frequently the dust storms caught up with us, and as we were grounded anyway, I started to photograph them. Thus I saw five dust-storm states from the air and from the ground.

In the last several years there have been droughts and sand storms and dusters, but they have been localized, and always one state could borrow from another. But this year the scourge assumes tremendous proportions. Dust storms are bringing distress and death to 300,000 square miles; they are blowing over all of Kansas, all of Nebraska and Wyoming, strips of the Dakotas, about half of Colorado, sections of Iowa and Missouri, the greater part of Oklahoma, and the northern panhandle of Texas, extending into the eastern parts of New Mexico.

Last year I saw farmers harvesting the Russian thistle. Never before had they thought of feeding thistles to cattle. But this prickly fodder became precious for food. This year even the Russian thistles are dying out and the still humbler soap weed becomes as vital to the farmer as the fields of golden grain he tended in the past. Last year's thistle-fed cattle dwindled to skin and bone. This year's herds on their diet of soap weed develop roughened hides, ugly growths around the mouth, and lusterless eyes.

Years of the farmers' and ranchers' lives have gone into the building up of their herds. Their herds were like their families to them. When AAA officials spotted cows and steers for shooting during the cattle-killing days of last summer, the farmers felt as though their own children were facing the bullets. Kansas, a Republican state, has no love for the AAA. This year winds whistled over land made barren by the drought and the crop-conservation program. When Wallace removed the ban on the planting of spring wheat he was greeted by cheers. But the wheat has been blown completely out of the ground. Nothing is left but soap weed, or the expensive cotton-seed cake, and after that—bankruptcy.

The storm comes up in a terrifying way. Yellow clouds roll. The wind blows such a gale that it is all my helper can do to hold my camera to the ground. The sand whips into my lens. I repeatedly wipe it away trying to snatch an exposure before it becomes completely coated again. The light becomes yellower, the wind colder. Soon there is no photographic light, and we hurry for shelter to the nearest farmhouse.

Three men and a woman are seated around a dust-caked lamp, on their faces grotesque masks of wet cloth. The children have been put to bed with towels tucked over their heads. My host greets us: "It takes grit to live in this country." They are telling stories: A bachelor harnessed the sandblast which ripped through the keyhole by holding his pots and pans in it until they were spick and span. A pilot flying over Amarillo got caught in a sand storm. His motor clogged; he took to his parachute. It took him six hours to shovel his way back to earth. And when a man from the next county was struck by a drop of water, he fainted, and it took two buckets of sand to revive him.

The migrations of the farmer have begun. In many of the worst-hit counties 80 per cent of the families are on relief. In the open farm country one crop failure follows another. After perhaps three successive crop failures the farmer can't stand it any longer. He moves in with relatives and hopes for a job in Arizona or Illinois or some neighboring state where he knows he is not needed. Perhaps he gets a job as a cotton picker, and off he goes with his family, to be turned adrift again after a brief working period.

We passed them on the road, all their household goods piled on wagons, one lucky family on a truck. Lucky, because they had been able to keep their truck when the mortgage was foreclosed. All they owned in the world was packed on it; the children sat on a pile of bureaus topped with mattresses, and the sides of the truck were strapped up with bed springs. The entire family looked like a Ku Klux Klan meeting, their faces done up in masks to protect them from the whirling sand.

Near Hays, Kansas, a little boy started home from school and never arrived there. The neighbors looked for him till ten at night, and all next day a band of two hundred people searched. At twilight they found him, only a quarter of a mile from home, his body nearly covered with silt. He had strangled to death. The man who got lost in his own ten-acre truck garden and wandered around choking and stifling for eight hours before he found his house considered himself lucky to escape with his life. The police and sheriffs are kept constantly busy with calls from anxious parents whose children are lost, and the toll is mounting of people who become marooned and die in the storms.

But the real tragedy is the plight of the cattle. In a rising sand storm cattle quickly become blinded. They run around in circles until they fall and breathe so much dust that they die. Autopsies show their lungs caked with dust and mud. Farmers dread the birth of calves during a storm. The newborn animals will die within twenty-four hours.

And this same dust that coats the lungs and threatens death to cattle and men alike, that ruins the stock of the storekeeper lying unsold on his shelves, that creeps into the gear shifts of automobiles, that sifts through the refrigerator into the butter, that makes housekeeping, and gradually life itself, unbearable, this swirling drifting dust is changing the agricultural map of the United States. It piles ever higher on the floors and beds of a steadily increasing number of deserted farmhouses. A half-buried plowshare, a wheat binder ruffled over with sand, the skeleton of a horse near a dirt-filled water hole are stark evidence of the meager life, the wasted savings, the years of toil that the farmer is leaving behind him.

Source: Margaret Bourke-White, "Dust Changes America," *The Nation*, Vol. 140, May 22, 1935, pp. 597–598. Reprinted with permission from the May 22, 1935 issue of *The Nation*.

13.5.   Republicans Attack New Deal Agricultural Policy (1936)

During the presidential campaign of 1936, the Republican Party conducted a zealous attack against the Democratic Party's New Deal policies under President Franklin Roosevelt. Although the campaign of Republican nominee Alf Landon endorsed certain social welfare measures, it focused its attack on the growth of the federal government at the expense of states' rights. The bitterness of the attack failed to upset the Democratic Party in the election, but it did bring attention to the waste of federal funds on a failed agricultural policy. Rather than continue to pour more funds into an untenable situation (Dust Bowl conditions and the Depression), Republicans recommended a return to smaller family farms and a better land use system. The following excerpt is from a 1936 Republican attack in the New York Times *several months before the election.*

Agriculture

... Our paramount object is to protect and foster the family type of farm, traditional in American life, and to promote policies which will bring about an adjustment of agriculture to meet the needs of domestic and foreign markets. As an emergency measure, during the agricultural depression, Federal benefit payments or grants in aid when administered within the means of the Federal Government are consistent with a balanced budget.

We propose:

1. To facilitate economical production and increased consumption on a basis of abundance instead of scarcity.

2. A national land-use program, including the acquisition of abandoned and non-productive farm lands by voluntary sale or lease subject to approval of the Legislative and Executive branches of the States concerned and the devotion of such land to appropriate public use, such as watershed protection and flood prevention, reforestation, recreation and conservation of wild life.

3. That an agricultural policy be pursued for the protection and restoration of the land resources, designed to bring about such a balance between soil-building and soil-depleting crops as will permanently insure productivity, with reasonable benefits to cooperating farmers on family-type farms, but so regulated as to eliminate the New Deal's destructive policy towards the dairy and live-stock industries.

4. To extend experimental aid to farmers developing new crops suited to our soil and climate.

5. To promote the industrial use of farm products by applied science.

6. To protect the American farmer against the importation of all livestock, dairy, and agricultural products, substitutes therefor, and derivatives therefrom, which will depress American farm prices.

Source: New York Times, June 12, 1936, reprinted in Avery Craven and Walter Johnson, eds., A Documentary History of the American People (Boston: Ginn and Co., 1951), pp. 743–744. Used by permission of the New York Times.

13.6.   Aftermath of the Drought (1936)

The following passages from the United States Department of Agriculture Report for 1936 seem unrealistically optimistic about the future of Great Plains farmers, predicting that there would not be "any general retreat of farming from even the worst affected areas." This pronouncement was not unlike the rosy pro-

jections offered by land boosters in earlier decades who lured
many farmers to the arid Great Plains with promises of bountiful
rain.

Weather conditions affecting agriculture in 1935 were in striking contrast with those of the preceding year. The general drought of 1934, which had prevailed over a great part of the country, came to an end. In the areas which had suffered worst, sufficient rain fell to check wind erosion, allay dust storms, and promote crop growth. The central valleys had too much rain, at any rate during the spring and early summer; and less than the usual percentage of the country suffered from deficient moisture. Of course somewhere or other in the cropped areas there is drought every year. This year, as if by way of compensation for her niggardliness in 1934, nature inflicted subnormal moisture conditions mostly on States which, nevertheless, still had sufficient moisture for crops.

The drought of 1934 began to break in the fall months, when timely rains relieved the acute situation in most regions and prepared the soil for winter cereals. Especially favored were the eastern and northern Great Plains, which had suffered tremendously during the crop-growing season. Only in the southwestern part of the Wheat Belt did the drought persist. Additional relief came to most areas in the spring of 1935, with the continued exception of the southwestern Great Plains. Early spring rains in the northern Great Plains, where dust storms had been severe in 1934, prevented widespread harmful soil drifting, and created favorable crop prospects. Finally, in May, heavy rains fell also in southwestern Kansas, southeastern Colorado, northwestern New Mexico, western Oklahoma, and the Panhandle of Texas, and ended the droughty, dusty conditions there.

However, the droughty conditions in a considerable southwestern area, including western Kansas, western Oklahoma, the Panhandle of Texas, and eastern Colorado, were only temporarily relieved by the heavy May rainfall. For following this, June and July again had marked deficient precipitation, and drought conditions became reestablished. In fact, at the close of July, scanty rainfall and high temperatures had produced drought conditions throughout the Plains and Rocky Mountain States. Some sections of the southwestern Plains received less than one-fourth of the normal rainfall in July, and high temperatures were persistent.

In the central valleys, where drought in 1934 approached the disaster point, rainfall in the spring and summer of 1935 was excessive and caused floods and serious crop damage. Frequent heavy rains delayed spring plantings and retarded crop growth. Most spring-planted crops in the interior valleys entered the summer much retarded. Considerable acreages intended for corn could not be planted to that crop, especially in the lower Ohio Valley, in Missouri, and in southern Iowa. Missouri farmers were able to plant only about two-thirds of their intended corn acreage. Many unplanted fields in the wet areas were later seeded to forage crops. Most States further west had ample irrigation water, mountain snowfall the previous winter having been heavier, and the irrigation water supply much greater than in 1934. In the area from Montana westward, however, the precipitation was insufficient.

. . .

Complicated and important likewise are the direct efforts on types of farming in the drought areas and the indirect effects in other regions. In normally droughty territory the drought caused a serious loss of topsoil through wind erosion, emphasized the necessity for returning certain tracts to grass, indicated the advantages of more diversification, and showed the unwisdom of prevailing tillage methods. Also, it completed the ruin of many farmers who had been unable even before the drought to make ends meet. These effects in combination may ultimately cause farmers in the normally droughty territory to change their methods greatly.

In territory not usually droughty the worst effects of the drought will be temporary. Disturbed crop rotations and damaged pastures and legumes will be restored. Meantime farmers will resort to emergency hay crops such as soybeans and Sudan grass. Probably a permanent result will be a higher percentage of grasses and legumes and a lower percentage of grain crops in the cropping systems. There may be important temporary shifts in livestock production. In the western Corn Belt, for example, farmers are turning generally to increased cattle raising. On the whole, the tendency in this region will be to return to normal both in crop production and livestock production.

. . .

It is improbable that there will be any general retreat of farming from even the worst affected areas. The Great Plains and adjacent regions suffered from drought in the years immediately preceding 1934 and bore also the handicap of low prices for their products. Many farmers in these areas had come almost to the end of their resources and had seen their debts mount and their lands and their equipment depreciate. But the soil of the Great Plains and of neighboring areas is well adapted on the whole to wheat production and poorly adapted to other types of farming. Notwithstanding the drought, the Great Plains States in 1934 raised 216,000,000 bushels of wheat, in comparison with 280,000,000 bushels produced in the States east of the western boundary of Minnesota, Iowa, and Missouri, and west of the Great Plains. Wheat production in the Great Plains will certainly not be abandoned, though it may be continued under cropping systems considerably modified and necessitating a higher percentage of feed crops and more livestock. It should be dropped, nevertheless, in certain localities where the conditions of soil and climate are demonstrably adverse. Research should differentiate the areas adapted to wheat production from those in which such farming seems hopeless, at any rate under the market conditions likely to prevail in the next few years.

This research must consider not merely the physical but the economic factors, as the physical and the economic phenomena interact. Their reciprocal influence affects productivity as well as production. Certain price conditions may encourage soil mining, and leave agriculture unable to withstand price recessions. Relatively high prices for wheat during and after the World War brought under the plow much land in the Great Plains that might better have been left in grass and exposed the soil to wind erosion. When prices and yields declined together in the drought years, thousands of farmers were unable to carry on. The problem now is to determine what types of farming should be substituted under the present economic conditions for the types that have failed. It is necessary, in other words, to recalculate the economic and physical balance and to reorganize farm production on a basis that can be maintained with the yields and the prices that may reasonably be expected. Yields that returned a profit before 1929 may be insufficient now.

Source: Yearbook of Agriculture 1936 (Washington, DC: U.S. Government Printing Office, 1936), pp. 40–43.

ANNOTATED SELECTED BIBLIOGRAPHY

Athearn, Robert G. *The Mythic West in Twentieth-Century America.* Lawrence: University Press of Kansas, 1986. Athearn examines the shifting perceptions of the West in the twentieth century.

Bonnifield, Matthew Paul. *The Dust Bowl: Men, Dirt, and Depression.* Albuquerque: University of New Mexico Press, 1979. A close study of the human and ecological costs of the Dust Bowl.

Frazier, Ian. *Great Plains.* New York: Farrar, Straus, Giroux, 1989. A journalist interweaves history, popular culture, and travelogue as he explores the Great Plains by automobile in the 1980s.

Gregory, James N. *American Exodus: The Dust Bowl Migration and Okie Culture in California.* New York: Oxford University Press, 1989. The transition of Oklahomans and their culture from the nation's heartland to California during the 1930s and 1940s.

Hurt, R. Douglas. *The Dust Bowl: An Agricultural and Social History.* Chicago: Nelson-Hall, 1981. A narrative of the agricultural and social history of the Dust Bowl.

Lookingbill, Brad D. *Dust Bowl USA: Depression America and the Ecological Imagination, 1929–1941.* Athens: Ohio University Press, 2000. Critical examination of the myths and memories that grew out of the hard times on the Great Plains.

Lowitt, Richard. *The New Deal and the West*. Bloomington: Indiana University Press, 1984. Lowitt takes the saga of western expansion into the 1930s as he examines the federal impact on the Great Plains and the Far West between 1932 and 1940.

Worster, Donald. *Dust Bowl: The Southern Plains in the 1930s*. New York: Oxford University Press, 1979. The story of the Dust Bowl migration from the southern plains to California.

General Bibliography

Adams, Alexander B. *The Disputed Lands: A History of the American West*. New York: G. P. Putnam's Sons, 1981.

Arrington, Leonard J. *Brigham Young: American Moses*. New York: Alfred A. Knopf, 1985.

Billington, Ray Allen. *Land of Savagery, Land of Promise: The European Image of the American Frontier in the Nineteenth Century*. New York: W. W. Norton, 1981.

Billington, Ray Allen, and Martin Ridge. *Westward Expansion: A History of the American Frontier*. 5th ed. New York: Macmillan, 1982.

Brown, Richard Maxwell. *No Duty to Retreat: Violence and Values in American History and Society*. Norman: University of Oklahoma Press, 1991.

Butler, Anne M. *Daughters of Joy, Sisters of Misery: Prostitutes in the American West, 1865–90*. Urbana: University of Illinois Press, 1985.

Cashion, Ty. *A Texas Frontier: The Clear Fork Country and Fort Griffin, 1849–1887*. Norman: University of Oklahoma Press, 1996.

Cleland, Robert Glass. *The Reckless Breed of Men: The Trappers and Fur Traders of the Southwest*. New York: Alfred A. Knopf, 1963.

Dary, David. *Cowboy Culture: A Saga of Five Centuries*. New York: Alfred A. Knopf, 1981.

———. *The Santa Fe Trail: Its History, Legends, and Lore*. New York: Alfred A. Knopf, 2000.

Durham, Philip, and Everett L. Jones. *The Negro Cowboys*. New York: Dodd, Mead, 1965.

Dykstra, Robert R. *The Cattletowns: A Social History of the Kansas Cattle Trading Centers Abilene, Ellsworth, Wichita, Dodge City and Caldwell, 1867 to 1885*. New York: Alfred A. Knopf, 1968.

Faragher, John Mack. *Women and Men on the Overland Trail*. New Haven: Yale University Press, 1979.

Holliday, J. S. *The World Rushed In: The California Gold Rush Experience*. New York: Simon and Schuster, 1981.

Jackson, Donald. *Custer's Gold: The United States Cavalry Expedition of 1874*. New Haven: Yale University Press, 1966.

Jeffrey, Julie Roy. *Frontier Women: The Trans-Mississippi West, 1840–1880*. New York: Hill and Wang, 1979.

Johnson, David Alan. *Founding the Far West: California, Oregon, and Nevada, 1840–1890*. Berkeley: University of California Press, 1992.

Kroeber, Theodora. *Ishi in Two Worlds: A Biography of the Last Wild Indian in North America*. Berkeley: University of California Press, 1976.

Lamar, Howard R. *The Far Southwest, 1846–1912*. New York: W. W. Norton, 1970.
———. *The New Encyclopedia of the American West*. New Haven: Yale University Press, 1998.

Larsen, Lawrence. *The Urban West at the End of the Frontier*. Lawrence: Regents Press of Kansas, 1978.

Limerick, Patricia N. *The Legacy of Conquest: The Unbroken Past of the American West*. New York: W. W. Norton, 1987.
———. *Something in the Soil: Legacies and Reckonings in the New West*. New York: W. W. Norton, 2000.

Marks, Paula Mitchell. *Precious Dust: The American Gold Rush Era, 1848–1900*. New York: William Morrow, 1994.

McGrath, Roger D. *Gunfighters, Highwaymen, and Vigilantes: Violence on the Frontier*. Berkeley: University of California Press, 1984.

Montgomery, M. R. *Jefferson and the Gun-Men: How the West Was Almost Lost*. New York: Crown, 2000.

Morgan, Dale L. *Jedediah Smith and the Opening of the West*. Lincoln: University of Nebraska Press, 1964.

Painter, Nell Irvin. *Exodusters: Black Migration to Kansas after Reconstruction*. New York: Alfred A. Knopf, 1976.

Reid, John Phillip. *Law for the Elephant: Property and Social Behavior on the Overland Trail*. San Marino, CA: Huntington Library, 1980.

Reps, John W. *Cities of the American West: A History of Urban Planning*. Princeton: Princeton University Press, 1979.

Roth, Mitchel. *Reading the American West: Primary Source Readings in American History*. New York: Longman, 1999.

Stallard, Patricia Y. *Glittering Misery: Dependents of the Indian Fighting Army*. Fort Collins, CO: Presidio Press, 1978.

Tate, Michael L. *The Frontier Army in the Settlement of the West*. Norman: University of Oklahoma Press, 1999.

Taylor, Quintard. *In Search of the Racial Frontier: African Americans in the West, 1528–1990*. New York: W. W. Norton, 1999.

Unruh, John D., Jr. *The Plains Across: The Overland Emigrants and the Trans-Mississippi West, 1840–60*. Urbana: University of Illinois Press, 1979.

Ward, Geoffrey C. *The West: An Illustrated History*. Boston: Little, Brown, 1996.

West, Elliott. *Growing Up with the Country: Childhood on the Far-Western Frontier.* Albuquerque: University of New Mexico Press, 1989.

White, Richard. *"It's Your Misfortune and None of My Own": A New History of the American West.* Norman: University of Oklahoma Press, 1991.

INTERNET WEB SITES

The Internet is a valuable repository of information on westward expansion. However, one must be wary when using this information, since many of the sites are not filtered or edited for content and authentication. The following sites are affiliated with either scholarly institutions of higher learning, research libraries, or well-respected historians and museums. Students should use the search words **American Western history, frontier history,** or **westward expansion** when looking for alternative sites.

One of the best sites is affiliated with the PBS television series on the West and can be found at http://www.pbs.org/weta/thewest/resources/archives. Here, at *New Perspectives on THE WEST,* students will find eight archives on the West beginning with Episode 1 (to 1806) and ending with Episode 8 (1887–1914). Each episode offers complete documents and memoirs from the era, photographs, paintings, lesson plans, and quizzes. The Library of Congress offers more than 30,000 photographs drawn from the holdings of the Western History and Genealogy Department at Denver Public Library. These photos were taken between 1860 and 1920 and can be located at http://memory.loc.gov/ammem/award97/codhtml/hawphone.html.

One of the most extensive sites on the Internet for teachers and students is located at http://cnug.clackesd.k12.or.us/oretrail/sites.html. Among the links are sites with maps of the major trails west, books and journals by surveyors and pioneers, interpretive centers, and links to major documentaries on the West.

Students who want to study the way the American West is portrayed in modern media and music can consult http://www.ukans.edu/~kansite/WEST/media.htm. Here one can find digital libraries, western documents and music, chatrooms, and information on popular western motion pictures. Also worth perusing is http://americanhistory.about.com/homework/americanhistory/cs/americanwest, which offers excerpts from pioneer diaries, a chronology of the conservation movement, and many interesting links to the Indian wars. For the story of westward expansion and the railroads see http://www.calhum.org/sfmoma-crossing/gallery.html and http://www.uprr.com/aboutup/history/. Anyone interested in mountain men and the fur trade should peruse the online Research Center sponsored by the American Mountain Men at http://www.xmission.com/~drudy/amm.html.

For information on the multicultural West, see http://www.wsu.edu/~amerstu/mw/home.html. Until recently many historians overlooked the contributions and roles of women, Latinos, Asians, Native Americans, and African Americans in the story of westward expansion. This source offers the best set of links to online documents, journals, popular culture sites, and other relevant materials on the West. See also http://www.coax.net/people/lwf/western.htm for more western links on the saga of minorities in the West.

VIDEOS AND CD-ROMs

Most textbooks now are supplemented by CD-ROMs. Two independent CD-ROMs that would be of value in class are *American Journey: Westward Expansion* (Woodbridge, CT: Primary Source Media, 1994) and *Lewis and Clark: The American Journal Series* (K–12 Micromedia Publishing, 1995). There is a wide selection of videotapes covering virtually every facet of westward expansion. One of the best is the almost thirteen-hour Ken Burns series, *The West* (1996), which primarily focuses on the period 1800–1915. There is a teaching edition in which each segment of tape is numbered and identified for use in the classroom. The film's lasting achievement is its interweaving of two distinct threads of western history—the triumph of westward expansion and the tragic dispossession of the Native Americans. Two of the best sources for videotapes on the West are the PBS episodes of *The American Experience* and the A&E series *The Real West*, the latter now marketed by the History Channel. Other PBS documentaries worth viewing include *Lewis and Clark—The Journey of the Corps of Discovery*, *The Donner Party*, *Surviving the Dust Bowl*, *Artists of the West*, *Last Stand at the Little Big Horn*, and the four-hour *U.S.-Mexican War*. Also helpful is Questar, Inc.'s (Chicago) six-part series, *America's Western Trails*.

The Native American side of westward expansion is also well told in a number of series. One of the most poignant and thought provoking is the seven-episode *How the West Was Lost*, which chronicles the Indian experience in the eighteenth and nineteenth centuries. This is now available from Facets Multi-Media.

Index

About the Author

MITCHEL ROTH is associate professor of criminal justice at Sam Houston State University. He is a historian of criminal justice and of the American West. He has written seven books including *Historical Dictionary of Law Enforcement* (Greenwood, 2000), *Historical Dictionary of War Journalism* (Greenwood, 1997), *Fulfilling a Mandate* (1997), *Reading the American West* (1999), and *Crime and Punishment: A History of Criminal Justice* (forthcoming 2002).